Robert Stephen Hawker, John G Godwin

Prose Works

Including Footprints of former men in far Cornwall. Carefully re-edited with

sketches never before published

.

Robert Stephen Hawker, John G Godwin

Prose Works
Including Footprints of former men in far Cornwall. Carefully re-edited with sketches never before published

ISBN/EAN: 9783337049294

Printed in Europe, USA, Canada, Australia, Japan

Cover: Foto ©Thomas Meinert / pixelio.de

More available books at **www.hansebooks.com**

THE PROSE WORKS

OF

REV. R. S. HAWKER

VICAR OF MORWENSTOW

*INCLUDING FOOTPRINTS OF FORMER MEN
IN FAR CORNWALL*

CAREFULLY RE-EDITED

WITH SKETCHES NEVER BEFORE PUBLISHED

WILLIAM BLACKWOOD AND SONS
EDINBURGH AND LONDON
MDCCCXCIII

PREFATORY NOTE.

THE following papers are, in the main, a reprint of Mr Hawker's contributions to 'Notes and Queries,' 'Household Words,' 'All the Year Round,' &c., collected and published by the author in 1870.

To some readers acquainted with Morwenstow and its church (*vide* p. 7), it may be of interest to know that a few years since a mural painting was discovered on the chancel wall representing St Bernard deriving nourishment from the breast of the Blessed Virgin.[1]

We are indebted to Miss Thorn, photographic artist, Bude, for kindly permitting us to copy her photograph depicting Morwenstow Church and Vicarage, which forms the frontispiece to this volume.

J. G. GODWIN.

[1] *Vide* Mrs Jameson's 'Legends of the Monastic Orders,' third edition, 1863, p. 145.

CONTENTS.

MORWENSTOW.[1]

THERE cannot be a scene more graphic in itself, or more illustrative in its history of the gradual growth and striking development of the Church in Keltic and Western England, than the parish of St Morwenna. It occupies the upper and northern nook of the county of Cornwall; shut in and bounded on the one hand by the Severn Sea, and on the other by the offspring of its own bosom, the Tamar river, which gushes, with its sister stream the Torridge, from a rushy knoll on the eastern wilds of Morwenstow.[2] Once, and in the first period of our history, it was one wide wild stretch of rocky moorland, broken with masses of dunstone and the sullen curve of the warrior's barrow, and flashing here and

---

[1] The foundations of this article first appeared in Mr Blight's 'Ancient Cornish Crosses,' Penzance, 1850; in an article entitled "A Cornish Churchyard," in 'Chambers's Journal,' 1852; also, as the "Legend of Morwenstow," in 'Willis's Current Notes,' 1856; and in its present extended form, in 'Footprints of Former Men in Far-Cornwall,' 1870, embodying the author's latest corrections and impressions.

[2] Willey Moor.

A

there with a bright rill of water or a solitary well.
Neither landmarks nor fences nor walls bounded or
severed the bold, free, untravelled Cornish domain.
Wheel-tracks in old Cornwall there were none; but
strange and narrow paths gleamed across the moorlands,
which the forefathers said, in their simplicity, were first .
traced by angels' feet. These, in truth, were trodden
and worn by religious men—by the pilgrim as he paced
his way toward his chosen and votive bourn, or by
the palmer, whose listless footsteps had neither a fixed
keblah nor a future abode. Dimly visible by the darker
hue of the crushed grass, these straight and narrow
roads led the traveller along from chapelry to cell, or
to some distant and solitary cave. On the one hand,
in this scenery of the past, they would guide us to the
"Chapel-piece of St Morwenna," a grassy glade along
the gorse-clad cliff, where to this very day neither will
bramble cling nor heather grow ; and, on the other, to
the walls and roof and the grooved stone for the water-
flow, which still survive, half-way down a headlong
precipice, as the relics of St Morwenna's Well. But
what was the wanderer's guidance along the bleak,
unpeopled surface of these Cornish moors? The wayside cross. Such were the crosses of St James and St
John, which even yet give name to their ancient sites
in Morwenstow, and proclaim to the traveller that, or
ever a church was reared or an altar hallowed here, the
trophy of old Syria stood in solemn stone, a beacon to
the wayfaring man, and that the soldiers of God's army
had won their honours among the unbaptised and barbarous people !

Here, then, let us stand and survey the earliest
scenery of pagan Morwenstow. Before us lies a
breadth of wild and rocky land; it is bounded by the

billowy Atlantic, with its arm of waters, and by the
slow lapse of that gliding stream of which the Keltic
proverb said, before King Arthur's day,—

> "Let Uter Pendragon do what he can,
> The Tamar water will run as it ran."

Barrows curve above the dead; a stony cross stands
by a mossed and lichened well; here and there glides
a shorn and vested monk, whose function it was, often
at peril of life and limb, to sprinkle the brow of some
hard-won votary, and to breathe the Gospel of the
Trinity on the startled ear of the Keltic barbarian.
Let us close this theme of thought with a few faint
echoes from the River of the West:—

> "Fount of a rushing river! wild flowers wreathe
>   The home where thy first waters sunlight claim,
> The lark sits hushed beside thee while I breathe,
>   Sweet Tamar spring, the music of thy name!
>
> On! through thy goodly channel, to the sea:
>   Pass amid heathery vale, tall rock, fair bough,
> But never more with footstep pure and free,
>   Or face so meek with happiness as now!
>
> Fair is the future scenery of thy days,
>   Thy course domestic, and thy paths of pride;
> `Depths that give back the soft-eyed violet's gaze—
>   Shores where tall navies march to meet the tide!
>
> Thine, leafy Tetcott, and those neighbouring walls,
>   Noble Northumberland's embowered domain:
> Thine, Cartha Martha, Morwell's rocky falls,
>   Storied Cotehele, and ocean's loveliest plain.
>
> Yet false the vision, and untrue the dream,
>   That lures thee from our native wilds to stray:
> A thousand griefs will mingle with that stream,
>   Unnumbered hearts shall sigh those waves away.

Scenes, fierce with men, thy seaward current laves,
　　Harsh multitudes will throng thy gentle brink ;
Back ! with the grieving concourse of thy waves ;
　　Home ! to the waters of thy childhood shrink !

Thou heedest not ! thy dream is of the shore ;
　　Thy heart is quick with life,—on ! to the sea !
How will the voice of thy far streams implore
　　Again, amid those peaceful weeds to be !

My soul! my soul! a happier choice be thine ;
　　Thine the hushed valley and the lonely sod—
False dream, far vision, hollow hope resign,
　　Fast by our Tamar spring—alone with God !"

Then arrived, to people this bleak and lonely boundary with the thoughts and doctrines of the Cross, the
piety and the legend of St Morwenna. This was the
origin of her name and place.

There dwelt in Wales in the ninth century a Keltic
king, Breachan by name—it was from him that the
words "Brecon" and "Brecknock" received origin ; and
Gladwys was his wife and queen. They had, according
to the record of Leland, the scribe, children twenty-and-
four. Now either these were their own daughters and
sons, or they were, according to the usage of those days,
the offspring of the nobles of their land, placed for loyal
and learned nurture in the palace of the king, and so
called the children of his house.

Of these Morwenna was one. She grew up wise,
learned, and holy above her generation ; and it was
evermore the strong desire of her soul to bring the barbarous and pagan people among whom she dwelt to
the Christian font. Now so it was that when Morwenna
was grown up to saintly womanhood there was a king
of Saxon England, and Ethelwolf was his noble name.
This was he who laid the endowment of his realm of

England on the altar of the Apostles at Rome, the first and eldest Church-king of the islands who occupied the English throne. He, Ethelwolf, had likewise many children; and while he intrusted to the famous St Swithun the guidance of his sons, he besought King Breachan to send to his court Morwenna, that she might become the teacher of the Princess Edith and the other daughters of his royal house. She came. She sojourned in his palace long and patiently; and she so gladdened King Ethelwolf by her goodness and her grace, that at last he was fain to give her whatsoever she sought.

Now the piece of ground, or the acre of God, which in those old days was wont to be set apart or hallowed for the site of a future shrine and church, was called the "station," or in native speech the "stowe," of the martyr or saint whose name was given to the altar-stone. So, on a certain day thus came and so said Morwenna to the king: "Largess, my lord the king, largess, for God's sake!" "Largess, my daughter?" answered Ethelwolf the king; "largess! be it whatsoever it may." Then said Morwenna: "Sir, there is a stern and stately headland in thy appanage of the Tamar-land, it is a boundary rugged and tall, and it looks along the Severn Sea; they call it in that Keltic region Hennacliff—that is to say, the Raven's Crag—because it hath ever been for long ages the haunt and the home of the birds of Elias. Very often, from my abode in wild Wales, have I watched across the waves until the westering sun fell red upon that Cornish rock, and I have said in my maiden vows, 'Alas! and would to God a font might be hewn and an altar built among the stones by yonder barbarous hill.' Give me, then, as I beseech thee, my lord the king, a station for a mes-

senger and a priest in that scenery of my early
prayer, that so and through me the saying of Esaias
the seer may come to pass, 'In the place of dragons,
where each lay, there may be grass with reeds and
rushes.'"

Her voice was heard; her entreaty was fulfilled.
They came at the cost and impulse of Morwenna; they
brought and they set up yonder font, with the carved
cable coiled around it in stone, in memory of the vessel
of the fishermen of the East anchored in the Galilæan
Sea. They built there altar and arch, aisle and device
in stone. They linked their earliest structure with
Morwenna's name, the tender and the true; and so it is
that notwithstanding the lapse of ten whole centuries
of English time, at this very day the bourn of many a
pilgrim to the West is the Station of Morwenna, or, in
simple and Saxon phrase, Morwenstow. So runs the
quaint and simple legend of our Tamar-side; and so
ascend into the undated era of the ninth or tenth age
the early Norman arches, font, porch, and piscina of
Morwenstow Church.

The endowment, in abbreviated Latin, still exists in
the registry of the diocese. It records that the monks
of St John at Bridgewater, in whom the total tithes and
glebe-lands of this parish were then vested, had agreed,
at the request of Walter Brentingham, the Bishop of
Exeter, to endow an altar-priest with certain lands,
bounded on the one hand by the sea, and on the other
by the Well of St John of the Wilderness, near the
church. They surrendered, also, for this endowment
the garbæ of two bartons of vills, Tidnacomb and Stanbury, the altarage, and the small tithes of the parish.
But the striking point in this ancient document is that,
whereas the date of the endowment is A.D. 1296, the

church is therein referred to by name as an old and
well-known structure. To such a remote era, therefore,
we must assign the Norman relics of antiquity which
still survive, and which, although enclosed within the
walls and outline of an edifice enlarged and extended at
two subsequent periods, have to this day undergone no
material change.

We proceed to enumerate and describe these features
of the first foundation of St Morwenna, and to which
I am not disposed to assign a later origin than from
A.D. 875 to A.D. 1000.

First among these is a fine Norman doorway at the
southern entrance of the present church. The arch-
head is semicircular, and it is sustained on either side
by half-piers built in stone, with capitals adorned with
different devices; and the curve is crowned with the
zigzag and chevron mouldings. This moulding is surmounted by a range of grotesque faces—the mermaid
and the dolphin, the whale, and other fellow-creatures
of the deep; for the earliest imagery of the primeval
hewers of stone was taken from the sea, in unison with
the great sources of the Gospel,—the Sea of Galilee,
the fishing men who were to haul the net, and the
"catchers of men." The crown of the arch is adorned
with a richly carved, and even eloquent, device: two
dragons are crouching in the presence of a lamb,
and underneath his conquering feet lies their passive
chain.

But it is time for us to unclose the door and enter in.
There stands the font in all its emphatic simplicity.
A moulded cable girds it on to the mother church; and
the uncouth lip of its circular rim attests its origin in
times of a rude taste and unadorned symbolism. For
wellnigh ten centuries the Gospel of the Trinity has

sounded over this silent cell of stone, and from the
Well of St John the stream has glided in, and the water
gushed withal, while another son or daughter has been
added to the Christian family. Before us stand the
three oldest arches of the Church in ancient Cornwall.
They curve upon piers built in channelled masonry, a
feature of Norman days which presents a strong contrast with the grooved pillars of solid or of a single
stone in succeeding styles of architecture. The western arch is a simple semicircle of dunstone from the
shore, so utterly unadorned and so severe in its design
that it might be deemed of Saxon origin, were it not
for its alliance with the elaborate Norman decoration
of the other two. These embrace again, and embody
the ripple of the sea and the monsters that take their
pastime in the deep waters. But there is one very
graphic "sermon in stone" twice repeated on the curve
and on the shoulder of the arch. Our forefathers called
it (and our people inherit their phraseology) "The
Grin of Arius." The origin of the name is this. It is
said that the final development of every strong and
baleful passion in the human countenance is a fierce
and angry laugh. In a picture of the Council of
Nicæa, which is said still to exist, the baffled Arius is
shown among the doctors with his features convulsed
into a strong and demoniac spasm of malignant mirth.
Hence it became one of the usages among the graphic
imagery of interior decoration to depict the heretic as
mocking the mysteries with that glare of derision and
gesture of disdain, which admonish and instruct, by the
very name of "The Grin of Arius." Thence were derived the lolling tongue and the mocking mouth which
are still preserved on the two corbels of stone in this
early Norman work. To this period we must also allot

the piscina, which was discovered and rescued from desecration by the present vicar.

The chancel wall one day sounded hollow when struck; the mortar was removed, and underneath there appeared an arched aperture, which had been filled up with jumbled carved work and a crushed drain. It was cleared out, and so rebuilt as to occupy the exact site of its former existence. It is of the very earliest type of Christian architecture, and, for aught we know, it may be the oldest piscina in all the land. At all events, it can scarcely have seen less than a thousand years. It perpetuates the original form of this appanage of the chancel; for the horn of the Hebrew altar, as is well known to architectural students, was in shape and in usage the primary type of the Christian piscina. These horns were four, one at each corner, and in outline like the crest of a dwarf pillar, with a cup-shaped mouth and a grooved throat, to receive and to carry down the superfluous blood and water of the sacrifices into a cistern or channel underneath. Hence was derived the ecclesiastical custom that, whenever the chalice or other vessel had been rinsed, the water was reverently poured into the piscina, which was usually built into a carved niche of the southward chancel wall. Such is the remarkable relic of former times which still exists in Morwenstow Church, verifying, by the unique and remote antiquity of its pillared form, its own primeval origin.

But among the features of this sanctuary none exceed in singular and eloquent symbolism the bosses of the chancel roof. Every one of these is a doctrine or a discipline engraven in the wood by some Bezaleel or Aholiab of early Christian days. Among these the Norman rose and the *fleur-de-lis* have frequent pre-eminence.

The one, from the rose of Sharon downward, is the
pictured type of our Lord; the other, whether as the
lotus of the Nile or the lily of the vale, is the type of
His Virgin Mother; and both of these floral decorations
were employed as ecclesiastical emblems centuries before they were assumed into the shields of Normandy
or England. Another is the double-necked eagle, the
bird of the Holy Ghost in the patriarchal and Mosaic
periods of revelation, just as the dove afterwards became in the days of the Gospel; and mythic writers
having asserted that when Elisha sought and obtained
from his master "a double portion of Elijah's spirit,"
this miracle was portrayed and perpetuated in architectural symbolism by the two necks of the eagle of Elisha.
Four faces cluster on another boss,—three with masculine features, and one with the softer impress of a female
countenance, a typical assemblage of the Trinity and the
Mother of God. Again we mark the tracery of that
"piety of the birds," as devout writers have named the
fabled usage of the pelican. She is shown baring and
rending her own veins to nourish with her blood her
thirsty offspring,—a group which so graphically inter-
prets itself to the eye and mind of a Christian man
that it needs no interpretation.

But very remarkable, in the mid-roof, is the boss of
the pentacle of Solomon. This was the five-angled
figure which was engraven on an emerald, and wherewith he ruled the demons; for they were the vassals of
his mighty seal, the five angles in their original myth-
icism, embracing as they did the unutterable name,
meant, it may be, the fingers of Omnipotence as the
symbolic Hand subsequently came forth in shadows on
Belshazzar's wall. Be this as it may, it was the con-
current belief of the Eastern nations that the sigil of

the Wise King was the source and instrument of his supernatural power. So Heber writes in his " Palestine "—

> " To him were known, so Hagar's offspring tell,
> The powerful sigil and the starry spell :
> Hence all his might, for who could these oppose ?
> And Tadmor thus and Syrian Balbec rose."

Hence it is that we find this mythic figure, in decorated delineation, as the signal of the boundless might of Him whose Church bends over all, the pentacle of Omnipotence! Akin to this graphic imagery is the shield of David, the theme of another of our chancel-bosses. Here the outline is six-angled : Solomon's device with one angle more, which, I would submit, was added in order to suggest another doctrine—the manhood taken into God, and so to become a typical prophecy of the Incarnation. The framework of these bosses is a cornice of vines. The root of the vines on each wall grows from the altar-side; the stem travels outward across the screen towards the nave. There tendrils cling and clusters bend, while angels sustain the entire tree.

> " Hearken ! there is in Old Morwenna's shrine,
> A lonely sanctuary of the Saxon days,
> Reared by the Severn Sea for prayer and praise,—
> Amid the carved work of the roof a vine.
> Its root is where the eastern sunbeams fall
> First in the chancel, then along the wall,
> Slowly it travels on—a leafy line,
> With here and there a cluster ; and anon
> More and more grapes, until the growth hath gone
> Through arch and aisle. Hearken ! and heed the sign ;
> See at the altar-side the steadfast root,
> . Mark well the branches, count the summer fruit.
> So let a meek and faithful heart be thine,
> And gather from that tree a parable divine ! "

A screen divides the deep and narrow chancel from the
nave. A scroll of rich device runs across it, wherein
deer and oxen browse on the leaves of a budding vine.
Both of these animals are the well-known emblems of
the baptised, and the sacramental tree is the type of the
Church grafted into God.

A strange and striking acoustic result is accomplished
by this and by similar chancel-screens: they act as the
tympanum of the structure, and increase and reverber-
ate the volume of sound. The voice uttered at the
altar-side smites the hollow work of the screen, and is
carried onward, as by some echoing instrument, into the
nave and aisles; so that the lattice-work of the chancel,
which at first thought might appear to impede the
transit of the voice, does in reality grasp and deliver
into stronger echo the ministry of tone.

Just outside the screen, and at the step of the nave,
is the grave of a priest. It is identified by the reversed
position of the carved cross on the stone, which also
indicates the self-same attitude in the corpse. The
head is laid down toward the east, while in all secular
interment the head is turned to the west. Until the
era of the Reformation, or possibly to a later date, the
head of the priest upon the bier for burial, and afterwards in the grave, was always placed " versus altare ";
and, according to all ecclesiastical usage, the discipline
was doctrinal also. The following is the reason as laid
down by Durandus and other writers. Because the
east, "the gate of the morning," is the keblah of Christian hope, inasmuch as the Messiah, whose symbolic
name was "The Orient," thence arrived, and thence,
also, will return on the chariots of cloud for the Judgment: we therefore place our departed ones with their
heads westward, and their feet and faces towards the

eastern sky, that at the outshine of the Last Day, and the sound of the archangel, they may start from their dust, like soldiers from their sleep, and stand up before the Son of man suddenly! But the apostles were to sit on future thrones and to assist at the Judgment: the Master was to arrive for doom amid His ancients gloriously, and the saints were to judge the world. These prophecies were symbolised by the burial of the clergy, and thence, in contrast with other dead, their posture in the grave. It was to signify that it would be their office to arise and to " follow the Lord in the air," when He shall arrive from the east and pass on-ward, gathering up His witnesses toward the west. Thus, in the posture of the departed multitudes, the sign is, " We look for the Son of man: ad Orientem Judah." And in the attitude of His appointed minis-ters, thus saith the legend on the tombs of His priests, " They arose and followed Him."

The eastern window of the chancel, as its legend records, is the pious and dutiful oblation of Rudolph, Baron Clinton, and Georgiana Elizabeth his wife. The central figure embodies the legend of St Morwenna, who stands in the attitude of the teacher of the Prin-cess Edith, daughter of Ethelwolf the Founder King; on the one side is shown St Peter, and on the other St Paul. The upper spandrels are filled with a Syrian lamb, a pelican with her brood, and the three first letters of the Saviour's name. The window itself is the recent offering of two noble minds; and while on this theme we may be pardoned for the natural boast that the patrons of this chancel have called by the name of Morwenna one of the fair and graceful daughters of their house. " Nomen, omen," was the Roman say-ing,—" Nomen, numen," be our proverb now ! But before we proceed to descend the three steps of the chancel floor, so obviously typical of Faith, Hope, and Charity, let us look westward through the tower-arch; and as we look we discover that the builders, either by chance or by design, have turned aside or set out of proportional place the western window of the tower. Is this really so, or does the wall of the chancel swerve? The deviation was intended, nor without an error could we render the crooked straight. And the reason is said to be this: when our Redeemer died, at the utterance of the word τετέλεσται, "It is done!" His head declined towards His right shoulder, and in that attitude He chose to die. Now it was to commemorate this drooping of the Saviour's head, to record in stone this eloquent gesture of our Lord, that the "wise in heart," who traced this church in the actual outline of a cross, departed from the precise rules of architect and carpenter.

The southern aisle, dedicated to St John the Baptist, with its granite and dunstone pillars, is of the later Decorated order, and is remarkable for its singular variety of material in stone. Granite pillars are surmounted by arches of dunstone; and, *vice versâ*, dunstone arches by pillared granite. This is again a striking example of doctrine proclaimed in structure, and is symbolic of the fact that the Spiritual Church gathered into one body every hue and kind of belief; whereas "Jew and Greek, Barbarian and Scythian, bond and free," were to be all one in Christ Jesus: so the material building personified, in its various and visible embrace, one Church to grasp, and a single roof to bend over all. This, the last addition to the ancient sanctuary of St Morwenna, bears on the capital of a pillar the date A.D. 1475, and thus the total structure stands a graphic monument of the growth and stature of a scene of ancient worship, which had been embodied and completed before the invention of printing and other modern arts had worked their revolution upon Western Europe.

The worshipper must descend three steps of stone as he enters into this aisle of St John; and this gradation is intended to recall the time and the place where the multitude went down into the river of Dan "at Beth-abara, beyond Jordan, where John was baptising."

The churchyard of Morwenstow is the scene of other features of a remote antiquity. The roof of the total church—chancel, nave, northern and southern aisles—is of wood. Shingles of rended oak occupy the place of the usual, but far more recent, tiles which cover other churches; and it is not a little illustrative of the antique usages of this remote and lonely sanctuary, that no change has been wrought, in the long lapse of ages, in this unique and costly, but fit and durable, roofing. It supplies a singular illustration of the Syriac version of the 90th Psalm, wherein, with prophetic reference to these commemorations of the deathbed of the Messias, it is written, "Lord, Thou hast been our roof from generation to generation."

The northern side of the churchyard is, according to ancient usage, devoid of graves. This is the common result of an unconscious sense among the people of the doctrine of regions—a thought coeval with the inspiration of the Christian era. This is their division. The east was held to be the realm of the oracles, the especial gate of the throne of God; the west was the domain of the people—the Galilee of all nations was there; the south, the land of the mid-day, was sacred to things heavenly and divine; but the north was the devoted

region of Satan and his hosts, the lair of the demon and
his haunt. In some of our ancient churches, and in
the church of Wellcombe, a hamlet bordering on Morwenstow, over against the font, and in the northern
wall, there is an entrance named the Devil's door: it
was thrown open at every baptism, at the Renunciation,
for the escape of the fiend; while at every other time
it was carefully closed. Hence, and because of the
doctrinal suggestion of the ill-omened scenery of the
northern grave-ground, came the old dislike to sepulture on the north side, so strikingly visible around this
church. The events of the last twenty years have
added fresh interest to God's acre, for such is the exact
measure of the grave-ground of St Morwenna. Along
and beneath the southern trees, side by side, are the
graves of between thirty and forty seamen, hurled by
the sea, in shipwreck, on the neighbouring rocks, and
gathered up and buried there by the present vicar and
his people. The crews of three lost vessels, cast away
upon the rocks of the glebe and elsewhere, are laid at
rest in this safe and silent ground. A legend for one
recording-stone thus commemorates a singular scene.
The figurehead of the brig Caledonia, of Arbroath, in
Scotland, stands at the graves of her crew, in the churchyard of Morwenstow :—

> " We laid them in their lowly rest,
>   The strangers of a distant shore ;
> We smoothed the green turf on their breast,
>   'Mid baffled ocean's angry roar !
> And there—the relique of the storm—
> We fixed fair Scotland's figured form.
>
> She watches by her bold—her brave—
>   Her shield towards the fatal sea ;

Their cherished lady of the wave
  Is guardian of their memory !
Stern is her look, but calm, for there
No gale can rend, or billow bear.

Stand, silent image, stately stand !
  Where sighs shall breathe and tears be shed ;
And many a heart of Cornish land
  Will soften for the stranger-dead.
They came in paths of storm—they found
This quiet home in Christian ground."

Half-way down the principal pathway of the churchyard is a granite altar-tomb. It was raised, in all likelihood, for the old "month's mind," or "year's mind,"
of the dead: and it records a sad parochial history of
the former time. It was about the middle of the sixteenth century that John Manning, a large landowner
of Morwenstow, wooed and won Christiana Kempthorne,
the vicar's daughter. Her father was also a wealthy
landlord of the parish in that day. Their marriage
united in their own hands a broad estate, and in the
midst of it the bridegroom built for his bride the manor-
house of Stanbury, and labelled the door-heads and the
hearths with the blended initials of the married pair.
It was a great and a joyous day when they were wed,
and the bride was led home amid all the solemn and
festal observances of the time. There were liturgical
benedictions of the mansion-house, the hearth, and the
marriage-bed ; for a large estate and a high place for
their future lineage had been blended in the twain.
Five months afterwards, on his homeward way from the
hunting field, John Manning was assailed by a mad
bull, and gored to death not far from his home. His
bride, maddened at the sight of her husband's corpse,
became prematurely a mother and died ! They were

B

laid, side by side, with their buried joys and blighted
hopes, underneath this altar-tomb—whereon the simple
legend records that there lie "John Manning and
Christiana his wife, who died A.D. 1546, without
living issue."

When the vicar of the parish arrived, in the year
1836, he brought with him, among other carved oak
furniture, a bedstead of Spanish chestnut, inlaid and
adorned with ancient veneer: and it was set up, unwittingly, in a room of the vicarage which looked out
upon the tombs. In the right-hand panel of the framework, at the head, was grooved in the name of John
Manning; and in the place of the wife, the left hand,
Christiana Manning, with their marriage date between.
Nor was it discovered until afterwards that this was the
very couch of wedded benediction, a relic of the great
Stanbury marriage, which had been brought back and
set up within sight of the unconscious grave; and thus
that the sole surviving records of the bridegroom and
the bride stood side by side, the bedstead and the tomb,
the first and the last scene of their early hope and their
final rest.

Another and a lowlier grave bears on its recording-
stone a broken snatch of antique rhythm, interwoven
with modern verse. A young man of this rural people,
when he lay a-dying, found solace in his intervals of
pain in the remembered echo of, it may be, some long-
forgotten dirge; and he desired that the words which
so haunted his memory might somehow or other be engraved on his stone. He died, and his parish priest
fulfilled his desire by causing the following death-verse
to be set up where he lies. We shall close our legends
of Morwenstow with these simple lines. The fragment

which clung to the dying man's memory was the first
only of these lines :—

> " ' Sing ! from the chamber to the grave !'
>   Thus did the dead man say,—
> ' A sound of melody I crave
>   Upon my burial-day.
>
> ' Bring forth some tuneful instrument,
>   And let your voices rise :
> My spirit listened as it went
>   To music of the skies !
>
> ' Sing sweetly while you travel on,
>   And keep the funeral slow:
> The angels sing where I am gone ;
>   And you should sing below !
>
> ' Sing from the threshold to the porch,
>   Until you hear the bell ;
> And sing you loudly in the church
>   The Psalms I love so well.
>
> ' Then bear me gently to my grave :
>   And as you pass along,
> Remember, 'twas my wish to have
>   A pleasant funeral-song !
>
> ' So earth to earth—and dust to dust—
>   And though my bones decay,
> My soul shall sing among the just,
>   Until the Judgment-day !' "

THE FIRST CORNISH MOLE.[1]

A MORALITY FROM THE ROCKY LAND.

A LONELY life for the dark and silent mole! Day is to her night. She glides along her narrow vaults, unconscious of the glad and glorious scenes of earth and air and sea. She was born, as it were, in a grave; and in one long, living sepulchre she dwells and dies. Is not existence to her a kind of doom? Wherefore is she thus a dark, sad exile from the blessed light of day? Hearken!

Here, in our bleak old Cornwall, the first mole was once a lady of the land. Her abode was in the far west, among the hills of Morwenna, beside the Severn Sea. She was the daughter of a lordly race, the only child of her mother; and the father of the house was dead: her name was Alice of the Combe. Fair was she and comely, tender and tall; and she stood upon the threshold of her youth. But most of all did men marvel at the glory of her large blue eyes. They were, to

---

[1] From 'Notes and Queries,' First Series, vol. ii. p. 225. 1850.

look upon, like the summer waters, when the sea is soft
with light. They were to her mother a joy, and to the
maiden herself, ah! *benedicite*, a pride. She trusted in
the loveliness of those eyes, and in her face and features
and form; and so it was that the damsel was wont to
pass the whole summer day in the choice of rich apparel
and precious stones and gold. Howbeit this was one of
the ancient and common usages of those old departed
days. Now, in the fashion of her stateliness and in the
hue and texture of her garments, there was none among
the maidens of old Cornwall like Alice of the Combe.
Men sought her far and near, but she was to them all,
like a form of graven stone, careless and cold. Her soul
was set upon a Granville's love, fair Sir Beville of Stowe
—the flower of the Cornish chivalry—that noble gentleman! That valorous knight! he was her star. And
well might she wait upon his eyes; for he was the gar-
land of the west. The loyal soldier of a Stuart king—
he was that stately Granville who lived a hero's life
and died a warrior's death! He was her star. Now
there was signal made of banquet in the halls of Stowe,
of wassail and dance. The messenger had sped, and
Alice of the Combe would be there. Robes, precious
and many, were unfolded from their rest, and the casket
poured forth jewel and gem, that the maiden might
stand before the knight victorious. It was the day—
the hour—the time—her mother sate at her wheel by
the hearth—the page waited in the hall—she came
down in her loveliness, into the old oak room, and stood
before the mirrored glass—her robe was of woven velvet,
rich and glossy and soft; jewels shone like stars in the
midnight of her raven hair, and on her hand there
gleamed afar off a bright and glorious ring! She stood
—she gazed upon her own fair countenance and form,

and worshipped! Now all good angels succour thee,
my Alice, and bend Sir Beville's soul! Fain am I to
greet thee wedded wife before I die! I do yearn to
hold thy children on my knee! Often shall I pray to-
night that the Granville heart may yield! Ay, thy
victory shall be thy mother's prayer. "Prayer!" was
the haughty answer: "now, with the eyes that I see in
that glass, and with this vesture meet for a queen, I
lack no trusting prayer!" Saint Juliot shield us! Ah!
words of fatal sound—there was a sudden shriek, a sòb,
a cry, and where was Alice of the Combe? Vanished,
silent, gone! They had heard wild tones of mystic
music in the air, there was a rush, a beam of light, and
she was gone, and that for ever! East sought they her,
and west, in northern paths and south; but she was
never more seen in the lands. Her mother wept till
she had not a tear left; none sought to comfort her, for
it was vain. Moons waxed and waned, and the crones
by the cottage hearth had whiled away many a shadowy
night with tales of Alice of the Combe. But at the
last, as the gardener in the pleasaunce leaned one day on
his spade, he saw among the roses a small round hillock
of earth, such as he had never seen before, and upon it
something which shone. It was her ring! It was the
very jewel she had worn the day she vanished out of
sight! They looked earnestly upon it, and they saw
within the border, for it was wide, the tracery of certain
small fine runes in the ancient Cornish tongue, which
said—

> " Beryan erde
> Oyn und perde ! "

Then came the priest of the place of Morwenna, a
grey and silent man ! He had served long years at his

lonely altar, a worn and solitary form. But he had
been wise in language in his youth, and men said that
he heard and understood voices in the air when spirits
speak and glide. He read and he interpreted thus the
legend on the ring,—

> " The earth must hide
> Both eyes and Pride ! "

Now as on a day he uttered these words, in the pleasaunce, by the mound, on a sudden there was among the
grass a low faint cry. They beheld, and oh, wondrous
and strange ! There was a small dark creature, clothed
in a soft velvet skin in texture and in hue like the Lady
Alice her robe, and they saw, as it groped into the earth,
that it moved along without eyes, in everlasting night !
Then the ancient man wept, for he called to mind many
things and saw what they meant ; and he showed them
how that this was the maiden, who had been visited
with a doom for her Pride ! Therefore her rich array
had been changed into the skin of a creeping thing ;
and her large proud eyes were sealed up, and she herself had become

THE FIRST MOLE OF THE HILLOCKS OF CORNWALL !

Ah, woe is me and well-a-day ! that damsel so stately
and fair, sweet Lady Alice of the Combe, should become,
for a judgment, the dark mother of the Moles ! Now
take ye good heed, Cornish maidens, how ye put on vain
apparel to win love ! And cast down your eyes, all ye
damsels of the west, and look meekly on the ground !
Be ye ever good and gentle, tender and true ; and when
ye see your own image in the glass, and ye begin to be
lifted up with the loveliness of that shadowy thing, call

to mind the maiden of the vale of Morwenna, her noble
eyes and comely countenance, her vesture of price, and
the glittering ring! Set ye by the wheel as of old they
sate, and when ye draw forth the lengthening wool, sing
ye evermore and say

> " Beryan erde
> Oyn und perde ! "

THE GAUGER'S POCKET.[1]

POOR old Tristram Pentire! How he comes up before me as I pronounce his name! That light, active, half-stooping form, bent as though he had a brace of kegs upon his shoulders still ; those thin, grey, rusty locks that fell upon a forehead seamed with the wrinkles of threescore years and five ; the cunning glance that questioned in his eye, and that nose carried always at half-cock, with a red blaze along its ridge, scorched by the departing footstep of the fierce fiend Alcohol, when he fled before the reinforcements of the coast-guard.

He was the last of the smugglers; and when I took possession of my glebe, I hired him as my servant-of-all-work, or rather no-work, about the house, and there he rollicked away the last few years of his careless existence, in all the pomp and idleness of "The parson's man." He had taken a bold part in every landing on the coast, man and boy, full forty years; throughout which time all kinds of men had largely trusted him

[1] From 'Household Words,' vol. vi. pp. 515-517. 1853.

with their brandy and their lives, and true and faithful
had he been to them, as sheath to steel.

Gradually he grew attached to me, and I could but
take an interest in him. I endeavoured to work some
softening change in him, and to awaken a certain sense
of the errors of his former life. Sometimes, as a sort of
condescension on his part, he brought himself to con-
cede and to acknowledge, in his own quaint, rambling
way—

"Well, sir, I do think, when I come to look back,
and to consider what lives we used to live,—drunk all
night and idle abed all day, cursing, swearing, fighting,
gambling, lying, and always prepared to shet [shoot] the
gauger,—I do really believe, sir, we surely was in sin!"

But, whatever contrite admissions to this extent were
extorted from old Tristram by misty glimpses of a moral
sense and by his desire to gratify his master, there were
two points on which he was inexorably firm. The one
was, that it was a very guilty practice in the authorities
to demand taxes for what he called run goods; and
the other settled dogma of his creed was, that it never
could be a sin to make away with an exciseman. Battles
between Tristram and myself on these themes were
frequent and fierce; but I am bound to confess that he
always managed, somehow or other, to remain master
of the field. Indeed, what Chancellor of the Exchequer
could be prepared to encounter the triumphant demand
with which Tristram smashed to atoms my suggestions
of morality, political economy, and finance? He would
listen with apparent patience to all my solemn and
secular pleas for the revenue, and then down he came
upon me with the unanswerable argument—

"But why should the king tax good liquor? If they
must have taxes, why can't they tax something else?"

My efforts, however, to soften and remove his doctrinal prejudice as to the unimportance, in a moral point of view, of putting the officers of his Majesty's revenue to death, were equally unavailing. Indeed, to my infinite chagrin, I found that I had lowered myself exceedingly in his estimation by what he called standing up for the exciseman.

"There had been divers passons," he assured me, "in his time in the parish, and very learned clergy they were, and some very strict; and some would preach one doctrine and some another; and there was one that had very mean notions about running goods, and said 'twas a wrong thing to do; but even he, and the rest, never took part with the gauger—never! And besides," said old Trim, with another demolishing appeal, "wasn't the exciseman always ready to put *us* to death when he could?"

With such a theory it was not very astonishing— although it startled me at the time—that I was once suddenly assailed, in a pause of his spade, with the puzzling inquiry, "Can you tell me the reason, sir, that no grass will ever grow upon the grave of a man that is hanged unjustly?"

"No, indeed, Tristram. I never heard of the fact before."

"Well, I thought every man know'd that from the Scripture: why, you can see it, sir, every Sabbath-day. That grave on the right hand of the path, as you go down to the porch-door, that heap of airth with no growth, not one blade of grass on it—that's Will Pooly's grave that was hanged unjustly."

"Indeed! but how came such a shocking deed to be done?"

"Why, you see, sir, they got poor Will down to

Bodmin, all among strangers, and there was bribery, and false swearing; and an unjust judge came down—and the jury all bad rascals, tin-and-copper-men—and so they all agreed together, and they hanged poor Will. But his friends begged the body and brought the corpse home here to his own parish; and they turfed the grave, and they sowed the grass twenty times over, but 'twas all no use, nothing would ever grow—he was hanged unjustly."

"Well but, Tristram, you have not told me all this while what this man Pooley was accused of: what had he done?"

"Done, sir! Done? Nothing whatever but killed the exciseman!"

The glee, the chuckle, the cunning glance, were inimitably characteristic of the hardened old smuggler; and then down went the spade with a plunge of defiance, and as I turned away, a snatch of his favourite song came carolling after me like the ballad of a victory:—

> " On, through the ground-sea, shove !
>   Light on the larboard bow !
> There's a nine-knot breeze above,
>   And a sucking tide below !
>
> Hush ! for the beacon fails :
>   The skulking gauger's by.
> Down with your studding-sails,
>   Let jib and foresail fly !
>
> Hurrah for the light once more !
>   Point her for Shark's-Nose Head ;
> Our friends can keep the shore,
>   Or the skulking gauger's dead.
>
> On, through the ground-sea, shove !
>   Light on the larboard bow !
> There's a nine-knot breeze above,
>   And a sucking tide below ! "

Among the " king's men," whose achievements haunted the old man's memory with a sense of mingled terror and dislike, a certain Parminter and his dog occupied a principal place. This officer appeared to have been a kind of Frank Kennedy in his way, and to have chosen for his watchword the old Irish signal "Dare!"

"Sir," said old Tristram once, with a burst of indignant wrath—"Sir, that villain Parminter and his dog murdered with their shetting-irons no less than seven of our people at divers times, and they peacefully at work in their calling all the while!"

I found on further inquiry that this man Parminter was a bold and determined officer, whom no threats could deter and no money bribe. He always went armed to the teeth, and was followed by a large, fierce, and dauntless dog, which he had thought fit to call Satan. This animal he had trained to carry in his mouth a carbine or a loaded club, which, at a signal from his master, Satan brought to the rescue. "Ay, they was bold audacious rascals—that Parminter and his dog—but he went rather too far one day, as I suppose," was old Tristram's chuckling remark, as he leaned on his spade, and I stood by.

"Did he, Trim; in what way?"

"Why, sir, the case was this. Our people had a landing down at Melluach, in Johnnie Mathey's hole, and Parminter and his dog found it out. So they got into the cave at ebb tide, and laid in wait, and when the first boat-load came ashore, just as the keel took the ground, down storms Parminter, shouting for Satan to follow. The dog knew better, and held back, they said, for the first time in all his life: so in leaps Parminter smash into the boat alone, with his cutlass drawn; but " (with a kind of inward ecstasy) "he didn't do much harm to the boat's crew——"

"Because," as I interposed, "they took him off to their ship?"

"No, not they; not a bit of it. Their blood was up, poor fellows; so they just pulled Parminter down in the boat, and chopped off his head on the gunwale!"

The exclamation of horror with which I received this recital elicited no kind of sympathy from Tristram. He went on quietly with his work, merely moralising thus —"Ay, better Parminter and his dog had gone now and then to the Gauger's Pocket at Tidnacombe Cross, and held their peace—better far.

The term "The Gauger's Pocket," in old Tristram's phraseology, had no kind of reference to any place of deposit in the apparel of the exciseman, but to a certain large grey rock, which stands upon a neighbouring moorland, not far from the cliffs which overhang the sea. It bears to this day, among the parish people, the name of the Witan-stone—that is to say, in the language of our forefathers, the Rock of Wisdom; because it was one of the places of usual assemblage for the Grey Eldermen of British or of Saxon times—a sort of speaker's chair or woolsack in the local parliaments. It was, moreover, there is no doubt, one of the natural altars of the old religion; and, as such, it is greeted with a fond and legendary reverence still. Hither Trim guided me one day, to show, as he told me, "the great rock set up by the giants, so they said—long, long ago, before there was any bad laws such as they make now." It was indeed a wild, strange, striking scene; and one to lift and fill, and, moreover, to subdue the thoughtful mind. Around was the wild, half-cultured moor; yonder, within reach of sight and ear, that boundless,

breathing sea, with that shout of waters which came
up ever and anon to recall the strong metre of the
Greek—

"Hark ! how old ocean laughs with all his waves !"

And there, before me, stood the tall, vast, solemn stone :
grey and awful with the myriad memorials of ancient
ages, when the white fathers bowed around the rocks
and worshipped !

"And now, sir," clashed in a shrill, sharp voice, "let
me show you the wonderfullest thing in all the place,
and that is, the Gauger's Pocket."

Accordingly I followed my guide, for it seems "I
had a dream that was not all a dream," as he led the
way to the back of the Witan-stone; and there, grown
over with moss and lichen, with a movable slice of
rock to conceal its mouth, old Tristram pointed out,
triumphantly, a dry and secret crevice, almost an arm's-
length deep. "There, sir," said he, with a joyous
twinkle in his eye,—"there have I dropped a little bag
of gold, many and many a time, when our people
wanted to have the shore quiet and to keep the exciseman out of the way of trouble; and there he
would go, if so be he was a reasonable officer, and the
byword used to be, when 'twas all right, one of us
would go and meet him, and then say, 'Sir, your
pocket is unbuttoned;' and he would smile and answer,
'Ay, ay! but never mind, my man, my money's safe
enough;' and thereby we knew that he was a just
man, and satisfied, and that the boats could take the
roller in peace; and that was the very way, sir, it came
to pass that this crack in the stone was called for evermore 'The Gauger's Pocket.'"

THE LIGHT OF OTHER DAYS.[1]

THE life and adventures of the Cornish clergy during
the eighteenth century would form a graphic volume
of ecclesiastical lore. Afar off from the din of the noisy
world, almost unconscious of the badge-words High
Church and Low Church, they dwelt in their quaint
grey vicarages by the churchyard wall, the saddened
and unsympathising witnesses of those wild, fierce
usages of the west which they were utterly powerless
to control. The glebe whereon I write has been the
scene of many an unavailing contest in the cause of
morality between the clergyman and his flock. One
aged parishioner recalls and relates the run—that is,
the rescue—of a cargo of kegs underneath the benches
and in the tower-stairs of the church. "We bribed
Tom Hockaday, the sexton," so the legend ran, "and
we had the goods safe in the seats by Saturday night.
The parson did wonder at the large congregation, for
divers of them were not regular church-goers at other
times; and if he had known what was going on he

---

[1] From 'Household Words,' vol. viii. pp. 305, 306. 1853.

could not have preached a more suitable discourse, for it was, 'Be not drunk with wine, wherein is excess.' One of his best sermons; but there it did not touch us, you see, for we never tasted anything but brandy or gin. Ah! he was a dear old man our parson, mild as milk; nothing ever put him out. Once I mind, in the middle of morning prayer, there was a buzz down by the porch, and the folks began to get up and go out of church one by one. At last there was hardly three left. So the parson shut the book and took off his surplice, and hé said to the clerk, 'There is surely something amiss.' And so there certainly was; for when we came out on the cliff there was a king's cutter in chase of our vessel, the Black Prince, close under the land, and there was our departed congregation looking on. Well, at last Whorwell, who commanded our trader, ran for the Gullrock (where it was certain death for anything to follow him), and the revenue commander sheered away to save his ship. Then off went our hats, and we gave Whorwell three cheers. So, when there was a little peace, the parson said to us all, 'And now, my friends, let us return and proceed with divine service.' We did return; and it was surprising, after all that bustle and uproar, to hear how Parson Trenowth went on, just as nothing had come to pass: 'Here beginneth the Second Lesson.'" But on another occasion, the equanimity and forbearance of the parson were sorely tried. He presided, as the custom was, at a parish feast, in cassock and bands, and had, with his white hair and venerable countenance, quite an apostolic aspect and mien. On a sudden, a busy whisper among the farmers at the lower end of the table attracted his notice, interspersed as it was by sundry nods and glances towards himself. At last one bolder than the rest ad-

C

dressed him, and said that they had a great wish to ask
his reverence a question if he would kindly grant them
a reply : it was on a religious subject that they had dis-
pute, he said. The bland old man assured them of his
readiness to yield them any information or answer in
his power.

"But what was the point in debate?"

"Why, sir, we wish to be informed if there were not
sins which God Almighty would never forgive?"

Surprised and somewhat shocked, he told them "that
he trusted there were no transgressions, common to
themselves, but, if repented of and abjured, they might
clearly hope to be forgiven." But, with a natural curiosity, he inquired what kind of iniquities they had dis-
cussed as too vile to look for pardon. "Why, sir,"
replied their spokesman, "we thought that if a man
should find out where run goods was deposited and
should inform the gauger, that such a villain was too
bad for mercy."

How widely the doctrinal discussions of those days
differed from our own! Let us not, however, suppose
that all the clergy were as gentle and unobtrusive as
Parson Trenowth. A tale is told of an adjacent parish,
situate also on the sea-shore, of a more stirring kind.
It was full sea in the evening of an autumn day when
a traveller arrived where the road ran along by a sandy
beach, just above high-water mark. The stranger, who
was a native of some inland town, and utterly unac-
quainted with Cornwall and its ways, had reached the
brink of the tide just as a "landing" was coming off.
It was a scene not only to instruct a townsman but also
to dazzle and surprise. At sea, just beyond the billows,
lay the vessel well moored with anchors at stem and
stern. Between the ship and the shore boats laden to

the gunwale passed to and fro. Crowds assembled on the beach to help the cargo ashore. On the one hand a boisterous group surrounded a keg with the head knocked in, for simplicity of access to the good cognac, into which they dipped whatsoever vessel came first to hand: one man had filled his shoe. On the other side they fought and wrestled, cursed and swore. Horrified at what he saw, the stranger lost all self-command, and, oblivious of personal danger, he began to shout, " What a horrible sight! Have you no shame? Is there no magistrate at hand? Cannot any justice of the peace be found in this fearful country ? "

" No—thanks be to God," answered a hoarse, gruff voice; " none within eight miles."

" Well, then," screamed the stranger, " is there no clergyman hereabout ? Does no minister of the parish live among you on this coast ? "

" Ay ! to be sure there is," said the same deep voice.

" Well, how far off does he live ? Where is he ? "

" That's he yonder, sir, with the lanthorn." And sure enough there he stood, on a rock, and poured, with pastoral diligence, the light of other days on a busy congregation.

THE REMEMBRANCES OF A CORNISH VICAR.[1]

IT has frequently occurred to my thoughts that the events which have befallen me since my collation to this wild and remote vicarage, on the shore of the billowy Atlantic sea, might not be without interest to the reader of a more refined and civilised region. When I was collated to the incumbency in 18—, I found myself the first resident vicar for more than a century. My parish was a domain of about seven thousand acres, bounded on the landward border by the course of a curving river, which had its source with a sister stream in a moorland spring within my territory, and, flowing southward, divided two counties in its descent to the sea. My seaward boundary was a stretch of bold and rocky shore, an interchange of lofty headland and deep and sudden gorge, the cliffs varying from three hundred to four hundred and fifty feet of perpendicular or gradual height, and the valleys gushing with torrents, which bounded rejoicingly towards the sea, and leaped at last, amid a cloud of spray,

[1] From 'All the Year Round,' vol. xiii. pp. 153-156. 1865.

into the waters. So stern and pitiless is this iron-bound coast, that within the memory of one man upwards of eighty wrecks have been counted within a reach of fifteen miles, with only here and there the rescue of a living man. My people were a mixed multitude of smugglers, wreckers, and dissenters of various hue. A few simple-hearted farmers had clung to the grey old sanctuary of the church and the tower that looked along the sea; but the bulk of the people, in the absence of a resident vicar, had become the followers of the great preacher of the last century who came down into Cornwall and persuaded the people to alter their sins. I was assured, soon after my arrival, by one of his disciples, who led the foray among my flock, that my "parish was so rich in resources for his benefit, that he called it, sir, the garden of our circuit." The church stood on the glebe, and close by the sea. It was an old Saxon station, with additions of Norman structure, and the total building, although of gradual erection, had been completed and consecrated before the middle of the fifteenth century. The vicarage, built by myself, stood, as it were, beneath the sheltering shadow of the walls and tower. My land extended thence to the shore. Here, like the Kenite, I had "built my nest upon the rock," and here my days were to glide away, afar from the noise and bustle of the world, in that which is perhaps the most thankless office in every generation, the effort to do good against their will to our fellow-men. Mine was a perilous warfare. If I had not, like the apostle, to "fight with wild beasts at Ephesus," I had to soothe the wrecker, to persuade the smuggler, and to "handle serpents," in my intercourse with adversaries of many a kind. Thank God! the promises which the clergy inherit

from their Founder cannot fail to be fulfilled. It was
never prophesied that they should be popular, or
wealthy, or successful among men ; but only that they
" should endure to the end," that " their generation
should never pass away." Well has this word been
kept !

Among my parishioners there were certain individuals
who might be termed representative men,—quaint and
original characters, who embodied in their own lives
the traditions and the usages of the parish. One of
these had been for full forty years a wrecker—that
is to say, a watcher of the sea and rocks for flotsam
and jetsam, and other unconsidered trifles which the
waves might turn up to reward the zeal and vigilance
of a patient man. His name was Peter Burrow, a man
of harmless and desultory life, and by no means identified with the cruel and covetous natives of the strand,
with whom it was a matter of pastime to lure a vessel
ashore by a treacherous light, or to withhold succour
from the seaman struggling with the sea. He was the
companion of many of my walks, and the witness with
myself of more than one thrilling and perilous scene.
Another of my parish notorieties, the hero of contra-
band adventure, and agent for sale of smuggled cargoes
in bygone times, was Tristam Pentire,[1] a name known
to the readers of these pages. With a merry twinkle
of the eye, and in a sharp and ringing tone, it was old
Tristam's usage to recount for my instruction such tales
of wild adventure and of " derring-do " as would make
the foot of an exciseman falter and his cheek turn pale.
But both these cronies of mine were men devoid of guile,
and in their most reckless of escapades innocent of mischievous harm. It was not long after my arrival in my

―――――――
[1] *Vide* p. 25 *et seq.*

new abode that I was plunged all at once into the midst
of a fearful scene of the terrors of the sea.   About
daybreak of an autumn day I was aroused by a knock
at my bedroom-door; it was followed by the agitated
voice of a boy, a member of my household, " Oh, sir,
there are dead men on vicarage rocks ! "

In a moment I was up, and in my dressing-gown and
slippers rushed out.   There stood my lad, weeping bitterly, and holding out to me in his trembling hands a
tortoise alive.   I found afterwards that he had grasped
it on the beach, and brought it in his hand as a strange
and marvellous arrival from the waves, but in utter
ignorance of what it might be.   I ran across my glebe,
a quarter of a mile, to the cliffs, and down a frightful
descent of three hundred feet to the beach.   It was
indeed a scene to be looked on once only in a human
life.   On a ridge of rock, just left bare by the falling
tide, stood a man, my own servant; he had come out to
see my flock of ewes, and had found the awful wreck.
There he stood, with two dead sailors at his feet, whom
he had just drawn out of the water stiff and stark.
The bay was tossing and seething with a tangled mass
of rigging, sails, and broken fragments of a ship; the
billows rolled up yellow with corn, for the cargo of the
vessel had been foreign wheat; and ever and anon
there came up out of the water, as though stretched
out with life, a human hand and arm.   It was the
corpse of another sailor drifting out to sea.   " Is there
no one alive ? " was my first question to my man.   " I
think there is, sir," he said, " for just now I thought I
heard a cry."   I made haste in the direction he pointed
out, and on turning a rock, just where a brook of fresh
water fell towards the sea, there lay the body of a man
in a seaman's garb.   He had reached the water faint

with thirst, but was too much exhausted to swallow or
drink. He opened his eyes at our voices, and as he
saw me leaning over him in my cassock-shaped dressing-
gown, he sobbed, with a piteous cry, " O mon père, mon
père !"   Gradually he revived, and when he had fully
come to himself with the help of cordials and food, we
gathered from him the mournful tale of his vessel and
her wreck.   He was a Jersey man by birth, and had
been shipped at Malta, on the homeward voyage of the
vessel from the port of Odessa with corn.   I had sent in
for brandy, and was pouring it down his throat, when
my parishioner, Peter Burrow, arrived.   He assisted,
at my request, in the charitable office of restoring the
exhausted stranger ; but when he was refreshed and
could stand upon his feet, I remarked that Peter did
not seem so elated as in common decency I expected
he would be.   The reason soon transpired.   Taking me
aside, he whispered in my ear, " Now, sir, I beg your
pardon, but if you'll take my advice, now that man
is come to himself, if I were you I would let him go
his way wherever he will.   If you take him into your
house, he'll surely do you some harm."   Seeing my surprise, he went on to explain.   " You don't know, sir,"
he said, " the saying on our coast—

> ' Save a stranger from the sea,
> And he'll turn your enemy.'

There was one Coppinger cast ashore from a brig that
struck up at Hartland, on the Point.   Farmer Hamlyn
dragged him out of the water and took him home, and
was very kind to him.   Lord, sir ! he never would leave
the house again !   He lived upon the folks a whole year,
and at last, lo and behold ! he married the farmer's
daughter Elizabeth, and spent all her fortin rollicking

. and racketing, till at last he would tie her to the bed-post and flog her till her father would come down with more money. The old man used to say he wished he'd let Coppinger lie where he was in the waves, and never laid a finger on him to save his life. Ay, and divers more I've heerd of that never brought no good to they that saved them."

"And did you ever yourself, Peter," said I, "being, as you have told me, a wrecker so many years—did you ever see a poor fellow clambering up the rock where you stood, and just able to reach your foot or hand, did you ever shove him back into the sea to be drowned ? "

" No, sir, I declare I never did. And I do believe, sir, if I ever had done such a thing, and given so much as one push to a man in such a case, I think verily that afterwards I should have been troubled and uncomfort-able in my mind."

" Well, notwithstanding your doctrine, Peter," said I, " we will take charge of this poor fellow ; so do you lead him into the vicarage and order a bed for him, and wait till I come in."

I returned to the scene of death and danger, where my man awaited me. He had found, in addition to the two corpses, another dead body jammed under a rock. By this time a crowd of people had arrived from the land, and at my request they began to search anxiously for the dead. It was, indeed, a terrible scene. The vessel, a brig of five hundred tons, had struck, as we afterwards found, at three o'clock that morning, and by the time the wreck was discovered she had been shattered into broken pieces by the fury of the sea. The rocks and the water bristled with fragments of mast and spar and rent timbers ; the cordage lay about in tangled masses. The rollers tumbled in volumes of corn, the wheaten cargo; and amidst it all the bodies of the helpless dead—that a few brief hours before had walked the deck the stalwart masters of their ship— turned their poor disfigured faces toward the sky, pleading for sepulture. We made a temporary bier of the broken planks, and laid thereon the corpses, decently arranged. As the vicar, I led the way, and my people followed with ready zeal as bearers, and in sad procession we carried our dead up the steep cliff, by a difficult path, to await, in a room at my vicarage which I allotted them, the inquest. The ship and her cargo were, as to any tangible value, utterly lost.

The people of the shore, after having done their best to search for survivors and to discover the lost bodies, gathered up fragments of the wreck for fuel, and shouldered them away,—not perhaps a lawful spoil, but a venal transgression when compared with the remembered cruelties of Cornish wreckers. Then ensued my interview with the rescued man. His name was Le Daine. I found him refreshed, and collected, and grateful. He told me his Tale of the Sea. The captain and all the crew but himself were from Arbroath, in Scotland. To that harbour also the vessel belonged. She had been away on a two years' voyage, employed in the Mediterranean trade. She had loaded last at Odessa. She touched at Malta, and there Le Daine, who had been sick in the hospital, but recovered, had joined her. There also the captain had engaged a Portuguese cook, and to this man, as one link in a chain of causes, the loss of the vessel might be ascribed. He had been wounded in a street-quarrel the night before the vessel sailed from Malta, and lay disabled and useless in his cabin throughout the homeward voyage. At Falmouth, whither they were bound for orders, the cook died. The captain and all the crew, except the cabin-boy, went ashore to attend the funeral. During their absence the boy, handling in his curiosity the barometer, had broken the tube, and the whole of the quicksilver had run out. Had this instrument, the pulse of the storm, been preserved, the crew would have received warning of the sudden and unexpected hurricane, and might have stood out to sea. Whereas they were caught in the chops of the Channel, and thus, by this small incident, the vessel and the mariners found their fate on the rocks of a remote headland in my lonely parish. I caused Le Daine to relate in detail the closing events.

"We received orders," he said, "at Falmouth to make for Gloucester to discharge. The captain, and mate, and another of the crew, were to be married on their return to their native town. They wrote, therefore, to Arbroath from Falmouth, to announce their safe arrival there from their two years' voyage, their intended course to Gloucester, and their hope in about a week to arrive at Arbroath for welcome there."

But in a day or two after this joyful letter, there arrived in Arbroath a leaf torn out of my pocket-book, and addressed "To the Owners of the Vessel," the Caledonia of Arbroath, with the brief and thrilling tidings, written by myself in pencil, that I wrote among the fragments of their wrecked vessel, and that the whole crew, except one man, were lost "upon my rocks." My note spread a general dismay in Arbroath, for the crew, from the clannish relationship among the Scots, were connected with a large number of the inhabitants. But to return to the touching details of Le Daine.

"We rounded the Land's End," he said, "that night

all well, and came up Channel with a fair wind. The captain turned in. It was my watch. All at once, about nine at night, it began to blow in one moment as if the storm burst out by signal; the wind went mad; our canvas burst in bits. We reeved fresh sails; they went also. At last we were under bare poles. The captain had turned out when the storm began. He sent me forward to look out for Lundy Light. I saw your cliff." (This was a bluff and broken headland just by the southern boundary of my own glebe.) " I sung out, 'Land!' I had hardly done so when she struck with a blow, and stuck fast. Then the captain sung out, 'All hands to the maintop!' and we all went up. The captain folded his arms, and stood by, silent."

Here I asked him, anxious to know how they expressed themselves at such a time, " But what was said afterwards, Le Daine?"

"Not one word, sir; only once, when the long-boat went over, I said to the skipper, 'Sir, the boat is gone!' But he made no answer."

How accurate was Byron's painting—

"Then shrieked the timid, and stood still the brave"!

"At last there came on a dreadful wave, mast-top high, and away went the mast by the board, and we with it, into the sea. I gave myself up. I was the only man on the ship that could not swim, so where I fell in the water there I lay. I felt the waves beat me and send me on. At last there was a rock under my hand. I clung on. Just then I saw Alick Kant, one of our crew, swimming past. I saw him lay his hand on a rock, and I sung out, 'Hold on, Alick!' but a wave rolled and swept him away, and I never saw his face more. I was beaten onward and onward among the

rocks and the tide, and at last I felt the ground with
my feet. I scrambled on. I saw the cliff, steep and
dark, above my head. I climbed up until I reached a
kind of platform with grass, and there I fell down flat
upon my face, and either I fainted away or I fell asleep.
There I lay a long time, and when I awoke it was just
the break of day. There was a little yellow flower just
under my head, and when I saw that I knew I was on
dry land." This was a plant of the bird's-foot clover,
called in old times Our Lady's Finger. He went on:
"I could see no house or sign of people, and the country
looked to me like some wild and desert island. At last
I felt very thirsty, and I tried to get down towards a
valley where I thought I should find water; but before
I could reach it I fell and grew faint again, and there,
thank God, sir, you found me."

Such was Le Daine's sad and simple story, and no
one could listen unmoved or without a strong feeling
of interest and compassion for the poor solitary sur-
vivor of his shipmates and crew. The coroner arrived,
held his 'quest, and the usual verdict of "Wrecked
and cast ashore" empowered me to inter the dead
sailors, found and future, from the same vessel, with
the service in the Prayer-book for the Burial of the
Dead. This decency of sepulture is the result of a
somewhat recent statute, passed in the reign of George
III. Before that time it was the common usage of
the coast to dig, just above high-water mark, a pit on
the shore, and therein to cast, without inquest or
religious rite, the carcasses of shipwrecked men. My
first funeral of these lost mariners was a touching and
striking scene. The three bodies first found were
buried at the same time. Behind the coffins, as they
were solemnly borne along the aisle, walked the soli-

tary mourner, Le Daine, weeping bitterly and aloud. Other eyes were moist, for who could hear unsoftened the greeting of the Church to these strangers from the sea, and the "touch that makes the whole earth kin," in the hope we breathed that we, too, might one day "rest as these our brethren did"? It was well nigh too much for those who served that day. Nor was the interest subdued when, on the Sunday after the wreck, at the appointed place in the service, just before the General Thanksgiving, Le Daine rose up from his place, approached the altar, and uttered, in an audible but broken voice, his thanksgiving for his singular and safe deliverance from the perils of the sea.

The text of the sermon that day demands its history. Some time before, a vessel, the Hero of Liverpool, was seen in distress, in the offing of a neighbouring harbour, during a storm. The crew, mistaking a signal from the beach, betook themselves to their boat. It foundered, and the whole ship's company, twelve in number, were drowned in sight of the shore. But the stout ship held together, and drifted on to the land so unshattered by the sea that the coast-guard, who went immediately on board, found the fire burning in the cabin. When the vessel came to be examined, they found in one of the berths a Bible, and between its leaves a sheet of paper, whereon some recent hand had transcribed verses the twenty-first, twenty-second, and twenty-third of the thirty-third chapter of Isaiah. The same hand had also marked the passage with a line of ink along the margin. The name of the owner of the book was also found inscribed on the fly-leaf. He was a youth of eighteen years of age, the son of a widow, and a statement under his name recorded

that the Bible was "a reward for his good conduct in
a Sunday-school." This text, so identified and enforced
by a hand that soon after grew cold, appeared strangely
and strikingly adapted to the funeral of shipwrecked
men; and it was therefore chosen as the theme for our
solemn day. The very hearts of the people seemed
hushed to hear it, and every eye was turned towards
Le Daine, who bowed his head upon his hands and
wept. These are the words: "But there the glorious
Lord will be unto us a place of broad rivers and
streams; wherein shall go no galley with oars, neither
shall gallant ship pass thereby. For the Lord is our
judge, the Lord is our lawgiver, the Lord is our king;
He will save us. Thy tacklings are loosed; they could
not well strengthen their mast, they could not spread
the sail: then is the prey of a great spoil divided; the
lame take the prey." Shall I be forgiven for the
vaunt, if I declare that there was not literally a single
face that day unmoistened and unmoved? Few, indeed, could have borne, without deep emotion, to see
and hear Le Daine. He remained as my guest six
weeks, and during the whole of this time we sought
diligently, and at last we found the whole crew, nine
in number. They were discovered, some under rocks,
jammed in by the force of the water, so that it took
sometimes several ebb-tides, and the strength of many
hands, to extricate the corpses. The captain I came
upon myself lying placidly upon his back, with his
arms folded in the very gesture which Le Daine had
described as he stood amid the crew on the maintop.
The hand of the spoiler was about to assail him when
I suddenly appeared, so that I rescued him untouched.
Each hand grasped a small pouch or bag. One contained his pistols; the other held two little log-reckoners

of brass; so that his last thoughts were full of duty to
his owners and his ship, and his latest efforts for rescue
and defence. He had been manifestly lifted by a billow
and hurled against a rock, and so slain; for the victims
of our cruel sea are seldom drowned, but beaten to
death by violence and the wrath of the billows. We
gathered together one poor fellow in five parts; his
limbs had been wrenched off, and his body rent. During our search for his remains, a man came up to me
with something in his hand, inquiring, " Can you tell
me, sir, what is this ? Is it a part of a man ? " It was
the mangled seaman's heart, and we restored it reverently to its place, where it had once beat high with
life and courage, with thrilling hope and sickening fear.
Two or three of the dead were not discovered for four
or five weeks after the wreck, and these had become
so loathsome from decay, that it was at peril of health
and life to perform the last duties we owe to our
brother-men. But hearts and hands were found for
the work, and at last the good ship's company—captain,
mate, and crew—were laid at rest, side by side, beneath
our churchyard trees. Groups of grateful letters from
Arbroath are to this day among the most cherished
memorials of my escritoire. Some, written by the
friends of the dead, are marvellous proofs of the good
feeling and educated ability of the Scottish people.
One from a father breaks off in irrepressible pathos,   .
with a burst of " O my son ! my son ! " We placed at
the foot of the captain's grave the figurehead of his
vessel. It is a carved image, life-size, of his native
Caledonia, in the garb of her country, with sword and
shield.

At the end of about six weeks Le Daine left my

house on his homeward way, a sadder and a richer man,
Gifts had been proffered from many a hand, so that
he was able to return to Jersey, with happy and grateful mien, well clothed, and with £30 in his purse.
His recollections of our scenery were not such as were
in former times associated with the Cornish shore; for
three years afterward he returned to the place of his
disaster accompanied by his uncle, sister, and affianced
wife, and he had brought them that, in his own joyous
words, "they might see the very spot of his great
deliverance:" and there, one summer day, they stood,
a group of happy faces, gazing with wonder and gratitude on our rugged cliffs, that were then clad in that
gorgeous vesture of purple and gold which the heather
and gorse wind and weave along the heights; and the
soft blue wave lapping the sand in gentle cadence, as
though the sea had never wreaked an impulse of
ferocity, or rent a helpless prey. Nor was the thank-
fulness of the sailor a barren feeling. Whensoever
afterward the vicar sought to purchase for his dairy
a Jersey cow, the family and friends of Le Daine re-
joiced to ransack the island until they had found the
sleekiest, loveliest, best of that beautiful breed; and it
is to the gratitude of that poor seaman and stranger
from a distant abode that the herd of the glebe has
long been famous in the land, and hence, as Homer
would have sung—hence came

"Bleehtab, and Lilith, Neelah, Evan Neelah, and Katy."

Strange to say, Le Daine has been twice shipwrecked
since his first peril—with similar loss of property, but
escape of life; and he is now the master of a vessel
in the trade of the Levant.

In the following year a new and another wreck was

D

announced in the gloom of night. A schooner under
bare poles had been watched for many hours from the
cliffs, with the steersman fastened at the wheel. All at
once she tacked and made for the shore, and just as she
had reached a creek between two reefs of rock, she foundered and went down. At break of day only her vane
was visible to mark her billowy grave. Not a vestige
could be seen of her crew. But in the course of the
day her boat was drifted ashore, and we found from the
name on the stern that the vessel was the Phœnix of St
Ives. A letter from myself by immediate post brought
up next day from that place a sailor who introduced
himself as the brother of a young man who had sailed
as mate in the wrecked ship. He was a rough plain-
spoken man, of simple religious cast, without guile or
pretence : one of the good old seafaring sort,—the men
who "go down to the sea in ships, and occupy their
business in great waters:" these, as the Psalmist
chants, " see the wonders of the Lord, and His glories in
the deep." At my side he paced the shore day after
day in weary quest of the dead. "If I could but get
my poor brother's bones," he cried out yearningly
again and again, "if I could but lay him in the earth,
how it would comfort dear mother at home!" We
searched every cranny in the rocks, and we watched
every surging wave, until hope was exchanged for
despair. A reward of meagre import, it is true, offered
by the Seaman's Burial Act, to which I have referred,
and within my own domain doubled always by myself,
brought us many a comrade in this sickening scrutiny,
but for long it was in vain. At last one day while we
were scattered over a broken stretch of jumbled rocks
that lay in huddled masses along the base of the cliffs,
a loud and sudden shout called me where the seaman

of St Ives stood.   He was gazing down into the broken
sea—it was on a spot near low-water mark—and there,
just visible from underneath a mighty fragment of rock,
was seen the ankle of a man and a foot still wearing a
shoe!   "It is my brother!" yelled the sailor, bitterly;
"it is our own dear Jem—I can swear to that shoe!"
We gathered around; the tide ebbed a very little
after this discovery, and only just enough to leave
dry the surface of the rock under which the body lay.
Soon the sea began again to flow, and very quickly we
were driven by the rising surges from the spot.   The
anguish of the mourner for his dead was thrilling to
behold and terrible to hear.   O my brother!   my
brother!" was his sob again and again; "what a burial-
place for our own dear merry boy!"   I tried to soothe
him, but in vain: the only theme to which he could be
brought to listen was the chance — and I confess it
seemed to my own secret mind a hopeless thought—
that it might be possible at the next ebb-tide, by skill
and strength combined, to move, if ever so little, the
monstrous rock, and so recover the corpse.   It was low
water at evening tide, and there was a bright Novem-
ber moon.   We gathered in numbers, for among my
parishioners there were kind and gentle-hearted men,
such as had "pity, tenderness, and tears," and all were
moved by the tale of the sailor, hurled and buried beneath a rock, by the strong and cruel sea.   The scene
of our first nightly assemblage was a weird and striking
sight.   Far, far above loomed the tall and gloomy headlands of the coast: around us foamed and raged the
boiling waves: the moon cast her massive lowering
shadows on rock and sea,—

"And the long moonbeam on the cold wet sand
Lay, like a jasper column, half upreared."

Stout and stalwart forms surrounded me, wielding their iron bars, pickaxes, and ropes. Their efforts were strenuous but unavailing. The tide soon returned in its strength, and drove us, baffled, from the spot before we had been able to grasp or shake the ponderous mass. It was calculated by competent judges that its weight was full fifteen tons : neither could there be a more graphic image of the resistless strength of the wrathful sea than the aspect of this and similar blocks of rifted stone, that were raised and rolled perpetually, by the power of the billows, and hurled, as in some pastime of the giants, along the shuddering shore! Deep and bitter was the grief of the sailor at our failure and retreat. His piteous wail over the dead recalled the agony of those who are recorded in Holy Writ, they who grieved for their lost ones, " and would not be comforted because they were not"! That night an inspiration visited me in my wakeful bed. At a neighbouring harbour dwelt a relative of mine, who was an engineer, in charge of the machinery on a breakwater and canal. To him at morning light I sent an appeal for succour, and he immediately responded with aidance and advice. Two strong windlasses, worked by iron chains, and three or four skilful men, were sent up by him next day with instructions for their work. Again at evening ebb we were all on the spot. One of our new assistants, a very Tubal-Cain in aspect and stature, and of the same craft with that smith before the Flood, plunged upon the rock as the water reluctantly revealed its upper side, and drilled a couple of holes in the surface with rapid energy to receive, each of them, that which he called a Lewis-wedge and a ring. To these the chains of the windlasses were fastened on. They then looped a rope around the ankle of the corpse and gave it as the post of honour to me to hold. It was on the evening of Sunday that all this was done, and I had deemed it a venial breach of discipline to omit the nightly service of the Church in order to suit the tide. A Puseyite bishop might have condemned my breach of Rubric and Ritual, but I exercise episcopal authority in my own parish, and accordingly I absolved myself. Forty strong parishioners, all absentees from evening prayer, manned the double windlass power; I intoned the pull; and by a strong and blended effort the rocky mass was slowly, silently, and gently upheaved: a slight haul at the rope, and up to our startled view, and to the sudden lights, came forth the altered, ghastly, flattened semblance of a man! "My brother! my brother!" shrieked a well-known voice at my side, and tears of gratitude and suffering gushed in mingled torrent over his rugged cheek. A coffin had been made ready, under the hope of final success, and therein we reverently laid the poor disfigured carcass of one who a little while before had been the young and joyous inmate of a fond and happy home. We had to clamber up a steep and difficult pathway along the cliff with the body, which was carried by the bearers in a kind of funeral train. The vicar of course led the way. When we were about half-way up a singular and striking event occurred, which moved us all exceedingly. Unobserved—for all were intent on their solemn task—a vessel had neared the shore; she lay to, and, as it seemed, had watched us with night-glasses from the deck, or had discerned us from the torches and lanterns in our hands. For all at once there sounded along the air three deep and thrilling cheers! And we could see that the crew on board had manned their yards. It was manifest that their loyal and hearty voices and gestures were intended to greet

and gratulate our fulfilment of duty to a brother mari-
ner's remains. The burial-place of the dead sailors in
this churchyard is a fair and fitting scene for their quiet
rest. Full in view and audible in sound for ever rolls
the sea. Is it not to them a soothing requiem that

> " Old Ocean, with its everlasting voice,
>   As in perpetual Jubilee, proclaims
>   The praises of the Almighty " ?

Trees stand, like warders, beside their graves; and the
Saxon and shingled church, " the mother of us all,"
dwells in silence by, to watch and wail over her safe
and slumbering dead. It recalls the imagery of the
Holy Book wherein we read of the gathered relics of
the ancient slain : " And Rizpah the daughter of Aiah
took sackcloth and spread it for her upon the rock from
the beginning of harvest until water dropped upon them
out of heaven, and suffered neither the birds of the air
to rest on them by day, nor the beasts of the field by
night." In such a shelter we laid our brother at rest,
rescued from the unhallowed sepulture of the rock ; and
there the faithful voice of the mourner breathed a last
farewell. " Good-bye," he said, " good-bye ! Safe and
quiet in the ground ! "

A year had passed away when the return of the
equinox admonished us again to listen for storms and
wrecks. There are men in this district whose usage it
is at every outbreak of a gale of wind to watch and
ward the cliffs from rise to set of sun. Of these my
quaint old parishioner, Peter Burrow, was one. On a
wild and dreary winter day I found myself seated on
a rock with Peter standing by, at a point that over-
hung the sea. We were both gazing with anxious
dismay at a ship which was beating to and fro in

the Channel, and had now drifted much too near to the surges and the shore. She had come into sight some hours before struggling with Harty Race, the local name of a narrow and boisterous run of sea between Lundy and the land, and she was now within three or four miles of our rocks. "Ah, sir," said Peter, "the coastmen say,

> ' From Padstow Point to Lundy Light,
>   Is a watery grave, by day or night.'

And I think the poor fellows off there will find it so." All at once, as we still watched the vessel labouring on the sea, a boat was launched over her side, and several men plunged into it one by one. With strained and anxious eyes we searched the billows for the course of the boat. Sometimes we caught a glimpse as it rode upon some surging wave; then it disappeared a while, and no trace was visible for long. At last we could see it no more. Meanwhile the vessel held down Channel, tacked and steered as if still beneath the guidance of some of her crew, although it must have been in sheer desperation that they still hugged the shore. What was to be done? If she struck, the men still on board must perish without help, for nightfall drew on; if the boat reappeared, Peter could make a signal where to land. In hot haste, then, I made for the vicarage, ordered my horse, and returned towards the cliffs. The ship rode on, and I accompanied her way along the shore. She reached the offing of a neighbouring haven and there grounded on the sand. No boatman could be induced to put off, and thick darkness soon after fell. I returned worn, heart-sick, and weary on my homeward way; there strange tidings greeted me,—the boat which we had watched so long had been rolled ashore by the billows empty. Peter Burrow had hauled her above high-water mark, and had found a name, " The Alonzo, of Stockton-on-Tees," on her stern. That night I wrote as usual to the owner, with news of the wreck, and the next day we were able to guess at the misfortuues of the stranded ship: a boat had visited the vessel, and found her freighted with iron from Gloucester for a Queen's yard round the Land's End. Her papers in the cabin showed that her crew of nine men had been reported all sound and well three days before. The owner's agent arrived, aud he stated that her captain was a brave and trusty officer, and that he must have beeu compelled by his men to join them when they deserted the ship. They must all have been swamped and lost not long after the launch of the boat, and while we watched for them in vain amid the waves. Then ensued what has long been with me the saddest and most painful duty of the shore : we sought and waited for the dead. Now there is a folk-lore of the beach that no corpse will float or be found until the ninth day after death. The truth is, that about that time the body proceeds to decompose, and as a natural result it ascends to the surface of the current, is brought into the shallows of the tide, and is there found. The owner's representative was my guest for ten days, and with the help of the ship's papers and his own per-sonal knowledge we were able to identify the dead. First of all the body of the captain came in ; he was a fine, stalwart, and resolute-looking man. His coun-tenance, however, had a grim and angry aspect, and his features wore somewhat of a fierce and reproach-ful look—just such an expression as would verify the truth of our suspicion that he had been driven by the violence of others to forsake his deck. The face of the dead man was as graphic a record of his living character as a physiognomist could portray. Then arrived the mate and three other men of the crew. None were placid of feature or calm and pleasant in look, as those usually are who are accidentally drowned or who die in their beds. But many of them had *that* awful expression of countenance which reminded me of a picture once described to me as the result of an experiment by certain artists in France. It was during the Revolution, and amid the anarchy of those times, that they bought a criminal who had been condemned to die, fastened him to a cross, and painted him for a crucifixion; but his face wore the aspect, not of the patient suffering which they intended to portray, but a strong expression of *reluctant agony.* Such has been the look that I myself have witnessed in many a poor disfigured corpse. The death-struggle of the conscious victim in the strong and cruel grasp of the remorseless sea was depicted in harsh and vivid lines on the brow of the dead.

But one day my strange old man, Peter Burrow, came to me in triumphant haste with the loud greeting, " Sir, we have got a noble corpse down on your beach ! We have just laid him down above high-water mark, and he is as comely a body as a man shall see !" I made haste to the spot, and there lay, with the light of a calm and wintry day falling on his manly form, a fine and stately example of a man : he was six feet two inches in height, of firm and accurate proportion throughout; and he must have been, indeed, in life a shape of noble symmetry and grace. On his broad smooth chest was tattooed a rood—that is to say, in artist phrase, our blessed Saviour on His cross, with, on the one hand,

His mother, and on the other St John the evangelist:
underneath were the initial letters of a name, P. B.
His arms also were marked with tracery in the same
blue lines.   On his right arm was engraved P. B. again,
and E. M., the letters linked with a wreath; and on his
left arm was an anchor, as I imagined the symbol of
hope, and the small blue forget-me-not flower.   The
greater number of my dead sailors—and I have myself
said the burial service over forty-two such men rescued
from the sea—were so decorated with some distinctive
emblem and name; and it is their object and intent,
when they assume these pictured signs, to secure
identity for their bodies if their lives are lost at sea,
and then, for the solace of their friends, should they be
cast on the shore and taken up for burial in the earth.
What a volume of heroism and resignation to a mournful probability in this calm foresight and deliberate
choice, to wear always on their living flesh, as it were,
the signature of a sepulchral name!   The symbolic
figures and the letters which were supposed to designate our dead were all faithfully transcribed and duly
entered in the vicar's book.   We carried the strangely
decorated man to his comrades of the deck, and gradually in the course of one month we discovered and
carefully buried the total crew of nine strong men.
These gathered strangers, the united assemblage from
many a distant and diverse abode, now calmly slept
among our rural and homely graves, the stout seamen
of the ship Alonzo, of Stockton-on-Tees!   The boat
which had foundered with them we brought also to the
churchyard, and there, just by their place of rest, we
placed her beside them keel upward to the sky, in token
that her work too was over and her voyage done.   There
her timbers slowly moulder still, and by-and-by her

dust will mingle in the scenery of death with the ashes
of those living hearts and hands that manned her, in
their last unavailing launch and fruitless struggle for
the mastery of life! But the history of the Alonzo is
not yet closed. Three years afterwards a letter arrived
from the Danish consul at a neighbouring seaport
town, addressed to myself as the vicar of the parish;
and the hope of the writer was that he might be able
to ascertain through myself, for two anxious and grieving parents in Denmark, tidings of their lost son. His
name, he said, was Philip Bengstein, and it was in the
correspondence that this strange and touching history
transpired. The father, who immediately afterward
wrote to my address, told me in tearful words that his
son, bearing that name, had gone away from his native
home because his parents had resisted a marriage which
he was desirous to contract. They found that he had
gone to sea before the mast, a position much below his
station in life; and they had traced him from ship to
ship, until at last they found him on the papers of the
Alonzo, of Stockton-on-Tees. Then their inquiry as to
the fate of that vessel had led them to the knowledge
through the owners that the vicar of a parish on the
seaboard of North Cornwall could in all likelihood
convey to them some tidings of their long-lost son. I
related in reply the history of the death, discovery, and
burial of the unfortunate young man. I was enabled
to verify and to understand the initial letters of his own
name, and of her who was not to become his bride—
although she still clung to his memory in loving loneli-
ness in that foreign land! Ample evidence, therefore,
verified his corpse, and I was proudly enabled to certify
to his parents the reverent burial of their child. A
letter is treasured among my papers filled to overflow-

ing with the strong and earnest gratitude of a stranger
and a Dane for the kindness we had rendered to one
who loved "not wisely," perchance, "but too well," to
that son who had been lost and was found too late:
one, too, "whose course of true love" had brought him
from distant Denmark to a green hillock among the
dead, beneath a lonely tower among the trees, by the
Cornish sea! What a picture was that which we saw
painted upon the bosom and the limbs of a dead man,
of fond and faithful love, of severed and broken hearts,
of disappointed hope, of a vacant chair and a hushed
voice in a far-away Danish home! Linked with such
themes as these which I have related in this Remembrance are the subjoined verses which were written on
a rock by the shore.

THE STORM.

War! 'mid the ocean and the land!
The battle-field Morwenna's strand,
Where rock and ridge the bulwark keep,
The giant warders of the deep!

They come! and shall they not prevail,
The seething surge, the gathering gale?
They fling their wild flag to the breeze,
The banner of a thousand seas!

They come, they mount, they charge in vain,
Thus far, incalculable main!
No more! thine hosts have not o'erthrown
The lichen on the barrier stone!

Have the rocks faith, that thus they stand
Unmoved, a grim and stately band,
And look, like warriors tried and brave,
Stern, silent, reckless, o'er the wave?

Have the proud billows thought and life
To feel the glory of the strife,
And trust one day, in battle bold,
To win the foeman's haughty hold ?

Mark, where they writhe with pride and shame,
Fierce valour, and the zeal of fame ;
Hear how their din of madness raves,
The baffled army of the waves !

Thy way, O God ! is in the sea ;
Thy paths where awful waters be :
Thy Spirit thrills the conscious stone ;
O Lord ! Thy footsteps are not known.

BLACK JOHN.[1]

A PICTURE hangs in my library—and it is one of
my · most treasured relics of old Cornwall—the
full-length and " counterfeit presentment," in oil, of a
quaint and singular dwarf. It exhibits a squat figure,
uncouth and original, just such a one as Frederick
Taylor would delight to introduce in one of his out-of-
door pieces of Elizabethan days, as an appendage to the
rural lady's state when she rode afield with her hawk
on her wrist. His height is under four feet, hump-
backed and misshapen; his head, with tangled elfy hair
falling wildly on his shoulders, droops upon his chest.
Negro features and a dark skin surround a loose and
flabby mouth, which teeth have long ceased to har-
monise and fill out. He is clad in a loose antique
russet gaberdine, the fashion of a past century: one
hand leans on a gnarled staff, and the other holds a
wide-brimmed felt hat, with humble gesture and look,
as though his master stood by.

The traditionary name of this well-remembered char-

[1] From 'All the Year Round,' vol. xiii. pp. 454-456. 1865.

acter on the Tamar-side is Black John. He lived from
the commencement to the middle of the eighteenth century in the household of an honoured name, Arscott of
Tetcott, an ancestor of one of the distinguished families
of Cornwall; and as his master was wellnigh the last of
the jovial open-housed squires of the West of England,
so was Black John the last of the jesters or makers of
mirth. When the feast was over, and the " wrath of
hunger " had been assuaged, while the hare's or fox's
head, the festive drinking-cup of silver, went round
with the nectar of the Georgian era, " strong punch for
strong heads," the jester was called in to contribute by
merry antic and jocose saying to the loud enjoyment of
the guests. Such were the functions sustained by my
pictured and storied dwarf, and many an anecdote still
survives around us in hearth and hall of the feats and
stories of the " Tetcott merry-man." Two of his usual
after-dinner achievements were better suited to the
rude jollity and coarse mirth of our forefathers than to
the refinements of our own time; although they are
said to exist here and there, among the " underground
men " and miners of Western Cornwall, even to this
day. These were " sparrow-mumbling " and swallowing
living mice, which were tethered to a string to ensure
their safe return to light and life. In the first of these
accomplishments, a sparrow, alive, was fastened to the
teeth of the artist with a cord, and he was expected to
mumble off the feathers from the fluttering and astonished bird, with his lips alone, until he was plucked
quite bare without the assistance or touch of finger or
hand. A couple of projecting tusks or fangs, such as
are called by the Italians Bourbon teeth, were of singular value as sparrow-holders to Black John; but these
were one day drawn by violence from his mouth by an

exasperated blacksmith, whose kitten had been slain, and who had been persuaded by a wretch, who was himself the actual assassin, that it was the jester who had guillotined the poor creature with his formidable jaws. The passage of the mouse was accomplished very often, amid roars of rude applause, down and up the gullet of the dwarf.

A tale is told of him, that one day, after he had for some time amused the guests, and had drank his full share of the ale, he fell, or seemed to fall, asleep. On a sudden he started up with a loud and terrified cry. Questioned as to the cause of his alarm, he answered, " O sir," to his master, " I was in a sog [sleep], and I had such a dreadful dream ! I thought I was dead, and I went where the wicked people go ! "

" Ha, John," said Arscott of Tetcott, in his grim voice, wide awake for a jest or a tale, " then tell us all about what you heard and saw."

" Well, master, nothing particular."

" Indeed, John ! "

" No, sir; things was going on just as they do upon airth—here in Tetcott Hall—the gentlefolks nearest the fire."

His master's house was surrounded with all kinds of tame animals and birds so bold and confiding, from long safety and intercourse, that the rooks would come down at a call and pick up food like pigeons at the very feet of a man. Among the familiar creatures of the Hall were two enormous toads : these were especial favourites with Mr Arscott, who was a very Chinese in his fondness for the bat and the toad, and who used to feed them very often with his own hands. One morning the family were aroused by sounds near the porch of battle and fight. A guest

from a distant town, who had arrived the night before
on a visit, was discovered prone upon the grass, and
over him stood as conqueror Black John, belabouring
him with his staff. His story was, when rescued and
set upon his feet, that on going out to breathe the
morning air he had encountered and slain a fierce and
venomous reptile—a big bloated creature that came
towards him with open mouth. It turned out to be
one of the enormous toads, an old and especial pet of
master and man, who had heard a sound of feet, and
came as usual to be fed, and was ruthlessly put to
death; not, however, unavenged, for a wild man of the
woods (so the townsman averred) had rushed upon him
and knocked him down. When Mr Arscott had heard
the story, he turned on his heel, and never greeted his
guest with one farewell word. Black John sobbed
and muttered vengeance in his den for many a day for
the death of "Old Dawty"—the household name of
the toad.

Black John's lair was a rude hut, which he had
wattled for a snug abode, close to the kennel. He
loved to retire to it, and sleep near his chosen companions, the hounds. When they were unkennelled,
he accompanied and ran with them afoot, and so
sinewy and so swift was his stunted form that he was
very often in their midst at the death. Then, with
the brush of the fox elaborately disposed as the crest
of his felt hat, John would make his appearance on
the following Sunday at church, where it was displayed,
and pompously hung up above his accustomed seat,
to his own great delight and the envy of many among
the congregation. When the pack found the fox, and
the huntsman's ear was gladdened by their shrill and
sudden burst into full cry, Black John's shout would

E

be heard in the field, with his standing jest, "There
they go! there they go! like our missus at home in
one of her storms!" As he grew older, and less equal
to the exertion of his strong and youthful days, John
took to wandering, gipsy-fashion, about the country-
side; and he found food and welcome at every cottage
and farmhouse. His usual couch was among the reeds
or fern of some sheltering brake or wood, and he slept,
as he himself used to express it, "rolled up, as warm as
a hedgeboar, round his own nose." One day, in bitter
snowy weather, he was found wanting from his accustomed haunts—"one morn they missed him on the
usual hill"—and after long search he was discovered
shrouded in snow, cold, stiffened, and to all outward
appearance dead. He was carried home, and in due
course was coffined and borne towards the grave. But
there, just as the clergyman who read the service had
reached the solemn words which commit the body to
the ground, a loud thumping noise was heard within
the coffin. The bystanders rent open the lid in hot
haste, and up started Black John alive, in amazement,
and in furious wrath. He had been in a long *de-
liquium*, or death-trance, from cold, and had been restored to life by the motion and warmth of his own
funeral ride. As he told the astonished mourners,
" He heard the words ' dust to dust,' and then," said he,
" I thought it was high time to bumpy." His words
passed into a proverb; and to this very day, when
Cornish men in these parts are placed in some sudden
extremity, and it becomes necessary to take strong and
immediate measures for extrication, the saying is, " It
is time to bumpy, as Black John said." In his anger
and mental confusion, Black John ever after attributed
his attempted burial to the conspiracy and ill-will

of the clergyman, whose words he had interrupted by his sudden resurrection. More than once the reverend gentleman was suddenly assaulted in his walks by a stone hurled at him from a hedge, followed by an angry outcry, in a well-known voice, of "Ha! old Dust-to-dust; here I be, alive and kicking!"

It may be easily believed that Black John was a very refractory subject for clerical interference and admonition. The result of frequent clerical attempts to reform his habits, was a rooted dislike on his part of the black coat and white neckcloth in all its shades and denominations. The visit of the first field-preacher to the precincts of the Hall was signalised by an exhibition of this feeling. John waylaid the poor unsuspecting man, and offered to guide him on his road by a short cut across the park, which, John alleged, would save him a "considerable bit of way." The treacherous guide led him along a narrow path into a paddock, wherein was shut up for safety Mr Arscott's perilous favourite bull. This animal had grown up from calf-hood the wanton but docile companion of Black John, whose wonderful skill in taming all manner of wild animals had made the "sire of the herd" so familiar with his strange warder, that he would follow him and obey his signals and voice like a dog. What took place between the bull and the preacher could only be guessed at. A rush was heard by a passer-by, and a yell; then the rustling of the branches of a tree, and finally a dead thud upon the grass. From the paddock-gate some little time after emerged Black John with a fragment of a white cravat in his hand, and this was all, so he steadfastly averred, that ever he could find of "the preacher's body." Actually, it was the sole relic of his arrival

and existence that survived in those wild parts. He
was never heard of more in that region. And although
there were rural sceptics who doubted that the bull
could have made such quick work of a full-grown
man, the story was fearful enough to scare away all
wandering preachers from that district while the dwarf
lived. On the Sunday following the terrific interview
between the preacher and the bull, John took his usual
place in church, but, to the astonishment of those who
were not in the secret, instead of the usual fox's
brush, a jaunty pennon of white rag floated as the
crest of the well-known felt hat.

Black John was long and fondly cherished by his
generous master. Mr Arscott lived like Adam in the
garden, surrounded by his animals and pets, each with
its familiar and household name; and no man ever
more fully realised the truth of the saying that "love
makes love," and that the surest way to kindle kindness is to be kind. Accurately has it been said of
him—

> " Oh, for the Squire ! that shook at break of morn
> Dew from the trees with echo of his horn !
> The gathering scene, where Arscott's lightest word
> Went, like a trumpet, to the hearts that heard ;
> The dogs, that knew the meaning of his voice,
> From the grim foxhound to my lady's choice :
> The steed that waited till his hand caressed :
> And old Black John that gave and bare the jest ! "

None, high or low, during the lifetime of the squire,
were allowed with impunity to injure or harass his
cross-grained jester, and many a mischievous escapade
was hushed up, and the sufferer soothed or pacified by
money or influence. When gout and old age had imprisoned Mr Arscott in his easy-chair, Black John

snoozed among the ashes of the vast wood-fires of the
hearth, or lay coiled upon his rug like some faithful
mastiff, watching every look and gesture of his master;
starting up to fill the pipe or the tankard of old ale,
and then crouching again.

> " This lasted long ; it fain would last
> Till autumn rustled on the blast."

And the good old squire in the language of the
Tamar-side, "passed out of it." At his death and
funeral, the agony of his misshapen retainer was un-
appeasable. He had to be removed by force from the
door of the vault, and then he utterly refused to depart
from the neighbourhood of the grave. He made himself another lair, near the churchyard wall, and there
he sobbed away the brief remnant of his days, in
honest and unavailing grief for the protector whom he
had so loved in life, and from whom in death he would
not be divided. Thus and there, not long after, he
died, as the old men of the parish used to relate, for
the "second and last time." He had what is called in
those parts a decent funeral, for his master had bequeathed to him an ample allowance for life and death
in his last will. The mourners ate of the fat and
drank of the strong, as their Celtic impulses would
suggest; and although some among them, who remembered John's former funeral, may have listened again
for a token or sign, poor Black John, alas for him !
had no master to come back to now, and declined "to
bumpy" any more.

A singular and striking circumstance attended the
final funeral of Black John. An aged crone, bent and
tottering, "worn Nature's mournful monument," was
observed following the bier, and the people heard her

muttering ever and anon, " Oh, is he really dead ? He came to life again once you know, and lived long after." When assured that all indeed was over, even her wild hope, she cried with a great sob, " O poor dear Johnny ! he was so good-looking and so steady till they spoilt him up at the Hall!" Her words recalled her to the memory of some old men who were there, and they knew her as a certain Aunty Bridget, who had been teased and worried, long years agone, at markets and fairs, as " Black John's sweetheart."

DANIEL GUMB'S ROCK.[1]

THERE is no part of our native country of England so little known, no region so seldom trodden by the feet of the tourist or the traveller, as the middle moorland of old Cornwall. A stretch of wild heath and stunted gorse, dotted with swelling hills, and interspersed with rugged rocks, either of native granite or rough-hewn pillar, the rude memorial of ancient art, spreads from the Severn Sea on the west to the tall ridge of Carradon on the east, and from Warbstow Barrow on the north to the southern civilisation of Bodmin and Liskeard. Throughout this district there is, even in these days, but very scanty sign of settled habitation. Two or three recent and solitary roads traverse the boundaries; here and there the shafts and machinery of a mine announce the existence of underground life; a few clustered cottages, or huts, for the shepherds, are sprinkled along the waste; but the vast and uncultured surface of the soil is suggestive of the bleak steppes of Tartary or the far wilds of Australia, and that in the very heart of modern England. Yet

[1] From 'All the Year Round,' vol. xv. pp. 206-210. 1866.

is there no scenery that can be sought by the antiquary or the artist that will so kindle the imagination
or requite the eye or the mind of the wanderer as this
Cornish solitude. If he travel from our storied Dundagel, eastward, Rowter, the Red Tor, so named from
its purple tapestry of heather and heath, and Brun-
guillie, the Golden Hill, crested with yellow gorse like
a crown, will win his approach and reward, with their
majestic horizon, the first efforts of his pilgrimage.
The summits and sides of these mountains of the west
are studded with many a logan-rock or shuddering-
stone of the old superstition. This was the pillar of
ordeal in Druid times, so poised that while it shook at
the slight faint touch of the innocent finger, it firmly
withstood the assailing strength of the guilty man.

Passing onward, the traveller will pause amid a
winding outline of unhewn granite pillars, and he will
gradually discover that these are set up to represent
the coils of a gigantic serpent, traced, as it were, in
stone. This is a memorial of the dragon-crest of a
Viking, or the demon-idol and shrine of an older antiquity. Not far off there gleams a moorland lake or
mimic sea, with its rippling laugh of waters—the
Dozmere Pool of many an antique legend and tale,
the mystic scene of the shadowy vessel and the Mort
d'Arthur of our living bard.[1] A sheep-track—for no
other visible path will render guidance along the moor
—leads on to Kilmarth Tor, from the brow of which
lofty crag the eye can embrace the expanse of the two
seas which are the boundaries of Cornwall on the
right and left. There, too, looms in the distance
rocky Carradon, with the valley of the Hurlers at its
foot. These tall shapes of granite, grim and gro-

[1] The late Lord Tennyson.

tesque, were once, as local legends say, nine bold upstanding Cornish men who disdained the Sabbath-day;
and as they pursued their daring pastime and "put the
stone " in spite of the warning of the priest, they were
changed, by a sudden doom, where they stood up to
play, and so were fixed for ever in monumental rock.
Above them lowers the Devil's Wring, a pile of granite
masses, lifted, as though by giant or demon strength,
one upon another; but the upper rocks vast and unwieldy, and the lower gradually lessening downward,
until they rest, poised, on a pivot of stone so slender
and small that it seems as though the wind sweeping
over the moor would overtopple it with a breath; and
yet centuries many and long have rolled over the
heath, and still it stands unshaken and unswerved.
Its name is derived from the similitude of the rocky
structure to the press wherein the ancient housewives
of rude Cornwall were accustomed to "wring" out the
milk from their cheese. Not far off from this singular
monument of "ages long ago" there is found to this
day a rough and rude assemblage of moorstone slabs,
some cast down and others erect, but manifestly
brought together and arranged by human hands and
skill. There is still traceable amid the fragments the
outline of a human habitation, once divided into cells,
and this was the origin and purpose of this solitary
abode. It was the work and the home of a remarkable
man—an eccentric and original character among the
worthies of the west—and the place has borne ever
since the early years of the last century the name of
Daniel Gumb's Rock. He was a native Cornishman,
born in a cottage that bordered on the moor, and in
the lowlier ranks of labouring life. In his father's
household he was always accounted a strange and

unsocial boy. In his childhood he kept aloof from all
pastime and play, and while his companions resorted
to their youthful amusements and sports, Daniel was
usually seen alone with a book or a slate whereon he
worked, at a very early age, the axioms of algebra or
the diagrams of Euclid. He had mastered with marvellous rapidity all the books of the country-side, and
he had even exhausted the instructions of the schoolmaster of the neighbouring town. Then it became his
chosen delight to wander on the moors with some
favourite volume in his hand, and a crust from his
mother's loaf in his bag; with his inseparable tools,
also, the chisel and the mallet, wherewithal to chip and
gather the geological specimens of his own district.
Often he would be absent whole nights, and when he
was questioned as to his place of shelter, he would
reply, " Where John the Baptist slept," or "At Roche,
in the hermit's bed ; " for the ruined cell of a Christian
anchorite stood, and yet stands, above the scenery of
the wanderings of that solitary boy.

But Daniel's principal ambition was to know and
name the planets and the stars. It was at the time
when the discoveries of foreign astronomers had peopled
the heavens with fresh imagery, and our own Newton
had given to the ethereal phenomena of the sky a " local
habitation and a name." It is very striking to discover
when the minds of any nation are flooded with new
ideas and original trains of thought, how soon the
strange tidings will reach the very skirts of the population, and borne, how we know not, will thrill the
hamlet and the village with the wonders that have
roused and instructed the far-off and civilised city.
Thus even Daniel's distant district became aware of
the novel science of the stars, and this intelligence

failed not to excite and foster the faculties of his original mind. Local legends still record and identify the tall and craggy places where the youthful "scholar" was wont to ascend and to rest all night with his face turned upward to the sky, "learning the customs of the stars," and "finding out by the planets things to come." Nor were his studies unassisted and alone. A master-mind of those days, Cookworthy of Plymouth, a learned and scientific man, still famous in the west, found out and fostered the genius of the intelligent youth. He gave him access to his library, and allowed him to visit his orrery and other scientific instruments; and the result of this kindness was shown in the tastes and future peculiarities of the mind of Gumb. The stern necessities of life demanded, in the course of time, that Daniel should fulfil the destiny of his birth, and win his bread by the sweat of his brow; for the meagre resources of his cottage-home had to be augmented by his youthful labour. In the choice of an occupation his early habits were not without their influence. He selected the craft of a hewer of stone, a very common calling on the surrounding moors; and there he toiled for several years of his succeeding life, amid the cyclopean models of the early ages. The pillared rocks of that wild domain were the monoliths of Celtic history, and the vast piles of the native moor were the heaped and unhewn pyramids of an ancient and nameless people. All these surrounding scenes acted on his tastes and impulses. "So the foundations of his mind were laid!" His father died, and Daniel became his own master, and had to hew his way through the rugged world by what the Cornish call "the pith of his bones." That he did so his future history will attest; but it was not unsoothed nor alone; nor was it without the usual incident of human existence. No man ever yet became happily great or joyfully distinguished without that kindling strength, the affectionate presence of a woman.

> " He who Joy would win,
> Must share it : Happiness was born a twin."

Such was the solace that arrived to soothe the dreary path of Daniel Gumb. He wooed and won a maiden of his native village, who, amid the rugged rocks and appellatives of Cornwall, had the soft Italian name of Florence. But where, amid the utter poverty of his position and prospects, could he find the peaceful and happy wedding-roof that should bend over him and his bride ? His friends were few, and they too poor and lowly to aid his start in life. He himself had inherited nothing save a strong head and heart, and two stalwart hands. He looked around him and afar off, and there was no avenue for house or home. Suddenly he recalled to mind his wandering days and his houseless nights, the scanty food, the absorbing meditation, and the kindly shelter of many a nook in the hollow places of the granite rock. He formed his plan, and made it known to his future and faithful bride; she assented with the full-hearted strength and trusting sacrifice of a woman's love. Then he went forth in the might of his simple and strong resolve,—his tools in his scrip, and a loaf or two of his accustomed household bread. He sought the well-known slope under Carradon, searched many a mass of Druid rock, and paced around cromlech and pillared stone of old memorial, until he discovered a primeval assemblage of granite slabs suited to his toil. One of these, grounded upon several others, the vast boulders of some diluvian flood, had the rude semblance of a roof. Underneath this shelving rock he scooped away the soil, finding, as he dug on, more than one upright slice of moorstone, which he left to stand as an inner and natural wall. At last, at the end of a few laborious days, Daniel stood before a large cavern of the rocks, divided into chambers by upstanding granite, and sheltered at a steep angle by a mountainous mass of stone. Nerved and sustained by the hopeful visions which crowded on his mind, and of which he firmly trusted that this place would be the future scene, he toiled on until he had finally framed a giant abode such as that wherein Cyclops shut in Ulysses and his companions, and promised to " devour No-man the last." Materials for the pavement and for closing up the inner walls were scattered abundantly around —nay, the very furniture for that mountain-home was at once ready for his hand ; for as Agag, king of the Amalekites, had his vaunted iron bed, so did Gumb frame and hew for himself and Florence, his wife, table and seat and a bedstead of native stone. Then he smoothed out and shot into a groove a thick and heavy door, so that, closed like an Eastern sepulchre, it demanded no common strength to roll away the stone. When all had been prepared, the bridegroom and the bride met at a distant church; the simple wedding feast was held at her father's house; and that night the husband led the maiden of his vows, the bride of his youth, to their wedding-rock ! If he had known the ode he might have chanted, in Horatian verse, that day—

" Nunc scio quid sit amor, duris in cotibus illum."

" Now know I what true love is ; in rugged dens he dwells."

Here the wedded pair dwelt in peace long and happy years, mingling the imagery of old romance with the sterner duties of practical life. As a far-famed hewer of stone, the skill and energy of this singular man never lacked employ, nor failed to supply the necessities of his moorland abode. Like a patriarch in his tent amid the solitudes of Syria, he was his own king, prophet, and priest. He paid neither rent, nor taxes, nor tithe. When children were born to him, he exercised unwittingly the power of lay-baptism which was granted in the primitive Church to the inhabitants of a wilderness, afar from the ministry of the priesthood, and his wife was content to be "churched" by her own cherished husband, among the altars of unhewn stone that surrounded their solitary cell. Who shall say that this simple worship of the father and the mother with their household, amid the paradise of hills, was not as sweet, with the balsam of the soul, as the incense-breathing psalm of the cathedral choir? Rightly or wrongly, it is known that Daniel entertained an infinite contempt for "the parsons" whose territories bordered on the moor. Not one of them, it was his wont to aver, could cross the Asses' Bridge of his favourite Euclid, a feat he had himself accomplished in very early youth; nor could the most learned among them all unravel the mysteries of his chosen companions, the wandering stars that travelled over Carradon every night. Long and frequent were his vigils for astronomical researches and delight. To this day the traveller will encounter on the face of some solitary rock a mathematical diagram carefully carved by some chisel and hand unknown; and while speculation has often been rife as to the Druidical origin of the mystic figure, or the scientific knowledge of the early Kelts, the local antiquary is aware that these are the simple records of the patient studies of Daniel Gumb.

When the writer of this article visited the neighbourhood in 183–, there still survived relics and remembrances of this singular man. There were a few written fragments of his thoughts and studies still treasured up in the existing families of himself and his wife. Here is a transcript: "Mr Cookworthy told me, when I saw him last, that astronomers in foreign parts, and our great man Sir Isaac here at home, had thought that the planets were so vast, and so like our earth in their ways, that they might have been inhabited by men; but he said, 'their elements and atmosphere are thought to be unfit for human life and breath.' But surely God would not have so wasted His worlds as to have made such great bright masses of His creation to roll along all barren, as it were, like desert places of light in the sky. There must be people of some kind there: how I should like to see them, and to go there when I die!"

Another entry on the same leaf: "Florence asked me to-day if I thought that our souls, after we are dead, would know the stars and other wise things better than we can now. And I answered her, Yes; and if I could—that is, if I was allowed to—the first thing I would try should be to square the circle true, and then, if I could, I would mark it and work it out somewhere hereabouts on a flat rock, that my son might find it there, and so make his fortune and be a great man. N.B.—Florence asked me to write this down."

On a thick sheet of pasteboard, with a ground-plan of a building on the other side, he had written: "*January 16, 1756.* — A terrible storm last night. Thunder and lightning and hail, with a tempest of wind. Saw several dead sheep on the moor. Ship-

wrecks, no doubt, at sea. A thought came into my
mind, Why should such harm be allowed to be done?
I read some reasons once in a book that Mr Cookworthy lent me, called 'The Origin of Evil'; but I
could not understand a word of it. My notion is, that
when evil somehow came into the world, God did not
destroy it at once, because He is so almighty that He
let it go on, to make manifest His power and majesty;
and so He rules over all evil things, and turns them
into good at the last. *N.B.*—The devil is called in the
Bible the Prince of the Powers of the Air: so he may
be, but he must obey his Master. The poor wretch is
but a slave after all!'"

On the fly-leaves of an old account-book the following strange statement appears: "*June 23, 1764.*—To-
day, at bright noon, as I was at my work upon the
moor, I looked up, and saw all at once a stranger
standing on the turf, just above my block. He was
dressed like an old picture I remember in the windows
of St Neot's Church, in a long brown garment, with a
girdle; and his head was uncovered and grizzled with
long hair. He spoke to me, and he said, in a low clear
voice, 'Daniel, that work is hard!' I wondered that
he should know my name, and I answered, 'Yes, sir;
but I am used to it, and don't mind it, for the sake of
the faces at home.' Then he said, sounding his words
like a psalm, 'Man goeth forth to his work and to his
labour until the evening; when will it be night with
Daniel Gumb?' I began to feel queer; it seemed to
me that there was something awful about the unknown
man. I even shook. Then he said again, 'Fear
nothing. The happiest man in all the earth is he that
wins his daily bread by his daily sweat, if he will but
fear God and do man no wrong.' I bent down my

head like any one confounded, and I greatly wondered who this strange appearance could be. He was not like a preacher, for he looked me full in the face; nor a bit like a parson, for he seemed very meek and kind. I began to think it was a spirit, only such ones always come by night, and here was I at noonday, and at work. So I made up my mind to drop my hammer and step up and ask his name right out. But when I looked up he was gone, and that clear out of my sight, on the bare wide moor suddenly. I only wish that I had gone forward at once and felt him with my hand, and found out if he was a real man or only a resemblance. What could it mean? Mem. to ask Mr C."

This event is recorded in a more formal and painful handwriting than the other MSS. which survive. Nothing could be further removed from superstition or fear than this man's whole character and mind. Hard as one of his native rocks, and accurate as a diagram, yet here is a tinge of that large and artless belief which is so inseparable from a Keltic origin, and which is so often manifested by the strongest and loftiest minds. Another paragraph, written on the blank page of an almanac, runs thus: "Found to-day, in the very heart of a slab rock that came out below the granite, the bony skeleton of a strange animal, or rather some kind of fish. The stone had never been broken into before, and looked ages older than the rocks above. Now, how came this creature to get in, and to die and harden there? Was it before Adam's time, or since? What date was it? But what can we tell about dates after all? Time is nothing but Adam's clock—a measurement that men invented to reckon by. This very rock with the creature in it was made, perhaps, before there was any such thing as time. In

F

eternity may be—that is, before there were any dates
begun.   At all events, when God did make the rock,
He must have put the creature there." This appears
to be a singular and rude anticipation of modern discovery, and a simple solution of a question of science
in our own and later time. It is to be lamented that
these surviving details of a thoughtful and original life
are so few and far between.

Gumb appears to have united in his native character the simplicity of an ancient hermit and the
stern contempt of the solitary student for the busy
hum of men, with the brave resolution and indepen-
dent energy of mind which have won success and fame
for some of our self-made sons of science and skill.
But his opportunities were few, and the severance of
his life and abode from contact with his fellow-men
forbade that access to the discoveries and researches
of his kind which might have rendered him, in other
days, the Hugh Miller of the rocks, or the Stephenson
or Watt of a scientific solitude. He and his wife
inhabited their wedded cell for many years and long.
The mother on her stony couch gladdened her anxious
husband with sons and daughters; but she had the
courage to brave her woman's trials alone, for neither
midwife nor doctor were ever summoned to "the rock."
These, as may well be imagined, were all literally
educated at home; but only one of their children—
his name was John — appears to have inherited his
father's habits or energy. He succeeded to the cav-
erned home after Daniel's death, and when his mother
had returned to her native village to die also, the
existence of John Gumb is casually seen recorded as
one of the skilful hewers of stone at the foot of
Carradon.   But Daniel died " an old man full of

days," and he was carried after all *ad plures,* and to the silent society of men, in the churchyard of the parish wherein stood afar off his rocky home. He won and he still deserves a nook of remembrance among the legendary sons of the west, " the giants " of Keltic race, " the mighty men that were of old, the men of renown." His mind, though rough-hewn, like a block of his native granite, must have been well balanced: resolute and firm reliance on a man's own resources, and disdain of external succour, have ever been a signal of native genius. To be able to live alone, according to the adage of an ancient sage, a man must be either an angel or a demon. Gumb was neither, but a simple, strong-hearted, and intellectual man. He had the "mens sana in corpore sano" of the poet's aspiration. A scenic taste and a mind "to enjoy the universe" he revealed in the very choice of his abode. In utter scorn of the pent-up city, and dislike for the reek of the multitude, he built like " the Kenite, his nest in the rock "; nor did he pitch his stony tent by chance, or in a casual place in the wild. He chose and he fixed his home where his eye could command and exult in a stretch of circumferent scenery a hundred and fifty miles in surrounding extent. In the east, he greeted the morning sun, as he mounted the rugged saddle of Dartmoor and Exmoor for his daily career. To the west, Roche, the rock of the ruined hermitage, lifted a bold and craggy crest to the sky, where long centuries before another solitary of more ascetic mind lay, like the patriarch on his pillow of granite, and reared a ladder to heaven by the energy of nightly prayer. Far, far away to the westward the haughty sun of England went into the storied Sea of Arthur and his knights, and touched caressingly the heights of

grim Dundagel with a lingering halo of light. These
were the visions that soothed and surrounded the
worker at his daily toil, and roused and strengthened
the energies of the self-sustaining man. The lessons of
the legend of Daniel Gumb are simple and earnest and
strong. The words of supernatural wisdom might be
graven as an added superscription on his rock, " Whatsoever thou doest, do it with all thine heart." If thou
be a man friendless and alone, the slave of the hammer
or the axe, and doomed to the sweat of labour day by
day till the night shall come that no man can work,
" aide-toi et Dieu t'aidera "—aid thyself and God will
succour thee.

ANTONY PAYNE, A CORNISH GIANT.[1]

ON the brow of a lofty hill, crested with stag-horned trees, commanding a deep and woodland gorge wherein " the Crooks of Combe " (the curves of a winding river) urge onward to the " Severn Sea," still survive the remains of famous old Stowe,—that historic abode of the loyal and glorious Sir Beville, the Bayard of old Cornwall, " sans peur et sans reproche," in the thrilling Stuart wars. No mansion on the Tamarside ever accumulated so rich and varied a store of association and event. Thither the sons of the Cornish gentry were accustomed to resort, to be nurtured and brought up with the children of Sir Beville Granville and Lady Grace; for the noble knight was literally the " glass wherein " the youth of those ancient times " did dress themselves." There their graver studies were relieved by manly pastime and athletic exercise. Like the children of the Persians, they were taught " to ride, to bend the bow, and to speak the truth." At hearth and hall every time-honoured usage and festive celebra-

[1] From ' All the Year Round,' vol. xvi. pp. 247-249. 1866.

tion was carefully and reverently preserved. Around
the walls branched the massive antlers of the red deer
of the moors, the trophies of many a bold achievement
with horse and hound. At the buttery-hatch hung a
tankard marked with the guests' and the travellers'
peg, and a manchet, flanked with native cheese, stood
ready on a trencher for any sudden visitant who might
choose to lift the latch; for the Granville motto was,
" An open door and a greeting hand." A troop of
retainers, servants, grooms, and varlets of the yard,
stood each in his place, and under orders to receive
with a welcome the unknown stranger, as well as their
master's kinsman and friend.

Among these, at the beginning of the seventeenth
century, appeared a remarkable personage. He was
the son of an old tenant on the estate, who occupied
the manor - house of Stratton, a neighbouring town.
His parents were of the yeoman rank in life, and pos-
sessed no singularity of personal aspect or frame, although both were comely. But Antony, their son, was
from his earliest years a wonderful boy. He shot up
into preternatural stature and strength. His propor-
tions were so vast that, when he was a mere lad, his
schoolmates were accustomed to " borrow his back,"
and, for sport, to work out their geography lessons or
arithmetic on that broad disc in chalk; so that, to his
mother's amazement and dismay, he more than once
brought home, like Atlas, the world on his shoulders,
for her to rub out. His strength and skill in every
boyish game were marvellous, and, unlike many other
large men, his mental and intellectual faculties increased with his amazing growth.

It was Antony Payne's delight to select two of his
stoutest companions, whom he termed " his kittens,"

and, with one under each arm, to climb some perilous
crag or cliff in the neighbourhood of the sea, " to show
them the world," as he said. He was called in the
school " Uncle Tony," for the Cornish to this day employ the names " uncle and aunt " as titles of endearment and respect. Another relic of his boyhood is
extant still : the country lads, when they describe anything of excessive dimensions, call it, " As long as
Tony Payne's foot."

He grew on gradually, and in accurate proportion of
sinews and thews, until, at the age of twenty-one, he
was taken into the establishment at Stowe. He then
measured seven feet two inches without his shoes, and
he afterwards added a couple of inches more to his
stately growth. Wide-chested, full-armed, and pillared
like a rock on lower limbs of ample and exact symmetry, he would have gladdened the critical eyes of
Queen Elizabeth, whose Tudor taste led her to exult in
" looking on a man." If his lot had fallen in later days,
he might have been hired by some wonder-monger to
astonish the provincial mind, or the intellect of cities,
as the Cornish Chang. But in good, old, honest, simple-
hearted England, they utilised their giants, and deemed
that when a cubit was added to the stature of a man,
it was for some wise good end, and they looked upon
their loftier brother with added honour and respect.

So for many years Payne continued to fulfil his
various duties as Sir Beville's chief retainer at Stowe.
He it was who was the leader and the authority in
every masculine sport. He embowelled and flayed
the hunted deer, and carried the carcass on his own
shoulders to the Hall, where he received as his guerdon
the horns and the hide. The antlers, cleansed and
polished, were hoisted as a trophy on the panelled

wall; and the skins, dressed and prepared, were shaped
into a jerkin for his goodly chest. It took the spoils
of three full-grown red deer to make the garment complete. His master's sons and their companions, the
very pride of the West, who were housed and instructed
at Stowe, when released from their graver studies, were
under his especial charge. He taught them to shoot,
and fish, and to handle arms. Tilt-yard and bowling-
green, and the hurler's ground, can still be identified at
Stowe. In the latter, the poising-place and the mark
survive, and a rough block of graywacke is called to
this day "Payne's cast"; it lies full ten paces beyond
the reach whereat the ordinary players could "put the
stone."

It is said that one Christmas-eve the fire languished
in the Hall. A boy with an ass had been sent to the
woodland for logs, and the driver loitered on his homeward way. Lady Grace lost patience, and was dis-
pleased. All at once a sudden outcry was heard at the
gate, and Sir Beville's Giant appeared with the loaded
animal on his mighty back. He threw down his burden
in triumph at the hearth-side, shouting merrily, "Ass
and fardel! ass and fardel for my lady's Yule!"
Another time he strode along the path from Kilkhampton village to Stowe with a bacon-hog of three
hundredweight thrown across his shoulders, and merely
because a taunting butcher had doubted his strength
for the feat. Among the excellences of Sir Beville's
Giant, it is told of him that he was by no means
clumsy or uncouth, as men of unusual size sometimes
are, but as nimble and elastic, and as capable of swift
and dexterous movement, as a light and muscular man.
Added to this, his was a strong and acute intellect; so
happy also in his language, and of such a ready wit,

that he was called by a writer of the last century, from his resemblance, in these points only, to Shakespeare's knight, "the Falstaff of the West."

But a great and sudden change was about to come over the happy halls of Stowe. The king and his Parliament were at fatal strife; and there could be but one place in the land for the true-hearted and chivalrous Sir Beville, and that was at his royal master's side. The well-known rallying cry went through the hills and valleys of Cornwall, "Granville's up!" and the hearts and hands of many a noble knight and man-at-arms turned towards old Stowe. Mounted messengers rode to and fro. Strange and stalwart forms arrived to claim a place in the ranks. Retainers were enrolled day and night; and the smooth sward of the bowling-green and the Fawn's Paddock were dinted by the hoofs of horses and the tread of serried men. Foremost among these scenes we find, as body-guard of his master, the bulky form of Antony Payne. He marshalled and manœuvred the rude levies from the western mines, "the underground men." He served out arms and rations, and established order, by the mere terror of his presence and strength, among the wild and mixed multitude that gathered "for the king and land."

Instead of the glad and hospitable scenery of former times, Stowe became in those days like a garrison surrounded by a camp. At last, one day tidings arrived that the battalions of the Parliament, led by Lord Stamford, were on their way northwards, and not many miles off. A picked and goodly company marched forth from the avenue of Stowe, and among them Payne, on his Cornish cob Samson, of pure Guinhilly breed. The next day, eight miles toward the south, the battle of

Stratton Hill was fought and won by the royal troops. The Earl of Stamford was repulsed, and fled, bequeathing, by a strange mischance, his own name, though the defeated commander, to the field of battle. It is called to this day Stamford Hill. Sir Beville returned that night to Stowe, but his Giant remained with some other soldiers to bury the dead. He had caused certain large trenches to be laid open, each to hold ten bodies side by side. There he and his followers carried in the slain. On one occasion they had laid down nine corpses, and Payne was bringing in another, tucked under his arm, like one of "the kittens" of his schoolboy days, when all at once the supposed dead man was heard pleading earnestly with him, and expostulating, "Surely you wouldn't bury me, Mr Payne, before I am dead?" "I tell thee, man," was the grim reply, "our trench was dug for ten, and there's nine in already ; you must take your place." "But I bean't dead, I say ; I haven't done living yet; be massyful, Mr Payne—don't ye hurry a poor fellow into the earth before his time." "I won't hurry thee: I mean to put thee down quietly and cover thee up, and then thee canst die at thy leisure." Payne's purpose, however, was kinder than his speech. He carried his suppliant carefully to his own cottage, not far off, and charged his wife to stanch, if possible, her husband's rebellious blood. The man lived, and his descendants are among the principal inhabitants of the town of Stratton to this day.

That same year the battle of Lansdown, near Bath, was fought. The forces of the Parliament prevailed, and Sir Beville nobly died. Payne was still at his side, and when his master fell, he mounted young John Granville, a youth of sixteen, whom he had always in charge, on his father's horse, and he led the Granville troop into the fight. A letter which the faithful retainer wrote to his lady at Stowe still survives. It breathes in the quaint language of the day a noble strain of sympathy and homage. Thus it ran:—

"HONOURED MADAM,—Ill news flieth apace. The heavy tidings no doubt hath already travelled to Stowe that we have lost our blessed master by the enemy's advantage. You must not, dear lady, grieve too much for your noble spouse. You know, as we all believe, that his soul was in heaven before his bones were cold. He fell, as he did often tell us he wished to die, in the great Stuart cause, for his country and his king. He delivered to me his last commands, and with such tender words for you and for his children as are not to be set down with my poor pen, but must come to your ears upon my best heart's breath. Master John, when I mounted him on his father's horse, rode him into the war like a young prince, as he is, and our men followed him with their swords drawn and with tears in their eyes. They did say they would kill a rebel for every hair of Sir Beville's beard. But I bade them remember their good master's word, when he wiped his sword after Stamford fight; how he said, when their cry was, 'Stab and slay!' 'Halt, men! God will avenge.' I am coming down with mournfullest load that ever a poor servant did bear, to bring the great heart that is cold to Kilkhampton vault. Oh, my lady, how shall I ever brook your weeping face? But I will be trothful to the living and to the dead.

"These, honoured madam, from thy saddest, truest servant, ANTONY PAYNE."

At the Restoration the Stowe Giant reappears upon

the scene, in attendance on his young master, John
Granville.   Sir Beville's son had been instrumental in
the return of the king, and had received from Charles
II. largess of money, great offices, and the earldom of
Bath.   Among other places of trust, he was appointed
Governor of the Garrison at Plymouth.   There Payne
received the appointment of Halberdier of the Guns,
and the king, who held him in singular favour, commanded his portrait to be painted by the Court artist,
Sir Godfrey Kneller.   The fate of this picture was one
of great vicissitude.   It hung in state for some years in
the great gallery at Stowe; thence, when that mansion
was dismantled at the death of the Earl of Bath, it
was removed to Penheale, another manor-house of the
Granvilles, in Cornwall; but it ceased to be highly
esteemed, from the ignorance of the people and the
oblivion of years, insomuch so that when Gilbert, the
Cornish historian, travelled through the county to
collect materials for his work, he discovered the portrait rolled up in an empty room, and described by the
farmer's wife as "a carpet with the effigy of a large
man upon it."   It was a gift to her husband, she said,
from the landlord's steward, and she was glad to sell it
as she did for £8!   When Gilbert died his collection of
antique curiosities was sold by auction at Devonport,
where he lived, and this portrait of Payne, which had
been engraved as the frontispiece to the second volume
of his 'History of Cornwall,' was bought by a stranger
who was passing through the town, and who had strolled
in to look at the sale, at the price of forty guineas.   The
value had been apparently enhanced by oil, and varnish,
and frame.   This stranger proved to be a connoisseur
in paintings: he conveyed it to London, and there it
was ascertained to be one of the masterpieces of Kneller;

it was resold for the enormous sum of £800. This picture, or even the engraving in Gilbert's work, reveals still to the eye the Giant of Old Stowe, "in his natural presentment" as he lived. There he stands before the eye, a stalwart soldier of the guard. One hand is placed upon a cannon, and the other wields the tall halberd of his rank and office as yeoman of the guns. By a strange accident this very weapon and a large flask or flagon, sheathed in wicker-work, which is said to have held "Antony's allowance," a gallon of wine, and which is placed in the picture on the ground at his feet—both these relics of the time and the man are now in the possession of the writer of this article, in the Vicarage House, near Stowe. It was in Plymouth garrison, and in his later days, that an event is recorded of Payne which testifies that even after long years "his eye had not grown dim, neither was his natural force abated." The Revolution had come and gone, and William and Mary had been enthroned. At the mess-table of the regiment in garrison, on the anniversary of the day when Charles I. had been beheaded, a sub-officer of Payne's own rank had ordered a calf's head to be served up in a "William-and-Mary dish." This, in those days of new devotion to the house of Hanover, was a coarse and common annual mockery of the beheaded king; and delf, with the faces of these two sovereigns for ornament, was a valued ware (the writer has one large dish). When Payne entered the room, his comrades pointed out to him the insulting and practical jest—to him, too, most offensive, for he was a Stuart man. With a ready and indignant gesture he threw out of the window the symbolic platter and its contents.

A fierce quarrel ensued and a challenge, and at break

of day Payne and his antagonist fought with swords
on the ramparts.   After a strong contest — for the
offender was a master of his weapon—Payne ran his
adversary through the sword-arm and disabled him.
He is said to have accompanied the successful thrust
with the taunting shout, "There's sauce for thy calf's
head!"   When the strong man at last began to bow
himself down at the approach of one stronger than he,
the Giant of Stowe obtained leave to retire.   He returned to Stratton, his native place, and found shelter
and repose in the very house and chamber wherein he
was born.

    After his death, neither the door nor the stairs would
afford egress for the large and coffined corpse.   The
joists had to be sawn through, and the floor lowered
with rope and pulley, to enable the Giant to pass out
towards his mighty grave.   Relays of strong bier-men
carried him to his rest, and the bells of the tower, by
his own express desire, "chimed him home."   He was
buried outside the southern wall of Stratton church.
When the writer was a boy, the sexton one day broke,
by accident, through the side wall of a vast but empty
sepulchre.   Many went to see the sight, and there,
marked by a stone in the wall, was a vault, like the
tomb of the Anakim, large enough in these days for
the interment of three or four of our degenerate dead.
But it was empty, desolate, and bare.   No mammoth
bones nor mysterious relics of the unknown dead.   A
massive heap of silent dust!

CRUEL COPPINGER.[1]

A RECORD of the wild, strange, lawless characters that roamed along the north coast of Cornwall during the middle and latter years of the last century would be a volume full of interest for the student of local history and semi-barbarous life. Therein would be found depicted the rough sea-captain, half smuggler, half pirate, who ran his lugger by beacon-light into some rugged cove among the massive headlands of the shore, and was relieved of his freight by the active and diligent "country-side." This was the name allotted to that chosen troop of native sympathisers who were always ready to rescue and conceal the stores that had escaped the degradation of the gauger's brand. Men yet alive relate with glee how they used to rush at some well-known signal to the strand, their small active horses shaved from forelock to tail, smoother than any modern clip, well soaped or greased from head to foot, so as to slip easily out of any hostile grasp ; and then, with a double keg or pack slung on

From 'All the Year Round,' vol. xvi. pp. 537-540. 1866.

to every nag by a single girth, away went the whole herd, led by some swift well-trained mare, to the inland cave or rocky hold, the shelter of their spoil. There was a famous dun mare—she lived to the age of thirty-seven, and died within legal memory—almost human in her craft and fidelity, who is said to have led a bevy of loaded pack-horses, unassisted by driver or guide, from Bossinney Haun to Roughtor Point. But beside these travellers by sea, there would be found ever and anon, in some solitary farmhouse inaccessible by wheels, and only to be approached by some treacherous foot-path along bog and mire, a strange and nameless guest —often a foreigner in language and apparel—who had sought refuge with the native family, and who paid in strange but golden coins for his shelter and food ; some political or private adventurer, perchance, to whom secrecy and concealment were safety and life, and who more than once lived and died in his solitary hiding-place on the moor.

There is a bedstead of carved oak still in existence at Trevotter—a farm among the midland hills—whereon for long years an unknown stranger slept. None ever knew his nation or name. He occupied a solitary room, and only emerged now and then for a walk in the evening air. An oaken chest of small size contained his personal possessions and gold of foreign coinage, which he paid into the hands of his host with the solemn charge to conceal it until he was gone thence or dead—a request which the simple - hearted people faithfully fulfilled. His linen was beautifully fine, and his garments richly embroidered. After some time he sickened and died, refusing firmly the visits of the local clergyman, and bequeathing to the farmer the contents of his chest. He wrote some words, they said, for his own tombstone, which, however, were not allowed to be engraved, but they were simply these—"H. De R. Equees & Ecsul." The same sentence was found, after his death, carved on the ledge of his bed, and the letters are, or lately were, still traceable on the mouldering wood.

But among the legends of local renown a prominent place has always been allotted to a personage whose name has descended to our times linked to a weird and graphic epithet—"Cruel Coppinger." There was a ballad in existence within human memory which was founded on the history of this singular man, but of which the first verse only can now be recovered. It runs—

> " Will you hear of the Cruel Coppinger ?
> He came from a foreign kind :
> He was brought to us by the salt-water,
> He was carried away by the wind."

His arrival on the north coast of Cornwall was signalised by a terrific hurricane. The storm came up Channel from the south - west. The shore and the heights were dotted with watchers for wreck—those daring gleaners of the harvest of the sea. It was just such a scene as is sought for in the proverb of the West—

> " A savage sea and a shattering wind,
> The cliffs before, and the gale behind."

As suddenly as if a phantom ship had loomed in the distance, a strange vessel of foreign rig was discovered in fierce struggle with the waves of Harty Race. She was deeply laden or water-logged, and rolled heavily in the trough of the sea, nearing the shore as she felt the tide. Gradually the pale and dismayed faces of the crew became visible, and among them one man of

G

herculeau height and mould, who stood near the wheel
with a speaking-trumpet in his hand. The sails were
blown to rags, and the rudder was apparently lashed
for running ashore. But the suck of the current and
the set of the wind were too strong for the vessel,
and she appeared to have lost her chance of reaching
Harty Pool. It was seen that the tall seaman, who
was manifestly the skipper of the boat, had cast off
his garments, and stood prepared upon the deck to
encounter a battle with the surges for life and rescue.
He plunged over the bulwarks, and arose to sight
buffeting the seas. With stalwart arm and powerful
chest he made his way through the surf, rode manfully
from billow to billow, until with a bound he stood at
last upright upon the sand, a fine stately semblance of
one of the old Vikings of the northern seas. A crowd
of people had gathered from the land, on horseback and
on foot, women as well as men, drawn together by the
tidings of a probable wreck. Into their midst, and to
their astonished dismay, rushed the dripping stranger :
he snatched from a terrified old dame her red Welsh
cloak, cast it loosely around him, and bounded suddenly
upon the crupper of a young damsel, who had ridden
her father's horse down to the beach to see the sight.
He grasped her bridle, and, shouting aloud in some
foreign language, urged on the double-laden animal
into full speed, and the horse naturally took his homeward way. Strange and wild were the outcries that
greeted the rider, Miss Dinah Hamlyn, when, thus
escorted, she reached her father's door in the very
embrace of a wild, rough, tall man, who announced
himself by a name — never afterwards forgotten in
those parts—as Coppinger, a Dane. He arrayed himself without the smallest scruple in the Sunday suit of

his host. The long-skirted coat of purple velveteen with large buttons, the embroidered vest, and nether garments to match, became him well. So thought the lady of his sudden choice. She, no doubt, forgave his onslaught on her and on her horse for the compliment it conveyed. He took his immediate place at the family board, and on the settle by the hearth, as though he had been the most welcome and long-invited guest in the land. Strange to say, the vessel disappeared immediately he had left her deck, nor was she ever after traced by land or sea. At first the stranger subdued all the fierce phases of his savage character, and appeared deeply grateful for all the kindness he received at the hands of his simple - hearted host. Certain letters which he addressed to persons of high name in Denmark were, or were alleged to be, duly answered, and remittances from his friends were supposed to be received. He announced himself as of a wealthy family and superior rank in his native country, and gave out that it was to avoid a marriage with a titled lady that he had left his father's house and gone to sea. All this recommended him to the unsuspecting Dinah, whose affections he completely won. Her father's sudden illness postponed their marriage. The good old man died to be spared much evil to come.

The Dane succeeded almost naturally to the management and control of the house, and the widow held only an apparent influence in domestic affairs. He soon persuaded the daughter to become his wife, and immediately afterwards his evil nature, so long smouldering, broke out like a wild beast uncaged. All at once the house became the den and refuge of every lawless character on the coast. All kinds of wild

uproar and reckless revelry appalled the neighbourhood day and night. It was discovered that an
organised band of desperadoes, smugglers, wreckers,
and poachers were embarked in a system of bold
adventure, and that "Cruel Coppinger" was their
captain. In those days, and in that unknown and
far-away region, the peaceable inhabitants were totally
unprotected. There was not a single resident gentleman of property or weight in the entire district; and
the clergyman, quite insulated from associates of his
own standing, was cowed into silence and submission.
No revenue officer durst exercise vigilance west of the
Tamar; and to put an end to all such surveillance at
once, it was well known that one of the "Cruel" gang
had chopped off a gauger's head on the gunwale of a
boat, and carried the body off to sea.

Amid such scenes Coppinger pursued his unlawful
impulses without check or restraint. Strange vessels
began to appear at regular intervals on the coast, and
signals were duly flashed from the headlands to lead
them into the safest creek or cove. If the ground-sea
were too strong to allow them to run in, they anchored
outside the surf, and boats prepared for that service
were rowed or hauled to and fro, freighted with illegal
spoil. Amongst these vessels, one, a full-rigged schooner,
soon became ominously conspicuous. She bore the
name of the Black Prince, and was the private property
of the Dane, built to his own order in a dockyard of
Denmark. She was for a long time the chief terror of
the Cornish Channel. Once with Coppinger on board,
when under chase, she led a revenue cutter into an in-
tricate channel near the Gull Rock, where, from knowledge of the bearings, the Black Prince escaped scath-
less, while the king's vessel perished with all on board.

In those times, if any landsman became obnoxious to Coppinger's men, he was either seized by violence or by craft, and borne away handcuffed to the deck of the Black Prince; where, to save his life, he had to enrol himself, under fearful oaths, as one of the crew. In 1835, an old man of the age of ninety-seven related to the writer that, when a youth, he had been so abducted, and after two years' service had been ransomed by his friends with a large sum. "And all," said the old man, very simply, "because I happened to see one man kill another, and they thought I should mention it."

Amid such practices ill-gotten gold began to flow and ebb in the hands of Coppinger. At one time he chanced to hold enough money to purchase a freehold farm bordering on the sea. When the day of transfer arrived, he and one of his followers appeared before the astonished lawyer with bags filled with various kinds of foreign coin. Dollars and ducats, doubloons and pistoles, guineas—the coinage of every foreign country with a seaboard—were displayed on the table. The man of law at first demurred to such purchase-money; but after some controversy, and an ominous oath or two of "that or none," the lawyer agreed to take it by weight. The document bearing Coppinger's name is still extant. His signature is traced in stern, bold, fierce characters, as if every letter had been stabbed upon the parchment with the point of a dirk. Underneath his autograph, also in his own writing, is the word "Thuro."

Long impunity increased Coppinger's daring. There were certain byways and bridle-roads along the fields over which he exercised exclusive control. Although every one had a perfect right by law to use these ways, he issued orders that no man was to pass over them by night, and accordingly from that hour none ever did. They were called " Coppinger's Tracks." They all converged at a headland which had the name of Steeple Brink. Here the cliff sheered off, and stood three hundred feet of perpendicular height, a precipice of smooth rock toward the beach, with an overhanging face one hundred feet down from the brow. There was a hollow entrance into the cliff, like a huge cathedral - door, crowned and surrounded with natural Saxon arches, curved by the strata of native stone. Within was an arched and vaulted cave, vast and gloomy; it ran a long way into the heart of the land, and was as large and tall—so the country-people said—as Kilkhampton church. This stronghold was inaccessible by natural means, and could only be approached by a cable-ladder lowered from above and made fast below on a projecting crag. It received the name of " Coppinger's Cave," and was long the scene of fierce and secret revelry that would be utterly inconceivable to the educated mind of the nineteenth century. Here sheep were tethered to the rock, and fed on stolen hay and corn till their flesh was required for a feast: kegs of brandy and hollands were piled around; chests of tea; and iron-bound sea-chests contained the chattels and the revenues of the Coppinger royalty of the sea. No man ever essayed the perilous descent into the cavern except the captain's own troop, and their loyalty was secured not only by their participation in his crimes but by a terrible oath.

The terror linked with Coppinger's name throughout the coast was so extreme that the people themselves, wild and lawless as they were, submitted to his sway as though he had been the lord of the soil and they his vassals. Such a household as Coppinger's was of course far from happy or calm. Although when his wife's

father died he had insensibly acquired possession of the
stock and farm, there remained in the hands of the
widow a considerable amount of money as her dower.
This he obtained from the poor helpless woman by in-
stalments; and when pretext and entreaty alike failed,
he resorted to a novel mode of levy. He fastened his
wife to the pillar of her oak bedstead, and called her
mother into the room. He. then explained that it was
his purpose to flog Dinah with the sea-cat, which he
flourished in his hand, until her mother had transferred
to him such an amount as he required of her reserved
property. This deed of atrocity he repeated until he
had utterly exhausted the widow's store. He had a
favourite mare, so fierce and indomitable that none but
Coppinger himself could venture on her back, and so
fleet and strong that he owed his escape from more than
one menacing peril by her speed and endurance. The
clergyman had spoken above his breath of the evil
doings in the cave, and had thus aroused his wrath and
vengeance. On a certain day he was jogging homeward
on his parish cob, and had reached the middle of a wide
and desolate heath. All at once he heard behind him
the clattering of horse-hoofs and a yell such as might
have burst from the throat of the visible demon when
he hurled the battle on the ancient saint. It was Cruel
Coppinger with his double-thonged whip, mounted on
his terrible mare. Down came the fearful scourge on
his victim's shuddering shoulders. Escape was impossible. The poor parson knew too well the difference
between his own ambling galloway, that never essayed
any swifter pace than a jog-trot, and that awful steed
behind him with footsteps like the storm. Circling,
doubling like a hare, twisting aside, crying aloud for
mercy,—all was vain. He arrived at last at his own

house, striped like a zebra, and as he rushed in at the
gate he heard the parting scoff of his assailant, " There,
parson, I have paid my tithe in full ; never mind the
receipt ! "

It was on the self-same animal that Coppinger performed another freak. He had passed a festive evening
at a farmhouse, and was about to take his departure,
when he spied at the corner of the hearth a little old
tailor of the country-side, who went from house to
house to exercise his calling. He was a half-witted,
harmless old fellow, and answered to the name of Uncle
Tom Tape.

" Ha, Uncle Tom ! " cried Coppinger; " we both travel
the same road, and I don't mind giving thee a hoist behind me on the mare."

The old man cowered in the settle. He would not
encumber the gentleman,—was unaccustomed to ride
such a spirited horse. But all his excuses were over-
borne. The other guests, entering into the joke, assisted
the trembling old man to mount the crupper of the
capering mare. Off she bounded, and Uncle Tom, with
his arms cast with the strong gripe of terror around his
bulky companion, held on like grim death. Unbuckling
his belt, Coppinger passed it around Uncle Tom's thin
haggard body, and buckled it on his own front. When
he had firmly secured his victim, he loosened his reins,
and urged the mare with thong and spur into a furious
gallop. Onward they rushed till they fled past the
tailor's own door at the roadside, where his startled
wife, who was on the watch, afterwards declared " she
caught sight of her husband clinging on to a rainbow."
Loud and piteous were the outcries of Tailor Tom, and
earnest his shrieks of entreaty that he might be told
where he was to be carried that night, and for what

doom he had been buckled on. At last, in a relaxation of their pace going up a steep hill, Coppinger made him a confidential communication.

"I have been," he said, "under a long promise to the devil that I would bring him a tailor to make and mend for him, poor man; and as sure as I breathe, Uncle Tom, I mean to keep my word to-night!"

The agony of terror produced by this revelation produced such convulsive spasms, that at last the belt gave way, and the tailor fell off like a log among the gorse at the roadside. There he was found next morning in a semi-delirious state, muttering at intervals, "No, no; I never will. Let him mend his breeches with his own drag-chain, as the saying is. I will never so much as thread a needle for Coppinger nor his friend."

One boy was the only fruit of poor Dinah's marriage with the Dane. But his birth brought neither gladness nor solace to his mother's miserable hearth. He was fair and golden-haired, and had his father's fierce, flashing eyes. But though perfectly well formed and healthful, he was born deaf and dumb. He was mischievous and ungovernable from his birth. His cruelty to animals, birds, and to other children was intense. Any living thing that he could torture appeared to yield him delight. With savage gestures and jabbering moans he haunted the rocks along the shore, and seemed like some uncouth creature cast up by the sea. When he was only six years old he was found one day upon the brink of a tall cliff, bounding with joy, and pointing downward towards the beach with convulsions of delight. There, mangled by the fall and dead, they found the body of a neighbour's child of his own age, who was his frequent companion, and whom, as it was inferred, he had drawn towards the steep precipice, and urged

over by stratagem or force. The spot where this occurred was ever afterwards his favourite haunt. He
would draw the notice of any passer-by to the place, and
then point downward where the murdered child was
found with fierce exultant mockery. It was a saying
evermore in the district, that, as a judgment on his
father's cruelty, his child had been born without a
human soul. He lived to be the pestilent scourge of
the neighbourhood.

But the end arrived. Money had become scarce, and
the resources of the cave began to fail. More than one
armed king's cutter were seen day and night hovering
off the land. Foreigners visited the house with tidings
of peril. So he " who came with the water went with
the wind." His disappearance, like his arrival, was
commemorated by a turbulent storm. A wrecker, who
had gone to watch the shore, saw, as the sun went down,
a full-rigged vessel standing off and on. By-and-by a
rocket hissed up from the Gull Rock, a small islet with
a creek on the landward side which had been the scene
of many a run of smuggled cargo. A gun from the ship
answered it, and again both signals were exchanged.
At last a well-known and burly form stood on the topmost crag of the island rock. He waved his sword, and
the light flashed back from the steel. A boat put off
from the vessel with two hands at every oar—for the
tide runs with double violence through Harty Race.
They neared the rocks, rowed daringly through the surf,
and were steered by some practised coxswain into the
Gull Creek. There they found their man. Coppinger
leaped on board the boat, and assumed the command.
They made with strong efforts for their ship. It was a
path of peril through that boiling surf. Still, bending
at the oar like chained giants, the man watched them

till they forced their way through the battling waters. Once, as they drew off the shore, one of the rowers, either from ebbing strength or loss of courage, drooped at his oar. In a moment a cutlass gleamed over his head, and a fierce stern stroke cut him down. It was the last blow of Cruel Coppinger. He and his boat's crew boarded the vessel, and she was out of sight in a moment, like a spectre or a ghost. Thunder, lightning, and hail ensued. Trees were rent up by the roots around the pirate's abode. Poor Dinah watched, and held in her shuddering arms her idiot-boy, and, strange to say, a meteoric stone, called in that country a storm-bolt, fell through the roof into the room at the very feet of Cruel Coppinger's vacant chair.

THOMASINE BONAVENTURE.[1]

THE aspect of rural England during the fifteenth and sixteenth centuries must have presented a strange and striking contrast, in the eye of a traveller, to the agricultural scenery of our own time. Thinly peopled —for the three millions of our chief city nowadays are in excess of the total population of the whole land of the Edwards and the Henrys—the inhabitants occupied hamlets few and far between, and a farm or grange signified usually a moated house amid a cluster of cultivated fields, gathered within fences from the surrounding forest or wold, and gleaming in the distance with rich or green enclosures, rescued from the wilderness, to give "fodder to the cattle, and bread to strengthen the heart of man." But the great domains of the land for the most part expanded into woodland and marsh and moor, with glades or grassy avenues here and there for access to the lair of the red deer or the wild boar, or other native game, which afforded in that day a principal supply of human food. Yonder in

[1] From 'All the Year Round,' vol. xvii. pp. 276-280. 1867.

the distance appeared ever and anon a beacon-tower,
which marked the place and ward for the warning of
hostile advances by night, and for the gathering rest of
the hobbelars or horsemen, whose office it was to scour
the country and to keep in awe the enemies of God and
the king. Wheel-roads, except in the neighbourhood
of cities or on the line of a royal progress, there were
none; and among the bridle-paths men urged their
difficult path in companies, for it was seldom safe for
an honest or well-to-do man to travel alone. Rivers
glided in silence to the sea without a sail or an oar to
ruffle their waters; and there were whole regions, that
now are loud with populous life, that might then have
been called void places of the uninhabited earth. But
more especially did this character of uncultured desola-
tion pervade the extreme borders of the west of England, the country between the Tamar and the sea.
There dwelt in scattered villages, or town-places as
they are called to this day, the bold and hardy Keltic
people, few in number, but, like the race of the Eastern
wild man, never taught to bear the yoke. Long after
other parts of England had settled into an improved
agriculture, and submitted to the discipline of more
civilised life, the Cornish were wont to hew their resources out of the bowels of their mother earth, or to
haul into their nets the native harvest of the sea.
Thus the merchandise of fish, tin, and copper became
the vaunted staple of their land. These, the rich pro-
ductions of their native county, were, even in remote
periods of our history, in perpetual request, and formed,
together with the wool of their moorland flocks, the
great trade of the Cornish people. From all parts, and
especially from that storied city whose merchants were
then, as now, princes of the land, men were wont to

encounter the perilous journey from the Thames to the
Tamar, to pursue their traffic with the "underground
folk," as they termed the inhabitants of Cornwall, that
rocky land of strangers, as, when literally interpreted,
is the exact meaning of its name.

It was in the year 1463, when Edward IV. occupied
the English throne, that a tall and portly merchant,
in the distinctive apparel of the times, rode along the
wilds of a Cornish moor. He sat high and firm upon
his horse, a bony gelding, with demipique saddle. A
broad beaver, or, as it was then called, a Flanders hat,
shaded a grave and thoughtful countenance, wherein
shrewdness and good-humour struggled for the mastery
and the latter prevailed, and his full brown beard was
forked—a happy omen, as it was always held, of prosperous life. His riding garb displayed that contrast of
colours which was then so valued by native taste, insomuch that the phrase "motley" had in its origin a
complimentary and not an invidious sound. Behind
him and near rode his servant, a stout and active-
looking knave, armed to the teeth.

The traveller had crossed the ford of a moorland
stream, when he halted and reined up at a scene that
greeted him on the bank. There, on a green and rushy
knoll and underneath a gnarled and wind-swept tree,
a damsel in the blossom of youth stood leaning on her
shepherd-staff: her companion, a peasant boy, drew
back, half shaded by a rock. Sheep of the native breed,
the long-forgotten Cornish Knott, gathered around. As
he drew nigh, the stranger discovered that the maiden
was tall and well formed, and that her rounded limbs
had the mould and movement of a natural grace that
only health and exercise could develop or bestow. The
sure evidence of her Keltic origin was testified by her

eyes of violet-blue and abundant hair of rich and radiant brown—the hue that Italian poets delight to describe as the colour of the ripe chestnut, or the stalks and fibres of the maidenhair fern. She had also the bashful nose that appears to retreat from the lip with the unmistakable curve of the Kelt. She was clad in a grey kirtle of native wool, and her bodice also was knitted at the hearth by homely hands. The merchant was first to speak.

" Be not scared," said he, " fair damsel, by a stranger's voice. My name is John Bunsby, of the city of London, and I am bound for the hostel of Wike St Marie, which must be somewhere nigh this moor. What did thy gossips call thee, maiden, at the font ? "

" My name, kind sir," she answered, modestly, " is Thomasine Bonaventure, and my father's house is hard by at Wike. These are my master's sheep."

" The evening falls fast," said the traveller; " I would fain hire safe guidance to yonder inn."

She beckoned to the youth and whispered a word in his ear, to which, however, he seemed to listen with reluctance or dislike, and then, with her crook still in her hand, she herself went on to guide the stranger on his way. They arrived in due course at the hostel-door, at the sign of the Rose : but it was the Rose, mere, and without an epithet; for mine host had wisely omitted, in those dangerous days, to designate the hue of that symbolic flower. The traveller dismounted at the door, thanked and requited his gentle guide, and signified that as soon as his leisure allowed he would find the way to her father's house. After a strict command to his own servant and the varlet of the stable that his horses should receive due vigilance and abundant food, Master Bunsby at last entered the inn. A

hecatomb of wood blazed on the hearth, shedding light
as well as heat around the panelled room—for in those
times of old simplicity a single apartment was allotted
for household purposes and for the entertainment of
guests. The traveller took an offered seat on the carved
oak settle, in the place of honour by the fire, and looked
on with interest at the homely but original scene. At
his right hand a vast oven, with an entrance not unlike
a church-door, was about to disgorge its manifold contents. Rye-loaves led the way, sweet and tasty to the
final crust (wheat was in those days a luxury unknown
in Cornwall); barley-bread and oaten cakes came forth
in due procession from the steaming cave; and, last of
all, the merchant's sight and nostrils were greeted by
the arrival of a huge and mysterious pie from its depths.
The achievements of the dame, who was both cook and
hostess in her own person, were duly and triumphantly
arrayed upon the board, and the stranger-guest took
the accustomed seat at the right hand of "mine host."
His eyes were fixed with curiosity and interest on the
hillock of brown dough which stood before him, and
reeked like a small volcano with steaming puffs of
savoury vapour. At last, when the massive crust which
lay like a tombstone over the mighty dish had been
broken up, the pie revealed its strange contents.
Conger-eels, pilchards, and oysters were mingled piece-
meal in the mass beneath, their intervals slushed with
melted better and clotted cream, and the whole well
seasoned, not without a savour of garlic, with spices,
pepper, and salt. The stranger's astonishment was
manifest in gesture and look, although he by no means
repulsed the trencher which came towards him loaded
with his bountiful share.

"Sir guest," said the host, "you doubtless know the

byword — ' The Cornish cooks make everything into
a pie.' Our grandames say that the devil never dared
cross the Tamar, or he would have been verily put
under a crust."

Satisfied with his fare, the merchant now inquired
for the dwelling-place of his guide. It was not far off.
The parents of the shepherdess inhabited a thatched
hut in the village, with the usual walls of beaten cob,
moulded of native clay: all within and without bespoke
extreme poverty and want, but there Master John
Bunsby soon found himself an honoured visitor seated
by the hearth, with a blazing fire of dry gorse gathered
from the moor to greet his arrival. There, while the
mother stood by her turn or wheel and span, and the
maiden's nimble fingers flashed her knitting-needles to
and fro by the fitful light of the fire, the old man her
father and the merchant conversed in a low voice far
into the night, on a theme of deep interest to both.
The talk was of Thomasine, the child of the house.
The merchant related his own prosperous affairs, and
spake of his goodly house in London, governed by a
thrifty and diligent wife: the household was one of
grave and decent demeanour, with good repute in the
vast city wherein dwelt the king. He had taken an
immediate interest, he declared, in the old man's
daughter, and desired to rescue her from the life she
led on the bleak unsheltered moor. He pledged himself, if they should consent, to convey her in safety to
London, and to place her in especial attendance on his
wife; and there, if her conduct were in unison with
her looks, he doubted not she would win many friends,
and secure a happy livelihood for the rest of her days.
He would await their decision at the inn, where he
should be detained by business two or three days.

H

Earnest and anxious were their thoughts and their
language in the cottage that night and the next day.
The aspect and speech of the rich patron were such
as invited confidence and trust; but there were the
love and fear of two aged hearts to satisfy and subdue. There was the fierce and stubborn repugnance
also of the youth, the companion of the maid, who stood
with her under the tree upon the moor. He was her
cousin, John Dineham, of Swannacote, and they had
grown up together from childhood, till, unconsciously
to themselves, the tenderness of kindred had strengthened into love. The damsel herself could not conceal
a natural longing to visit the great city, where they
said, but it might be untrue, "that the houses were
stuck as close together as Wike St Marie church and
tower;" but she would at all events behold for once
in her life the dwelling-place of the king. "She would
store up every coin, and come back with money enow
to buy a flock of sheep of her own, which she and John
would tend together, as aforetime, on the moor." All
this shook the scale.

When the merchant arrived to seek their decision,
it was made, and in favour of his wish. A pillion or
padded seat was obtained from some neighbouring
farm, and belted behind the saddle of the merchant's
man. Thereon, with a small fardel in her hand, which
held all her worldly goods and gear, mounted Thomasine Bonaventure, while all the villagers came around
to bid her farewell—all but one, and it was her cousin
John. He had gone, as he had told her, to the moor,
and there among the branches of the tree which
marked the greeting-place of Master Bunsby the youth
waited to watch her out of sight. He lifted up his
hand and waved it as she passed on with a gesture of

warning, but which she interpreted and returned as a silent caress.

The travellers arrived at their journey's end after being only a fortnight on the road—a speed so satisfactory and unusual, that it was Dame Bunsby's emphatic remark that she verily thought they must have flown.

Her mistress received Thomasine with a kind and hearty welcome, and ratified, by her everyday approval, her husband's choice of the Cornish maid. When she was first told that her name was Bonaventure, and her husband explained that it signified good luck, she said, "Well, sweetheart, when I was a girl they used to say that the name was a fore-sign of the life, and God grant that thine may turn out [so] to be."

Time passed on, and in a year or two the wild Cornish lass had grown into a frame of thorough symmetry, firmness, and health. Her strong thews, of country origin, rendered her capable of long and active labour, and she had acquired with gradual ease the habits and appliances of city life. She was very soon the favoured and the favourite manager of the household. Her mistress, born and reared in a town, had been long a frail and delicate woman ; and life in London in those days, as now, was fraught with the manifold perils of pestilent disease. To one of those ancient scourges of the population, the sweating - sickness, Dame Bunsby succumbed. Her death drew nigh, and, with the touching simplicity of the times, she told her true and tender husband, with smiling tears, that she thought he could not do better than, if they so agreed to put Thomasine in her place when she was gone "Tell her it was my last wish."

This gentle desire so uttered—her strong and grateful

feelings towards the master who had taken her, as she expressed it in her rural speech, lean from the moor, and fed her, so that her very bones belonged to him— her happy home, and the power she would acquire to make the latter days in the cottage at Wike St Marie prosperous and calm,—all these impulses flocked into Thomasine's heart, and controlled for the time even the remembrance of Cousin John. That poor young man, when the tidings came that she was about to become her master's wedded wife, suddenly disappeared, and for a while the place of his retreat was unknown; but it afterwards transpired that he had crossed the moor to a "house of religious men" called the White Monks of St Cleer, and pleaded for reception there as a needy novice of the gate. His earnest entreaties had prevailed; and six months after his first love, and his last, had put on her silks as a city dame, and begun her rule as the mistress of a goodly house in London, her cousin had taken the vows of his noviciate, and received the first tonsure of St John.

Her married life did not, however, long endure. Three years after the master became the husband, he took the "plague sore," and died. They were childless; but he bequeathed "all his goods and chattel property, and his well-furnished mansion, to his dear wife Thomasine Bonaventure, now Bunsby;" and the maid of the moor became one of the wealthy widows of London city. Among the MSS. which still survive, there is a letter which announces the event of her husband's death and bequest, and then proceeds to notify her solemn donation, as a year's-mind of Master Bunsby, of ten marks to the Reeve of Wike St Marie, "to the intent that he shall cause skeelful masons to build a bridge at the Ford of Green-a-Moor; yea, and

with stout stonework well laid; and see," she wrote,
" that they do no harm to that tree which standeth fast
by the brook, neither dispoyle they the rushes and
plants that grow thereby; for there did I passe many
goodly hours when I was a simple mayde, and there
did I first see the kind face of a fathful frend." But
in another missive to her mother, about the same date,
there is a touch of tenderness which shows that her
woman's nature survived all changes, and was strong
within her still. She writes: " I know that Cousin
John is engaged to the monks of St Cleer. Hath he
been shorn, as they do call it, for the second time ?
Inquire, I beseech, if he seeketh to dispart from that
cell ? And will red gold help him away ? I am pros-
pered in pouch and coffer, and he need not shame
to be indebted unto me, that owe so much to him."
But this frank and kindly effort—" the late remorse
of love "—did not avail. John had broken the last
link that bound him to the world, and was lost to
love and her. Reckless thenceforward therefore, if
not fancy-free, and it may be somewhat schooled by
the habits and associations of city life, she did not wear
the widow's wimple long. After an interval of years,
we find her the honoured wife " of that worshipful
merchant-adventurer, Master John Gall of St Law-
rence, Milk Street."

Gall was very rich, and he appears to have emptied
his money-bags into his wife's lap, as the gossip of the
city ran, for it is on record that soon after her second
marriage she manifested her prosperity like a true-
hearted Cornish woman by ample " gifts " and largess
to the borough of St Marie, " my native place."
Twenty acres of woodland copse in the neighbourhood
were bought and conveyed by that kind and gracious

lady, Dame Thomasine Gall, to feoffees and trust-men
for the perpetual use of the poor of the paroche, "for
fewel to be hewn in parcels once a-year, and justly
and equally divided for evermore on the vigil of St
Thomas the twin." To her mother she sends by " a
waggon which has gone on an enterprise into Cornwall
for woollen merchandise, a chest with array of clothing,
fair weather and foul, head-gear and body raiment to
boot, all the choice and costly gifts to my loving parents of my goodman Gall, and in remembrance, as
he chargeth me to say, that ye have reared for him a
kindly and loving wife." But the graphic and touching passage in this letter is the message which suc-
ceeds: "Lo! I do send you also herewithal in the
coffer a litel boke: it is for a gift to my Cousin John.
Tell him it is not written as the whilom usage was
and he was wont to teach me my Christ Cross Rhime;
but it is what they do call emprinted with a strange
device of an iron engin brought from forrin parts.
Bid him not despise it, for although it is so small that
it will lie on the palm of your hand, yet it did cost me
full five marks in exchange." But her marriage life
was doomed to bring her only brief and transitory intervals of wedded happiness. Five years after the
date of her letter above quoted, she was again alone
in the house. Master Gall died, but not until he had
endowed his " tender wife with all and singular his
moneys and plate, bills, bonds, and ventures now at
sea," &c., with a long inventory of the "precious things
beneath the moon," too long to rehearse, but each and
all to the sole use, enjoyment, and behoof of Dame
Thomasine, whose maiden name of Bonaventure was
literally interpreted and fulfilled in every successive
change of station.

We greet her then once more as a rich and buxom widow of city fame. Her wealth, added to her comeliness—for she was still in the prime of life—brought many "a potent, grave, and reverend seignor" to her feet, and to sue for her hand. Nor did she long linger in her choice. The favoured suitor now was Sir John Perceval, goldsmith and usurer—that is to say, banker, in the phrase of that day ; very wealthy, of high repute, alderman of his ward, and in such a position of civic advancement that he would have been described in modern language as next the chair. He wooed and won the " Golden Widow "—for so, because of her double inheritance of the wealth of two rich husbands, she was merrily named. Their wedding was a kind of public festival, and the bride, in acknowledgment of her own large possessions, was invested with a stately dower at the church-door. One year after their marriage her husband, Sir John, was elected to that honourable office which is still supposed by foreign nations to be only second in rank to that of the monarch on the throne, Lord Mayor of the city of London.

Thus, by a strange succession of singular events, the barefooted shepherdess of a Cornish moorland became the Lady Mayoress of metropolitan fame; and the legend of Thomasine Bonaventure—for it was now well known—was the popular theme of royal and noble interest among the lords and ladies of the Court. She demeaned herself bravely and decorously in her ascent among the great and lofty ones of the land. Like all noble natures, her spirit rose with her personal elevation, and took equal place with her compeers of each superior rank. Nor did her true and simple woman's nature undergo any depreciation or change. It breathes and survives in every sentence of her family letters, transcripts of which have been perpetuated and preserved to our own times. One part of her personal history is illustrative of a scene of life and manners when Henry VII. was king.

"Sweet mother," she wrote, "thy daughter hath seen the face of the king. We were bidden to a banket at the royal palace, and Sir John and I dared not choose but go. There was such a blaze of lords and ladies in silks and samite, and jewels and gold, that it was like the city of New Jerusalem in the Scriptures; and I, thy maid Thomasine, was arrayed so fine, that they brought up the saying that I was dressed like an altar. When we were led into the chamber of dais, where his highness stood, the king did kiss me on the cheek, as the manner is, and he seemed gentle and kind. But then did he turn to my good lord and husband, and say, with a look stark and stern enow, ' Ha, Sir John ! see to it that thy fair dame be liege and true, for she comes of the burly Cornish kind, and they be ever rebels in blood and bone. Even now they be one and all for that knave Warbeck, who is among them in the West.' You will gesse, dear mother, how my heart did beat. But withal the king did drink to me at the banket, and did merrily call, 'Health to our Lady Mayoress, Dame Thomasine Perceval, which now feedeth her flock in the rich pastures of our city of London.' And thereat they did laugh, and fleer, and shout, and there was flashing of tankards and jingling of cups all down the hall."

With increase of wealth came also many a renewed token of affectionate regard and sterling bounty to her old and well-beloved dwelling-place of Wike St Marie. As her wedding-gift of remembrance she directed that "a firm and steadfast road should be laid down with

stones," at her whole cost, along the midst of Green-a-
Moor, and fit for man and beast to travel on, with their
lawful occasions, from Lanstaphadon to the sea. At
another time, and for a New Year's gift, she gave the
sum of forty marks towards the building of a tower for
St Stephen's church, above the causeway of Dunheved;
and it was her desire that they should carry their
pinnacles so tall that "they might be seen from Swannacote Cross, by the moor, to the intent that they who
do behold it from the Burgage Mound may remember
the poor maid which is now a wedded dame of London
citie."

During her three marriages she had no children, and
it was her singular lot to survive her third husband,
Sir John: it was in long widowhood after him that she
lived and died. Her will, bearing date the vigil of the
Feast of Christmas, A.D. 1510, is a singular document,
for therein the memory and the impulses of her early
life are recalled and condensed. She bequeaths large
sums of money to be laid out and invested in land for
the welfare of the village borough, whereto, amid all
the strange vicissitudes of her existence, her heart had
always clung with fond and lingering regret. She
directs that a chantry with cloisters was to be built
near the church of Wike St Marie, at the discretion
and under the control of her executor and cousin, John
Dincham, the unforgotten priest. She endows it with
thirty marks by the year, and provides that there shall
be established therein "a schole for young children
born in the paroche of Wike St Marie; and such to be
always preferred as are friendless and poor." They are
to be "taught to read with their fescue from a boke of
horn, and also to write, and both as the manner was in
that country when I was young." The well-remem-

bered days of her girlhood appear to tinge every line
of her last will. Her very codicil is softened with a
touch of her first and fondest love. In it she gives to
the priest of the church, where she well knew that her
cousin John would serve and sing, "the silver chalice
gilt, which good Master Maskelyne the goldsmith had
devised for her behoof, with a leetle blue flower which
they do call a forget-me-not wrought in Turkess at the
bottom of the bowl, to the intent that whensoever it is
used the minister may remember her who was once a
simple shepherd-maid by the wayside of Wike St Marie,
and who was so wonderfully brought by many great
changes to be the Mayoress of London citie before she
died."

THE BOTATHEN GHOST.[1]

THERE was something very painful and peculiar in the position of the clergy in the west of England throughout the seventeenth century. The Church of those days was in a transitory state, and her ministers, like her formularies, embodied a strange mixture of the old belief with the new interpretation. Their wide severance also from the great metropolis of life and manners, the city of London (which in those times was civilised England, much as the Paris of our own day is France), divested the Cornish clergy in particular of all personal access to the master-minds of their age and body. Then, too, the barrier interposed by the rude rough roads of their country, and by their abode in wilds that were almost inaccessible, rendered the existence of a bishop rather a doctrine suggested to their belief than a fact revealed to the actual vision of each in his generation. Hence it came to pass that the Cornish clergyman, insulated within his own limited sphere, often without even the presence of a country squire (and un-

---

[1] From 'All the Year Round,' vol. xvii. pp. 501-504. 1867.

checked by the influence of the Fourth Estate—for until
the beginning of this nineteenth century, 'Flindell's
Weekly Miscellany,' distributed from house to house
from the pannier of a mule, was the only light of the
West), became developed about middle life into an original mind and man, sole and absolute within his parish
boundary, eccentric when compared with his brethren
in civilised regions, and yet, in German phrase, "a
whole and seldom man " in his dominion of souls. He
was " the parson," in canonical phrase—that is to say,
The Person, the somebody of consequence among his
own people. These men were not, however, smoothed
down into a monotonous aspect of life and manners by
this remote and secluded existence. They imbibed,
each in his own peculiar circle, the hue of surrounding
objects, and were tinged into distinctive colouring and
character by many a contrast of scenery and people.
There was "the light of other days," the curate by the
sea-shore, who professed to check the turbulence of the
" smugglers' landing " by his presence on the sands, and
who "held the lantern" for the guidance of his flock
when the nights were dark, as the only proper ecclesiastical part he could take in the proceedings. He was
soothed and silenced by the gift of a keg of hollands or
a chest of tea. There was the merry minister of the
mines, whose cure was honeycombed by the underground men. He must needs have been artist and poet
in his way, for he had to enliven his people three or
four times a-year by mastering the arrangements of a
"guary," or religious mystery, which was duly performed
in the topmost hollow of a green barrow or hill, of
which many survive, scooped out into vast amphi-
theatres and surrounded by benches of turf, which held
two thousand spectators. Such were the historic plays,

"The Creation" and "Noe's Flood," which still exist in the original Celtic as well as the English text, and suggest what critics and antiquaries Cornish curates, masters of such revels, must have been,—for the native language of Cornwall did not lapse into silence until the end of the seventeenth century. Then, moreover, here and there would be one parson more learned than his kind in the mysteries of a deep and thrilling lore of peculiar fascination. He was a man so highly honoured at college for natural gifts and knowledge of learned books which nobody else could read, that when he "took his second orders" the bishop gave him a mantle of scarlet silk to wear upon his shoulders in church, and his lordship had put such power into it that when the parson had it rightly on, he could "govern any ghost or evil spirit," and even "stop an earthquake."

Such a powerful minister, in combat with supernatural visitations, was one Parson Rudall, of Launceston, whose existence and exploits we gather from the local tradition of his time, from surviving letters and other memoranda, and indeed from his own "Diurnal," which fell by chance into the hands of the present writer. Indeed the legend of Parson Rudall and the Botathen Ghost will be recognised by many Cornish people as a local remembrance of their boyhood.

It appears, then, from the diary of this learned master of the grammar-school—for such was his office as well as perpetual curate of the parish—"that a pestilential disease did break forth in our town in the beginning of the year A.D. 1665; yea, and it likewise invaded my school, insomuch that therewithal certain of the chief scholars sickened and died." "Among others who yielded to the malign influence was Master John Eliot, the eldest son and the worshipful heir of

Edward Eliot, Esquire of Trebursey, a stripling of sixteen years of age, but of uncommon parts and hopeful
ingenuity. At his own especial motion and earnest
desire I did consent to preach his funeral sermon." It
should be remembered here that, howsoever strange
and singular it may sound to us that a mere lad should
formally solicit such a performance at the hands of his
master, it was in consonance with the habitual usage of
those times. The old services for the dead had been
abolished by law, and in the stead of sacrament and
ceremony, month's mind and year's mind, the sole substitute which survived was the general desire "to par-
take," as they called it, of a posthumous discourse,
replete with lofty eulogy and flattering remembrance
of the living and the dead. The diary proceeds:—

"I fulfilled my undertaking, and preached over the
coffin in the presence of a full assemblage of mourners
and lachrymose friends. An ancient gentleman, who
was then and there in the church, a Mr Bligh of
Botathen, was much affected with my discourse, and
he was heard to repeat to himself certain parentheses
therefrom, especially a phrase from Maro Virgilius,
which I had applied to the deceased youth, 'Et puer
ipse fuit cantari dignus.'

"The cause wherefore this old gentleman was thus
moved by my applications was this: He had a first-
born and only son—a child who, but a very few months
before, had been not unworthy the character I drew of
young Master Eliot, but who, by some strange accident,
had of late quite fallen away from his parent's hopes,
and become moody, and sullen, and distraught. When
the funeral obsequies were over, I had no sooner come
out of church than I was accosted by this aged parent,
and he besought me incontinently, with a singular

energy, that I would resort with him forthwith to his
abode at Botathen that very night; nor could I have
delivered myself from his importunity, had not Mr
Eliot urged his claim to enjoy my company at his own
house. Hereupon I got loose, but not until I had
pledged a fast assurance that I would pay him, faithfully, an early visit the next day."

"The Place," as it was called, of Botathen, where old
Mr Bligh resided, was a low-roofed gabled manor-house
of the fifteenth century, walled and mullioned, and
with clustered chimneys of dark-grey stone from the
neighbouring quarries of Ventor-gan. The mansion
was flanked by a pleasaunce or enclosure in one space,
of garden and lawn, and it was surrounded by a solemn
grove of stag-horned trees. It had the sombre aspect
of age and of solitude, and looked the very scene of
strange and supernatural events. A legend might well
belong to every gloomy glade around, and there must
surely be a haunted room somewhere within its walls.
Hither, according to his appointment, on the morrow,
Parson Rudall betook himself. Another clergyman, as
it appeared, had been invited to meet him, who, very
soon after his arrival, proposed a walk together in the
pleasaunce, on the pretext of showing him, as a stranger,
the walks and trees, until the dinner-bell should strike.
There, with much prolixity, and with many a solemn
pause, his brother minister proceeded to "unfold the
mystery."

"A singular infelicity," he declared, "had befallen
young Master Bligh, once the hopeful heir of his parents
and of the lands of Botathen. Whereas he had been
from childhood a blithe and merry boy, 'the gladness,'
like Isaac of old, of his father's age, he had suddenly,
and of late, become morose and silent—nay, even

austere and stern—dwelling apart, always solemn, often
in tears. The lad had at first repulsed all questions as
to the origin of this great change, but of late he had
yielded to the importunate researches of his parents,
and had disclosed the secret cause. It appeared that
he resorted, every day, by a pathway across the fields,
to this very clergyman's house, who had charge of his
education, and grounded him in the studies suitable to
his age. In the course of his daily walk he had to pass
a certain heath or down where the road wound along
through tall blocks of granite with open spaces of
grassy sward between. There in a certain spot, and
always in one and the same place, the lad declared that
he encountered, every day, a woman with a pale and
troubled face, clothed in a long loose garment of frieze,
with one hand always stretched forth, and the other
pressed against her side. Her name, he said, was
Dorothy Dinglet, for he had known her well from his
childhood, and she often used to come to his parents'
house; but that which troubled him was, that she had
now been dead three years, and he himself had been
with the neighbours at her burial; so that, as the
youth alleged, with great simplicity, since he had seen
her body laid in the grave, this that he saw every day
must needs be her soul or ghost. 'Questioned again
and again,' said the clergyman, 'he never contradicts
himself; but he relates the same and the simple tale
as a thing that cannot be gainsaid. Indeed the lad's
observance is keen and calm for a boy of his age.
The hair of the appearance, sayeth he, is not like anything alive, but it is so soft and light that it seemeth
to melt away while you look; but her eyes are set, and
never blink—no, not when the sun shineth full upon
her face. She maketh no steps, but seemeth to swim

along the top of the grass; and her hand, which is stretched out alway, seemeth to point at something far away, out of sight. It is her continual coming; for she never faileth to meet him, and to pass on, that hath quenched his spirits; and although he never seeth her by night, yet cannot he get his natural rest.'

"Thus far the clergyman; whereupon the dinner clock did sound, and we went into the house. After dinner, when young Master Bligh had withdrawn with his tutor, under excuse of their books, the parents did forthwith beset me as to my thoughts about their son. Said I, warily, 'The case is strange, but by no means impossible. It is one that I will study, and fear not to handle, if the lad will be free with me, and fulfil all that I desire.' The mother was overjoyed, but I perceived that old Mr Bligh turned pale, and was downcast with some thought which, however, he did not express. Then they bade that Master Bligh should be called to meet me in the pleasaunce forthwith. The boy came, and he rehearsed to me his tale with an open countenance, and, withal, a modesty of speech. Verily he seemed 'ingenui vultus puer ingenuique pudoris.' Then I signified to him my purpose. 'To-morrow,' said I, 'we will go together to the place; and if, as I doubt not, the woman shall appear, it will be for me to proceed according to knowledge, and by rules laid down in my books.' "

The unaltered scenery of the legend still survives, and, like the field of the forty footsteps in another history, the place is still visited by those who take interest in the supernatural tales of old. The pathway leads along a moorland waste, where large masses of rock stand up here and there from the grassy turf, and clumps of heath and gorse weave their tapestry of golden

I

and purple garniture on every side. Amidst all these, and winding along between the rocks, is a natural foot-way worn by the scant, rare tread of the village traveller. Just midway, a somewhat larger stretch than usual of green sod expands, which is skirted by the path, and which is still identified as the legendary haunt of the phantom, by the name of Parson Rudall's Ghost.

But we must draw the record of the first interview between the minister and Dorothy from his own words. "We met," thus he writes, "in the pleasaunce very early, and before any others in the house were awake; and together the lad and myself proceeded towards the field. The youth was quite composed, and carried his Bible under his arm, from whence he read to me verses, which he said he had lately picked out, to have always in his mind. These were Job vii. 14, 'Thou scarest me with dreams, and terrifiest me through visions;' and Deuter-onomy xxviii. 67, 'In the morning thou shalt say, Would to God it were evening, and in the evening thou shalt say, Would to God it were morning; for the fear of thine heart wherewith thou shalt fear, and for the sight of thine eyes which thou shalt see.'

"I was much pleased with the lad's ingenuity in these pious applications, but for mine own part I was somewhat anxious and out of cheer. For aught I knew this might be a *dæmonium meridianum*, the most stub-born spirit to govern and guide that any man can meet, and the most perilous withal. We had hardly reached the accustomed spot, when we both saw her at once gliding towards us; punctually as the ancient writers describe the motion of their 'lemures, which swoon along the ground, neither marking the sand nor bend-ing the herbage.' The aspect of the woman was exactly that which had been related by the lad. There was the

pale and stony face, the strange and misty hair, the
eyes firm and fixed, that gazed, yet not on us, but on
something that they saw far, far away; one hand and
arm stretched out, and the other grasping the girdle of
her waist. She floated along the field like a sail upon
a stream, and glided past the spot where we stood,
pausingly. But so deep was the awe that overcame me,
as I stood there in the light of day, face to face with a
human soul separate from her bones and flesh, that my
heart and purpose both failed me. I had resolved to
speak to the spectre in the appointed form of words,
but I did not. I stood like one amazed and speechless,
until she had passed clean out of sight. One thing remarkable came to pass. A spaniel dog, the favourite
of young Master Bligh, had followed us, and lo! when
the woman drew nigh, the poor creature began to yell
and bark piteously, and ran backward and away, like
a thing dismayed and appalled. We returned to the
house, and after I had said all that I could to pacify
the lad, and to soothe the aged people, I took my leave
for that time, with a promise that when I had fulfilled
certain business elsewhere, which I then alleged, I
would return and take orders to assuage these disturb-
ances and their cause.

"*January 7, 1665.*—At my own house, I find, by my
books, what is expedient to be done; and then, Apage,
Sathanas!

"*January 9, 1665.*—This day I took leave of my wife
and family, under pretext of engagements elsewhere,
and made my secret journey to our diocesan city,
wherein the good and venerable bishop then abode.

"*January 10.*—*Deo gratias*, in safe arrival at Exeter;
craved and obtained immediate audience of his lordship; pleading it was for counsel and admonition on a

weighty and pressing cause; called to the presence;
made obeisance; and then by command stated my case
—the Botathen perplexity—which I moved with strong
and earnest instances and solemn asseverations of that
which I had myself seen and heard.   Demanded by his
lordship, what was the succour that I had come to entreat at his hands?   Replied, licence for my exorcism,
that so I might, ministerially, allay this spiritual visitant, and thus render to the living and the dead release
from this surprise.   'But,' said our bishop, 'on what
authority do you allege that I am intrusted with faculty
so to do?   Our Church, as is well known, hath abjured
certain branches of her ancient power, on grounds of
perversion and abuse.'   'Nay, my lord,' I humbly answered, 'under favour, the seventy-second of the canons
ratified and enjoined on us, the clergy, anno Domino
1604, doth expressly provide, that " no minister, *unless
he hath* the licence of his diocesan bishop, shall essay to
exorcise a spirit, evil or good."   Therefore it was,' I did
here mildly allege, 'that I did not presume to enter on
such a work without lawful privilege under your lordship's hand and seal.'   Hereupon did our wise and
learned bishop, sitting in his chair, condescend upon the
theme at some length with many gracious interpreta-
tions from ancient writers and from Holy Scripture,
and I did humbly rejoin and reply, till the upshot was
that he did call in his secretary and command him to
draw the aforesaid faculty, forthwith and without further delay, assigning him a form, insomuch that the
matter was incontinently done; and after I had dis-
bursed into the secretary's hands certain moneys for
signiary purposes, as the manner of such officers hath
always been, the bishop did himself affix his signature
under the *sigillum* of his see, and deliver the document

into my hands. When I knelt down to receive his benediction, he softly said, 'Let it be secret, Mr R. Weak brethren! weak brethren!'"

This interview with the bishop, and the success with which he vanquished his lordship's scruples, would seem to have confirmed Parson Rudall very strongly in his own esteem, and to have invested him with that courage which he evidently lacked at his first encounter with the ghost.

The entries proceed: "*January 11, 1665.*—Therewithal did I hasten home and prepare my instruments, and cast my figures for the onset of the next day. Took out my ring of brass, and put it on the index-finger of my right hand, with the *scutum Davidis* traced thereon.

"*January 12, 1665.*—Rode into the gateway at Botathen, armed at all points, but not with Saul's armour, and ready. There is danger from the demons, but so there is in the surrounding air every day. At early morning then, and alone,—for so the usage ordains,—I betook me towards the field. It was void, and I had thereby due time to prepare. First, I paced and measured out my circle on the grass. Then did I mark my pentacle in the very midst, and at the intersection of the five angles I did set up and fix my crutch of *raun* [rowan]. Lastly, I took my station south, at the true line of the meridian, and stood facing due north. I waited and watched for a long time. At last there was a kind of trouble in the air, a soft and rippling sound, and all at once the shape appeared, and came on towards me gradually. I opened my parchment-scroll, and read aloud the command. She paused, and seemed to waver and doubt; stood still; then I rehearsed the sentence again, sounding out every syllable like a chant. She drew near my ring, but halted at first outside, on the brink. I sounded again, and now at the third time I gave the signal in Syriac — the speech which is used, they say, where such ones dwell and converse in thoughts that glide.

" She was at last obedient, and swam into the midst of the circle, and there stood still, suddenly. I saw, moreover, that she drew back her pointing hand. All this while I do confess that my knees shook under me, and the drops of sweat ran down my flesh like rain. But now, although face to face with the spirit, my heart grew calm, and my mind was composed. I knew that the pentacle would govern her, and the ring must bind, until I gave the word. Then I called to mind the rule laid down of old, that no angel or fiend, no spirit, good or evil, will ever speak until they have been first spoken to. *N.B.*—This is the great law of prayer. God Himself will not yield reply until man hath made vocal entreaty, once and again. So I went on to demand, as the books advise; and the phantom made answer, willingly. Questioned wherefore not at rest? Unquiet, because of a certain sin. Asked what, and by whom? Revealed it; but it is *sub sigillo*, and therefore *nefas dictu;* more anon. Inquired, what sign she could give that she was a true spirit and not a false fiend? Stated, before next Yule-tide a fearful pestilence would lay waste the land and myriads of souls would be loosened from their flesh, until, as she piteously said, 'our valleys will be full.' Asked again, why she so terrified the lad? Replied: 'It is the law: we must seek a youth or a maiden of clean life, and under age, to receive messages and admonitions.' We conversed with many more words, but it is not lawful for me to set them down. Pen and ink would degrade and defile

the thoughts she uttered, and which my mind received
that day. I broke the ring, and she passed, but to
return once more next day. At even-song, a long discourse with that ancient transgressor, Mr B. Great
horror and remorse; entire atonement and penance;
whatsoever I enjoin; full acknowledgment before
pardon.

"*January 13, 1665.*—At sunrise I was again in the
field. She came in at once, and, as it seemed, with
freedom. Inquired if she knew my thoughts, and
what I was going to relate? Answered, ' Nay, we
only know what we perceive and hear; we cannot see
the heart.' Then I rehearsed the penitent words of
the man she had come up to denounce, and the satis-
faction he would perform. Then said she, ' Peace in
our midst.' I went through the proper forms of dis-
missal, and fulfilled all as it was set down and written
in my memoranda; and then, with certain fixed rites,
I did dismiss that troubled ghost, until she peacefully
withdrew, gliding towards the west. Neither did she
ever afterward appear, but was allayed until she shall
come in her second flesh to the valley of Armageddon
on the last day."

These quaint and curious details from the " diurnal "
of a simple-hearted clergyman of the seventeenth century appear to betoken his personal persuasion of the
truth of what he saw and said, although the statements
are strongly tinged with what some may term the
superstition, and others the excessive belief, of those
times. It is a singular fact, however, that the canon
which authorises exorcism under episcopal licence, is
still a part of the ecclesiastical law of the Anglican
Church, although it might have a singular effect on
the nerves of certain of our bishops if their clergy were

to resort to them for the faculty which Parson Rudall obtained. The general facts stated in his diary are to this day matters of belief in that neighbourhood; and it has been always accounted a strong proof of the veracity of the Parson and the Ghost, that the plague, fatal to so many thousands, did break out in London at the close of that very year. We may well excuse a triumphant entry, on a subsequent page of the " diurnal," with the date of July 10, 1665: " How sorely must the infidels and heretics of this generation be dismayed when they know that this black death, which is now swallowing its thousands in the streets of the great city, was foretold six months agone, under the exorcisms of a country minister, by a visible and suppliant ghost! And what pleasures and improvements do such deny themselves who scorn and avoid all opportunity of intercourse with souls separate, and the spirits, glad and sorrowful, which inhabit the unseen world !"

A RIDE FROM BUDE TO BOSS.[1]

BY TWO OXFORD MEN.[2]

DEAR old Oxford! amid the brawl and uproar of the
latter days, and with many a frailty in the curtains of the Ark which the weapons of the Philistines
have found and pierced, yet *alma mater*, mother mild,
like our native England, "with all thy faults I love
thee still." And when I recall my own undergraduate
life of thirty years and upwards agone, I feel, notwithstanding modern vaunt, the *laudator temporis acti*
earnest within me yet and strong. Nowadays, as it
seems to me, there is but little originality of character
in the still famous University; a dread of eccentric
reputation appears to pervade College and Hall; every
"Oxford man," to adopt the well-known name, is subdued into sameness within and without, controlled as
it were into copyism and mediocrity by the smoothing-

---

[1] From 'Belgravia,' vol. iii. pp. 328-337. 1867.
[2] The author in company with Rev. Dr Jeune, afterwards Bishop of
Peterborough.

iron of the nineteenth century. Whereas in my time,
and before it, there were distinguished names, famous
in every mouth for original achievements and "deeds
of daring-do." There were giants in those days—men
of varied renown—and they arose and won for themselves in strange fields of fame, record and place.
Each became in his day a hero of the 'Iliad' or
'Odyssey' of Oxford life—a kind of Homeric man.
Once and again in the course of every term, the whole
University would ring with some fearless and practical
jest, conceived and executed with a dash of original
genius which betokened future victories in the war of
wit and the world of men. How well do I remember
a bold travesty of discipline which once set the com-
mon-rooms in a roar, and even among "mine ancients,"
made it

> "merry in hall
> Where beards wagged all"!

A decree had been issued by the "authorities" of a
well-known College (it was in the pre-ritual days) that
no undergraduate should present himself at morning
chapel service with his scarlet hunting-coat underneath
his surplice—a costume neither utterly secular nor
completely ecclesiastical, and therefore a motley garb
which it did not seem unjust or unreasonable to forbid
in a sacred place. However, the order was implicitly
obeyed at the ensuing matins, with solemn and suspi-
cious exactitude. Alas! it was "the torrent's smooth-
ness ere it dash below"; for on the third morning,
when the College servants arrived to take down the
shutters and to light the fires, they discovered that
"a change had come over the spirit of their dream."
Every one of the panelled doors throughout the Quad-

rangle of the Canons, the very seat of hoar and reverend authority, had been artistically painted during the
night with the hue of Nimrod, a glowing hunter's red !
The gates were immediately closed and barred, and
every member of the College convened before a grand
divan of the Dons, to undergo immediate scrutiny on
the origin of that which some of the undergraduates
irreverently termed this ultra-observance of the rubric
(their wit would be obscure to those who are unaware
that *rubrica,* the etymon of our Church rules, signifies
ruddy or red). The authors of this outrage escaped
detection, although every painter in Oxford was summoned for examination, and all the dealers in colours
and oils. It was subsequently whispered among the
initiated that the artist, with his brushes and materials,
had been brought down from London in a post-
chaise-and-four, secretly introduced through an unnoted postern, and when his work was done, hospitably
feasted and paid, and then sent back at full speed
through the night to town.

Another " merrie jest," but with a lowlier scene and
an humbler *dramatis personæ,* raised the laugh of many
a common-room and wine-party about the same period
of my own undergraduate recollections. There was
an ancient woman, blear-eyed and dim-sighted, " worn
nature's mournful monument," who had the far and
wide repute of witchcraft among the College servants
and the " baser sort " in the suburbs of the town ; but
in reality she was a mere " wreck of eld," a harmless
and helpless old creature, who stood at more than one
college - gate for alms. Her well - known name was
Nanny Heale. Her cottage, or rather decayed old hut,
leaned against a steep mound by the castle-wall, and
was so hugged in by the ground that, from a path

along the ramparts a passer-by might cast a bird's-
eye look down Nanny's chimney, and watch well her
hearth and home.   One winter evening certain frolic-
some wights, out of College in search of a channel for
the exuberant spirits of their age, were pacing, like
Hardicanute, the wall east and west, when a glance
down the witch's chimney revealed a quaint and simple
scene of humble life.   There she crouched, close by the
smoking embers, peering into the fire; and before her
very nose there hung, just over the fire, a round iron
vessel, called in the western counties a crock, filled to
the brim with potatoes, and without a cover or lid.
This utensil was suspended by its swing-handle to an
iron bar, which went from side to side of the chimney-
wall.   To see and to assail the weak point in a field of
battle is evermore the signal of a great captain.   The
onslaught was instantly planned.   A rope, with a hook
of iron at the end, was slowly and noiselessly lowered
down the chimney, and, unnoted by poor Nanny's blink-
ing sight, the handle of the iron pot was softly grasped
by the crook, and the vessel with its mealy contents
began to ascend in silent majesty towards the upper
air.   Thoroughly roused by this unnatural and ungrate-
ful demeanour of her lifelong companion of the hearth,
old Nanny arose from her stool, peered anxiously upward to watch the ascent, and shouted at the top of her
voice:—

   "Massy 'pon my sinful soul! art gwain off—taties
and all?"

   The vessel was quietly grasped, carried down in hot
haste, and planted upright outside the cottage-door.   A
knock, given for the purpose, summoned the inmate,
who hurried out and stumbled over, as she afterwards
interpreted the event, her penitent crock.

"So then," was her joyful greeting — "so then! thcer't come back to holt, then! Ay, 'tis a cold out o' doors."

Good came out of evil; for her story, which she rehearsed again and again, with all the energy and firm persuasion of truth, at last reached the ears of the parish authorities, and they, on inquiry into the evidence, forthwith decreed the addition of a shilling a-week to poor old Nanny's allowance, on the plea that her faculties had quite failed her, and that she required greater charity because of her wandering mind. Yet the fact which she testified met the criterion of evidence demanded by Hume, for the event occurred within the experience of the witness herself.

It was by outbreaks of animal spirits such as these that the monotony of collegiate life in those days was relieved, for the University supplied but little excitement of mental kind. The battle-cries of High Church and Low Church—" that bleating of the sheep and that lowing of the oxen " which nowadays we hear—had not yet begun to rouse the Oxford mind; and the only war about vestments that I recollect was our hot fierce struggle after a festive assembly to get first out into the lobby, and to grasp as a spoil the best caps and gowns one by one, until the unhappy freshman who arrived last had to put up with such ragged specimens of University costume as would hardly have satisfied the veriest Puritan for the performance of divine service.

Well, for us two—the subjects of this paper—the life of Oxford, with its freaks and its discipline, for a time was over; we had each passed the final examination so graphically named " the Great Go"; and that so as to be, what man so seldom is in this world, satisfied. In high heart, and with spirits running over, my friend

and I appointed a tryst in a small watering-place on
the north coast of Cornwall as the starting-point for a
ride " all down the thundering shores of Bude and Boss."
In due time, and on a glorious summer day, we mounted
our " Galloway nags," and, like the knights of ancient
ballad, " we laughed as we rode away." The start was
from Bude, and we made our first halt at a place twelve
miles towards the south-west; a scene of general local
renown, and which bears the parochial name of Warbstow Barrow. It stands upon a lofty hill that soars and
swells upward into a vast circular mound, enthroned, as
it were, amid a wild and boundless stretch of heathy
and gorsy moorland. It was soothing to the sight to
look down and around on the tapestry of purple and
gold intermingled in natural woof, and flowing away
in free undulation on every side. The view from this
mountain-top was of wonderful extent, but wild, desolate, and bare. Beneath, on three sides, spread the
moor, dotted here and there with a grey old church,
that crouched toward the shadow of its low Saxon
battlemented tower, as if it still sought shelter, after so
many ages, from the perils of surrounding barbarism.
On the fourth side swelled the sea. But the brow of
this hill, like that of many others in the west, dropped
into the shape of a mighty circular bowl—a kind of
hollow valley turfed with grass, and surrounded by a
rim; an amphitheatre, however, large enough to hold
five thousand people at once. On the flat level floor of
this round crater, and in the exact midst, still swells up
uninjured the outline of a viking's grave, unlike other
burial-mounds so common in Cornwall and elsewhere,
" where the brown barrow curves its sullen breast above
the bones of some dead gentile's soul," and that on
every hillside and plain. The shape of the great hillock

at Warbstow is neither oval nor round, but survives
the exact image of the dragon-ship of northern piracy
and war. Moreover, not the shape only, but the size
of the ancient vessel of the dead, is perpetuated here.
Measured and graduated by scale, this oblong, curved,
and narrow grave would yield the dimensions of a boat
of fifty tons, which would be about the weight of a
Scandinavian serpent of the sea.

We saw that an effort had been made to open this
barrow at one of the ends; but an old woman, whom
we found at a cottage not far off, assured us " that they
that tried it were soon forced to give up their digging
and flee, for the thunders came for 'em, and the light-
nings also."

We endeavoured to sound the local mind of our in-
formant as to the history of the place and origin of the
grave; but all we could drag out of her, after questions
again and again, was " great warriors, supposing, in old
times." Such was the dirge of the mighty dead, and
their requiem, at Warbstow Barrow. But the sun had
begun to lean, and we were bound for Boscastle, the
breviate of Bottreau Castle, and the abode of the earls
of that name.

Strange, striking, and utterly unique is the first
aspect of this village by the sea. The gorge or valley
lies between two vast and precipitous hills, that yawn
asunder as though they had been cleft by the spells of
some giant warlock of the West, like the Eildon Hill
by Michael Scott. As you descend the hill from the
north you discover on the opposite side clusters of
quaint old-fashioned houses, grotesque and gabled, that
appear as though they clung together for mutual sup-
port on the slope of that perilous cliff. Between the
houses, and sheer down the mountain-side, descended,

or rather fell, a steep and ugly road; which led, however, to the " safety of the vale," and landed the traveller at last in a deep cut or gash between the hills,
where the creek ebbed and flowed, which was called by
strangers in their courtesy, and by the inhabitants, with
aboriginal pride, "the Harbour"— *Cornice* "Hawn."
There "went the ships," so that they did not exceed
sixty tons in freight; and thither arrived, at certain
intervals, coals and timber in bulk and quantity,
which can be ascertained, no doubt, by the return of
imports laid before Parliament by the Chancellor of
the Exchequer.

We reached in safety our bourn for the night at the
bottom of the hill, and discovered the hostelry by the
sign which swung above the door. This appeared to us
to represent a man's shoe; but when we had read the
legend, we found that it signified the Ship Inn, and
was the "actual effigy" of a vessel which belonged to
the port. Here we received a smiling welcome from
the hostess, a ruddy-visaged widow,—Joan Treworgy
was her Keltic name—fubby and interjectional in figure,
and manifestly better adapted for her abode at the foot
of the hill than at any mansion farther up. She was
born, as she afterwards related, two doors off; and,
except that she had travelled up the hill to Forraburry
church to be married there, it appeared that a diameter
of five yards would have defined the total circumference
of her wandering life.

As soon as we arrived, she called up from some vasty
deep underneath her house a grim and shaggy shape,
who answered to the name of Tim, but whom we identified as Caliban on the spot, and charged him to take
proper care of the Captains' horses (for by that title all
strangers in sound garments and whole hats are saluted

in the land of the quarry and the mine), and to be sure
that they had plenty of whuts. She then invited us to
enter her "parrolar," a room rather cosy than magnifi-
cent; for when our landlady had followed in her two
guests, and stood at the door, no one beside could have
forced an entrance, any more than a cannon-ball could
cleave through a feather-bed. We then proceeded to
confer about beds for the night, and, not without misgiving, inquired if she could supply a couple of those
indispensable places of repose. A demur ensued. All
the gentry in the town, she declared, were accustomed
to sleep "two in a bed," and the officers that travelled
the country, and stopped at her house, would mostly
do the same; but, however, if we commanded two beds
for only two people, two we must have; only, although
they were both in the same room, we must certainly
pay for two, and sixpence apiece was her regular price.
We assented, and then went on to entreat that we
might dine. She graciously agreed; but to all questions as to our fare her sole response was, "Meat—
meat and taties." "Some call 'em," she added, in a
scornful tone, "'purtaties,' but we always say 'taties'
here." The specific differences between beef, mutton,
veal, &c., seemed to be utterly or artfully ignored, and
to every frenzied inquiry her calm inexorable reply
was, "Meat—nice wholesome meat and taties."

In due time we sat down in that happy ignorance
as to the nature of our viands which a French cook is
said to desire; and although we both made a not un-
satisfactory meal, it is a wretched truth that by no effort
could we ascertain what it was that was roasted for us
that day by widow Treworgy, hostess of the Ship, and
which we consumed. Was it a piece of Boscastle baby?
as I suggested to my companion in the midst of his

K

enjoyment; and the question caused him to arise and
rush out to inquire once again, and insist on knowing
the whole truth; but he soon came back baffled, and
shouting, "Meat and taties!" There was not a vestige
of bone nor any outline that could identify the joint,
and the not unsavoury taste was something like tender
veal. It was not until years afterwards that light was
thrown on our mysterious dinner that day by a passage
which I accidentally turned up in an ancient history of
Cornwall. Therein I read "that the sillie people of
Bouscastle and Boussiney do catch in the summer seas
divers young soyles [seals], which, doubtful if they be
fish or flesh, conynge housewives will nevertheless roast,
and do make thereof very savoury meat." "Ay, ay,"
said my friend and fellow-traveller, when I had transcribed and sent him this extract—"Ay! clear as day
—meat and taties; how I wish I had old mother Treworgy now by the throat! I would make her walk
up that hill every day for a month, and stop her meat
and taties till she was the size of other people."
When the hour arrived that should have been the
time of rest, we mounted a cabin-ladder, which our
hostess assured us was "the stairs." We found the
two beds which had been allotted to us, but, as it was
foretold, in one small, hot, stuffy room. As we entered
the narrow door, a solitary casement twinkled on one
side of the opposite wall, flanked by a glazed cupboard-
door, paned to match, on the other. This latter, the
false light, my friend opened by mistake—he was near-
sighted, and our single dip was dim—to sniff, as he
said, the evening air; but he shut it up again in quick
disgust, declaring that the whole atmosphere of the
village was impregnated with onions and cheese. To
bed, but not to rest. Every cubic inch of ozone was

exhausted long before midnight, and, as the small hours
struck on the kitchen-clock below, we found that
"Boscastle had murdered sleep, and therefore Oxford
could sleep no more." With the first faint glimmer
of day we arose and stole gently out into the dawn.
Before us stood the one-arched bridge spanning the
river-bed. Lower down the creek the mast and rigging
of a sloop at anchor was visible, like network traced
upon the morning sky. But the lowly level had no
attraction for our path: there lay the sluggish mist of
night, and it seemed to our distempered fancy like the
dull heavy breath of the snorers in that village glen;
but above and upwards stretched the tall ascending
road, like Jacob's ladder resting on the earth and
reaching to the sky. Surely on the brow of that
mountain-top there must be breath and room. We
turned, therefore, to climb, and for once "vaulting
ambition did not o'erleap itself." Slow and difficult
was the way, but cooler and more bracing the air every
yard that we achieved.

We stood at last on the brow of the vast gorge, and
full five hundred feet above the sea, where church and
tower crowned the cliff like a crest. The scene we
looked upon was indeed exhilarating, stately, and
grand. On the right hand, and to the west, arose
and stood the craggy heights of Dundagel, island and
main, ennobled by the legends of old historic time.
To the left, a boundless reach of granite-sprinkled
moor, where barrow, logan rock, and cromlech stood,
the mute memorials of Keltic antiquity. Beneath,
and afar off, the sea, at that silent hour, like some
boundless lake, "its glad waves murmuring all around
the soul;" near, and at our feet, the jumbled village,
crouching on either side of the steepy road, and cling-

ing to its banks as if the inhabitants sought to secure
access for escape when the earthquake should rend or
the volcano pour. We prepared to return and descend; but this was by no means an easy feat, from
the extreme angle at which the roadway fell. At the
first look on the inclined plane it seemed easier to sit
down and slide; but on the whole we thought it
better to walk and pause and creep.

Another and a new feature in the scene now met
our gaze. Annexed to every human abode a small hut
had been stuck on to the walls for the home of the
"gentleman" that, in Cornwall as in Ireland, pays the
rent—*Keltice*, the pig. The hovels of these bristly
vassals, like the castles of their lords, were cabined
and circumscribed in the extreme. There was just
room enough to breathe, but not to snore without
impediment of tone. A sudden inspiration awoke in
our minds. Surely it would be an act of humanity
and kindness to enable these poor suffocating creatures once in their lives to taste the balmy breath of
a summer morning. It will be to us, we said and
thought, a personal delight to see them emerge from
their close and festering abodes and rush out in the
free, soft radiance of the dawn! Action followed
close on thought. Hastily, busily, every rude rough
bar was drawn back, door and substitute for door un-
closed; and a general jail-delivery of imprisoned swine
was ruled and accomplished on the spot. Undetected
by a single human witness, without interruption from
slumbering master or lazy hind, the total deed was
done. Gradually descending the hill, and scattering,
like ancient heroes and modern patriots, freedom and
deliverance as we went, never did the children of
liberty so exult in their unshackled deliverance as

these Boscastle hordes. There was one result, however, which we had not foreseen, and its perilous consequences had quite escaped anticipation. The inmates of every sty, as soon as their opportunities of
egress had been ascertained by marching out of their
prison-doors and arriving unchecked at the roadside—
when they looked upward and surveyed the steep and
difficult ascent, and counted mentally the cost of
attempting to surmount the steep, they all, as with
one hoof and mind, turned down the hill. Sire and
dam, lean and corpulent, farrow and suckling, all *uno
impetu*, selected and rushed down the *facilis descensus
Averni;* and although, in all likelihood, they had never
pondered the contrast of the Roman poet, yet they
spontaneously moved and seconded, and carried the
unanimous resolution that *revocare gradum, hic labor,
hoc opus est.* The consequence of this choice of way
was too soon apparent. Just as we had drawn the
last bar, and were approaching the bottom of the
steep, we looked back and saw that we were pursued,
and should speedily be surrounded, by a mixed multitude of porcine advocates for free discussion in the
open air, such as might have gladdened the heart of
any critic on the original and cultivated breeds of the
west of England. Prominent among them the old
Cornish razor-back asserted its pre-eminence of height
and bone, nor were punchy representatives of the
Berkshire and Suffolk genealogies absent on this
festive occasion. Growing now apprehensive of the
consequences of discovery, if an early rising owner
should ascertain the authors of this daring effort to
" deliver their dungeons from the captive," we hastened
to secure ourselves in the shelter of our hostelry of
the Ship, and fortunately found, on reaching our " little

chamber on the wall," that the widow and her household were still fast asleep. We fastened the door and
listened for results. The outcries and yells were fearful. By-and-by human voices began to mingle with
the tumult; there were shouts of inquiry and surprise,
then sounds of apparent expostulation and entreaty,
and again a "storm of hate and wrath and wakening
fear." Many a battle of soldiers must have fought and
ended with less uproar. At last the tumult pierced
even the ears of our hostess Joan Treworgy. We
heard her puff and blow, and call for Tim. At last,
after waiting a prudent time, we thought it best to
call aloud for shaving-water, and to inquire with
astonishment into the cause of that horrible disturb-
ance which had roused us from our morning sleep.
This brought the widow in hot haste to our door.

"Why, they do say, Captain," was her doleful response, "that all the pegs up-town have a-rebelled, and
they've a-be, and let one the wother out, and they be
all a-gwain to sea huz-a-muz, bang!"

Although this statement was somewhat obscure in
its phraseology, and the Keltic byword at the close,
wherein the "sense is kindred to the sound," yet we
understood too well that the main facts of the history
were as true as if Macaulay had recorded them; so we
pretended to dress in great haste, and hurried down to
see the war. It was indeed an original scene;

> "For chief intent on deeds of strife,
>   Or bard of martial lay,
> 'Twere worth ten years of peaceful life,
>   One glance at their array!"

Here a decently dressed woman made many fruitless
endeavours to coax out of the brawl five or six squeal-

ing farrows, the offspring of a gaunt old dam that, like
the felon sow of Rokeby, was "so distraught with
noise" that "her own children she mought clean devour." There a stalwart quarryman, finding all other
efforts fruitless, had seized his full-grown porker by
the legs and hoisted him on his shoulders to ride home
pickaback, uttering all the while yells of fierce expostulation and defiance. One hot little man, with a red
face and gesticulating hands, had grasped a long pole,
and laid about him in mad fury, promiscuously, until
a tall and bristly hog rushed at him from behind, and
carried him off down the hill seated at full charge like
a knight of King Arthur's Court, with "semblance of
a spear," and tilted him at last head over heels in the
bed of the stream. But some way up the hill we came
suddenly upon a scene which demanded all our sympathy; help there was none. A panting old woman
had singled out her hog and separated him from the
crowd; and a fine fat animal he was—four hundredweight at least—and so unfitted for the slightest exertion, that unless he had resorted to sliding and rolling,
it was difficult to conceive how he had accomplished
even his down-hill journey from the sty. But up hill
—as his obdurate mistress appeared to propose,—no,
no. There was a look in his eye, as he glanced back
at his despairing owner, that seemed to suggest a grunt
in strong German emphasis, *das geht nicht.* He had
thrust his snout and half his nose through the bars of
a gate; and there he stuck, and manifestly meant to
stick fast, while she belaboured him with strokes like
a flail. She paused as we approached the spot, and
with an appealing look for our assent, she piteously
exclaimed, "My peg's surely mazed, maister, or he's
ill-wished; some ennemie hath a-dond it!" My

thought responded to her charge; it was certainly no
enemy of the pig that "dond it," whatsoever he might
be to his owner.

We left "her alone in her glory," and returned to
the inn, communing as we went on the store of legend,
tale, and history we had laid up for future generations
in thus opening a field of achievement for the Boscastle
swine.   What themes of marvel would travel down by
the cottage hearth, there to be rehearsed by wrinkled
eld !—the wondrous things always the more believed
as they became more incredible.   Doubtless the local
event would very soon be resolved into demoniac
agency, because, ever since the miracle of Gadara, the
people have always linked the association of demons
and swine; and they refer to the five small dark punc-
tures always visible on the hoof of the hog as the points
of entrance and departure for the fiend.

Once in after-life did this fitful freak recur to our
minds.   We separated, my companion of this ride and
myself—I to a country cure, and my friend back to
Oxford, " to climb the steep where fame's proud temple
shines afar."   He ascended step by step until he became Dean of the College to which we both belonged.
In course of time, after the usual interval, I went up
to take my M.A. degree.   Now the custom was, and is,
that the Dean takes the candidate by the hand, leads
him up to the chair of the Vice-Chancellor, and presents him for his degree in a Latin speech.   We were all
assembled in the appointed place, the Dean, my friend,
taking us up in turn one by one.   Among the group
was a stout burly man, a gentleman commoner, sleek
and fat, and manifestly well-to-do in life.   With him
the Dean had trouble; unwieldy and confused and
slow, it was difficult to get him through the crowd

and up to his place in time. They passed me in a
kind of struggle,—the Dean leading and endeavour-
ing to guide, the candidate hanging back and getting
pitched in the throng. Just then I managed to
whisper—

"Why, your peg's surely mazed, maister!"

I was hardly prepared for the result when I "struck
the electric chain wherewith we are darkly bound."
The association came back; the words called up the
scene among the swine; and when the crowd gave way,
there stood the Dean before the Vice-Chancellor's chair,
greeting him, not with a Latin form, but in spasms of
uncontrollable laughter!

To return to the original scene. We ordered Caliban
with our ponies to be ready at the door, and we in the
meanwhile called on our hostess to produce her bill.
She hum'd and ha'd and hesitated, and seemed at a loss
to produce the "little dockyment," which is usually
supposed to be a matter of very fluent composition at
an inn. It was not until we had again and again explained that we desired her to state in writing what
we had to pay, that she seemed at last to comprehend.
A deal of scuffling about the kitchen ensued. There
was quick passing to and fro, in and out; there were
several muttered discussions of the lower house; a
neighbour, who appeared to be a glazier, was sent for;
and at last the door opened, and our red pursy little
hostess bustled in, bobbed a curtsey, and presented for
our perusal her small account, chalked upon the upper
lid of the kitchen bellows, which she gracefully held
towards us by the snout. Poor old Joan Treworgy!
how utterly did thy rough simplicity put to shame
the vaunting tariff and the "establishment charges"
of this nineteenth century of Messrs Brag and Sham!

The bill, which we duly transcribed, and which was then paid and rubbed out, thus ran:—

CAPTENS.

		s.	d.
T for 2		0	6
Sleep for 2		1	0
Meat and Taties and Bier . . .		1	6
Bresks		1	6

Four shillings and sixpence for bed and board for two wolfish appetites for a night and a day, to say nothing of the pantomime performed gratuitously for our behoof, at a very early hour, by Boscastle amateurs! Good day, Mrs Treworgy! good day! "To-morrow to fresh woods and pastures new."

HOLACOMBE.[1]

THERE is a small outlying hamlet in my parochial charge, about two miles from my vicarage, with a population of about two hundred souls, inhabiting a kind of plateau shut in by lofty hills and skirted by the sea. These rural and simple-hearted people, secluded by their remote place of abode from the access of the surrounding world, present a striking picture of old and Celtic England such as it existed two or three hundred years ago. A notion of their solitude and simplicity may be gathered from the fact that, whereas they have no village postman or office, their only mode of intercourse with the outer life of their kind is accomplished through the weekly or other visit of their clergyman. He carries their letters, which contain short but simple annals of the poor, and he receives and returns their weekly and laborious literary compositions to edify and instruct their distant and more civilised correspondents. The address on each

[1] Welcombe, to which Mr Hawker became curate in 1850, and which he continued to serve until his death.—ED.

letter is often such as to baffle all ordinary curiosity, and unless deciphered by the skill of the experts of the post-office, must often furnish hieroglyphics for the study of the Postmaster-General as obscure, if not so antique, as the legends on a pyramid or Rosetta stone. A visit to a distant market-town is an achievement to render a man an authority or an oracle among his brethren; and one who has accomplished that journey twice or thrice is ever regarded as a daring traveller, and consulted about foreign countries with a feeling of habitual respect.

They have amongst them no farrier for their cattle, no medical man for themselves, no beerhouse, no shop; a man who travels for a distant town supplies them with tea by the ounce, or sugar in smaller quantities still. Not a newspaper is taken in throughout the hamlet, although they are occasionally astonished and delighted by the arrival from some almost forgotten friend in Canada of an ancient copy of the 'Toronto Gazette.' This publication they pore over to weariness, and on Sunday they will worry the clergyman with questions about Transatlantic places and names of which he is obliged to confess himself utterly ignorant, a confession which consciously lowers him in their veneration and respect. An ancient dame once exhibited her prayer-book, very nearly worn out, printed in the reign of George II., and very much thumbed at the page from which she assiduously prayed for the welfare of Prince Frederick, without one misgiving that she violated the article of our Church which forbids prayer for the dead.

Among the singular traits of character which are developed amid these, whom I may designate in the German phrase as my mossy parishioners, there is one which I should define, in their extreme simplicity, as exuberant belief, or rather faith in excess. I do not, however, intend by this term any kind of religious peculiarity of tenet or creed, but only a prostration of the intellect before certain old traditionary and inherited impulses of the human mind. They share and they embrace those instinctive tendencies of their Celtic nature which in all ages have led their race to cherish a credence in the existence and power of witches, fairies, and the force of charms and spells. It is well known that all such supernatural influences on ordinary life are singularly congenial to the ancient and the modern Cornish mind. I do not exaggerate when I affirm at all events my own persuasion, that two-thirds of the total inhabitants of Tamar-side implicitly believe in the power of the *Mal Occhio*, as the Italians name it, or the Evil Eye. Is this incredible in a day when the spasms and raps and bad spelling of a familiar spirit are received with acquiescent belief in polished communities, and even in intellectual London? The old notion that a wizard or a witch so became by a nefarious bargain with the enemy of man, and by a surrender of his soul to his ultimate grasp, although still held in many a nook of our western valleys, and by the crooning dame at her solitary hearth, appears to have been exchanged in my hamlet of Holacombe (for such is its name) for a persuasion that these choosers of the slain inherit their faculty from their birth. Whispers of forbidden ties between their parents, and of monstrous and unhallowed alliances of which these children are the issue, largely prevail in this village. There it is held that the witch, like the poet, is so born. I have been gravely assured that there are well-known marks which distinguish the ill-wishers from

all beside. These are black spots under the tongue; in
number five, diagonally placed: " Like those, sir, which
are always found in the feet of swine," and which,
according to the belief of my poor people, and which,
as a Scriptural authority, I was supposed unable to
deny, were first made in the unclean animals by the
entrance of the demons into the ancestral herd at
Gadara. A peculiar kind of eyeball, sometimes bright
and clear, and at others covered with a filmy gauze,
like a gipsy's eye, as it is said, by night; or a double
pupil, ringed twice; or a larger eye on the left than on
the right side ; these are held to be tokens of evil omen,
and accounted to indicate demoniac power, and certain
it is that a peculiar glare or a glance of the eye does
exist in those persons who are pointed out as in possession of the craft of the wizard or witch. But an ancient
man, who lived in a lone house in a gorge near the
church, once actually disclosed to me in mysterious
whispers, and with many a gesture of alarm and dread,
a plan which he had heard from his grandfather, and
by which a person evilly inclined, and anxious for more
power than men ought to possess, might at any time
become a master of the Evil Eye.

"Let him go to chancel," said he, "to sacrament, and
let him hide and bring away the bread from the hands
of the priest; then, next midnight let him take it and
carry it round the church, widdershins—that is, from
south to north, crossing by east three times : the third
time there will meet him a big, ugly, venomous toad,
gaping and gasping with his mouth opened wide, let
him put the bread between the lips of the ghastly
creature, and as soon as ever it is swallowed down his
throat he will breathe three times upon the man, and he
will be made a strong witch for evermore."

I did not fail to express the horror and disgust with which I had listened to this grandsire's tale, and to assure him that any man capable of performing such an atrocious ceremony for such a purpose, must be by his very nature fit for every evil desire, and prepared, of his own mere impulse, to form the most unhallowed wishes for the harm of his fellow-creatures, such as a demon only could delight to fulfil. But the feats which are supposed to be achieved by the witch—for the question proposed by the sapient King Jamie has been solved by the Cornish people, whether the Devil doth not oftener dally with ancient women than men —are invariably deeds of loss and harm: Some felon sow like her of Rokeby, becomes the grunting mother of a large family of farrows; all at once, like Medea, she hates her own offspring with a fiendish hatred, and spurns them all away from her milk. They pine and squeal, and at last sit upright on their hinder parts like pleading children, put their little paws together in piteous fashion, and die one by one. All this would never have come to pass had not the dame, the day before, refused a bottle of milk to one who " should have been a woman," " but that her beard forbade them to interpret that such she were." What graphic tales of " things ill-wished " have I not heard around and within this wild and lonely hamlet! All at once a flock or herd would begin to pine away with some strange and nameless disease, the shepherd's ewes yeaned dead lambs, and were found standing over their lost offspring aghast. Or his cows, " the milky mothers of the herd," would rush from field to field, " quite mad," with their tails erect towards the sky, like the bare poles of a ship in distress scudding before the gale ; or the brown mare would refuse to be har-

nessed, and signify her intention to remain in the stall
on a busy day, to her master's infinite disgust. In the
more civilised part of my parish the well-to-do farmer
would have a remedy. He would mount his horse one
break of day on some secret expedition, and be absent
for another day or two. Then he returns armed with
a packet of white powders, which he scatters carefully,
one at every gate on his farm, and his men hear him as
he goes muttering in solemn fashion some strange set
words, which turn out, when the scroll is submitted to
the schoolmaster afterwards, to contain the blessings of
the twenty-eighth chapter of Deuteronomy, copied in
writing for his use. He has paid a visit, it appears, to
a distant town, and been closeted with a well-known
public character of the west, popularly called the White
Witch, and it is he who has not only exposed the name
and arts of the parish practitioner of evil, but has supplied an antidote in the shape of baffling powders and
" charms of might."

Some years agone a violent thunderstorm passed over
the hamlet of Holacombe, and wrought great damage in
its course. Trees were rooted up, cattle killed, and a
rick or two set on fire. It so befell that I visited, the
day after, one of the chief agricultural inhabitants of
the village, and I found the farmer and his men standing by a ditch wherein lay, heels upward, a fine young
horse quite dead. " Here, sir," he shouted, as I came
on, " only please to look! is not this a sight to see?"
I looked at the poor animal, and uttered my sympathy
and regret at the loss.

" One of the fearful results," I happened to say, " of
the storm and lightning yesterday." " There, Jem,"
said he to one of his men, triumphantly, " didn't I say
the parson would find it out? Yes, sir," he said, " it is

as you say: it is all that wretched old Cherry [1] Parnell's doing, with her vengeance and her noise!" I
stared with astonishment at this unlooked-for interpretation which he had put into my mouth, and waited
for him to explain. "You see, sir," he went on to say,
"the case was this: old Cherry came up to my place,
tottering along and mumbling that she wanted a fagot
of wood. I said to her, 'Cherry,' says I, 'I gave you
one only two days agone, and another two days before
that, and I must say that I didn't make up my wood-
rick altogether for you.' So she turned away, looking
very grany, and muttering something about 'Hotter for
me hereafter.' Well, sir, last night I was in bed, I and
my wife, and all to once there bursted a thunderbolt,
and shaked the very room and house. Up we started,
and my wife says, 'O father, old Cherry's up! I wish
I had gone after her with that there fagot.' I confess I
thought in my mind I wish she had; but it was too
late then, and I would try to hope for the best. But
now, sir, you see with your own eyes what that re-
vengeful old woman hath been and done. And I do
think, sir," he went on to say, changing his tone to a
kind of indignant growl—"I *do* think that when I call
to mind how I've paid tithe and rates faithfully all these
years, and kept my place in church before your reverence every Sabbath-day, and always voted in the vest-
ries that what hath a be ought to be, and so on, I do
think that such ones as old Cherry Parnell never ought
to be allowed to meddle with such things as thunder
and lightning." What could I—what could any man
in his senses—say to this?

The great charmer of charms in this strange corner
of the world is a seventh son born in direct succession

---

[1] *Charity* is the full name.

L

from one father and one mother. Find such a person, and you have "the sayer of good words" always at your command. He is called in our folk-lore the doctor of the district. There is such an old man in my hamlet, popularly called Uncle Tony Cleverdon. He was baptised Anthony; but this has been changed by kindly village parlance and the usage of the West. For with us the pet name is generally the short name, and any one venerable from age and amiable in nature is termed, without relationship, but merely for endearment, "uncle" and "aunt." Uncle Tony has inherited this endowment in a family of thirteen children, he being the seventh born. He often says that his lucky birth has been as good as "a fortin" to him all his life; for although he is forbidden by usage and tradition to take money for the exercise of his functions, nothing has hindered that he should always be invited to sit as an honoured guest at the table furnished with good things in the houses of his votaries. Uncle Tony allowed me, as a vast favour, to take down from his lips some of his formularies: they had never been committed to writing before, he said; not, as I believe, for more than three centuries, for they smack of the middle ages. He very much questioned whether their virtue would not be utterly destroyed when he was gone, by their being "put into ink."

Uncle Tony was like an ancient augur in the science of birds. "Whenever you see one magpie alone by himself," said he, with a look of inimitable sagacity, "that bird is upon no good: spit over your right shoulder three times, and say—

> ' Clean birds by sevens,
> Unclean by twos,
> The dove in the heavens
> Is the one I choose ! ' "

Among the myriads of sea and land birds that throng this coast, the raven is king of the rock. The headland and bulwark of the slope of Holacombe is a precipice of perpendicular rock. There, undisturbed (for no bribe would induce a villager to slay them, old or young), the ravens dwell, revel, and reign. One day, as we watched them in their flapping flight, said Uncle Tony to me, "Sometimes, sir, these wild creatures will be so merciful that they will even save a man's life.' "Indeed! how?" "Why, sir, it came to pass on this wise. There was once a noted old wrecker called Kinsman: he lived in my father's time; and when no wreck was onward, he would get his wages by raising stone in a quarry by the sea-shore. Well, he was to work one day over yonder, half way down Tower Cliff, and all at once he heard a buzz above him in the air, and he looked up, and there were two old ravens flying round and round very near his head. They kept whirling and whirling and coming so nigh, and they seemed so knowing, that the old man thought verily they were trying to speak, as they made a strange croak; but after some time they went away, and old Kinsman went on with his work. Well, sir, by-and-by they both came back again, flying above and round as before; and then at last, lo and behold! the birds dropped right down into the quarry two pieces of wreck-candle just at the old man's feet." (Very often the wreckers pick up Neapolitan wax-candles from vessels in the Mediterranean trade that have been lost in the Channel.) "So when Kinsman saw the candles, he thought in his mind, ' There is surely wreck coming in upon the beach :' so he packed his tools together and left them just where he stood, and went his way wrecking. He could find no jetsam, however, though he searched far and wide, and he used

to say he verily believed that the ravens must have had
the candles at hand in their holt, to be so ready with
them as they were.   Next day he went back to quarry
to his work, and he always used to say it was as true
as a proverb: there the tools were all buried deep
out of sight, for the craig above had given way and
fallen down, and if he had tarried only one hour longer
he must have been crushed to death !   So you see, sir,
what knowledge those ravens must have had; how well
they knew the old man, and how fond he was of wreck;
how crafty they were to hit upon the only plan that
would ever have slocked him away: and the birds,
moreover, must have been kind creatures, and willing
to save a poor fellow's life.   There is nothing on airth
so knowing as a bird is, unless it may be a snake.   Did
you ever hear, sir, how I heal an adder's bite ?   You
cut a piece of hazelwood, sir, and you fasten a long bit
and a short one together into the form of a cross; then
you lay it softly upon the wound, and you say, thrice,
blowing out the words aloud like one of the commandi-
ments—

> ' Underneath this hazelin mote
> There's a Braggoty worm with a speckled throat,
>   Nine double is he :
> Now from nine double to eight double,
> And from eight double to seven double,
> And from seven double to six double,
> And from six double to five double,
> And from five double to four double,
> And from four double to three double,
> And from three double to two double,
> And from two double to one double,
> And from one double to no double,
>   No double hath he !'

"There, sir," said Uncle Tony, "if David had known

that charm he never would have wrote the verse in the
Psalms about the adder that was so deaf that she would
not hear the voice of the charmer, charm he never so
wisely. I never knew that charm fail in all my life!"
Tony added, after a pause—" Fail! of course, sometimes
a body may fail, but then 'tis always from people's
obstinacy and ignorance. I daresay, sir, you've heard
the story of Farmer Colly's mare, how she bled herself
to death ; and they say he puts the blame on me. But
what's the true case? His man came rapping at my
door after I was in bed. I got up and opened the casement and looked out, and I asked what was amiss?
' O Tony,' says he, ' master's mare is blooding streams,
and I be sent over to you to beg you to stop it.' ' Very
well,' I said, ' I can do it just as well here as if I came
down and opened the door : only just tell me the name
of the beast, and I'll proceed.' ' Name,' says he, ' why,
there's no name that I know by ; we allus call her the
black mare.' ' No name?' says I ; ' then how ever can I
charm her? Why, the name's the principal thing!
Fools! never to give her a name to rule the charm by.
Be off! be off! I can't save her.' So the poor old thing
died in course." "And what may your charm be, Tony?"
said I. "Just one verse in Ezekiel, sir, beginning, ' I
said unto thee when thou wast in thy blood, Live.'
And so on. I say it only twice, with an outblow
between each time. But the finest by-word that I
know, sir, is for the prick of a thorn." And here it
follows from my diary in the antique phraseology
which Uncle Tony had received from his forefathers
through descending generations :—

> "Happy man that Christ was born !
> He was crownèd with a thorn :

He was piercèd through the skin,
For to let the poison in;
But His five wounds, so they say,
Closed before He passed away.
In with healing, out with thorn :
Happy man that Christ was born !"

Another time Uncle Tony said to me, "Sir, there is
one thing I want to ask you, if I may be so free, and it
is this, Why should a merry-maid" (the local name for
mermaid), "that will ride about upon the waters in such
terrible storms, and toss from sea to sea in such ruxles
as there be upon the coast—why should she never lose
her looking-glass and comb?" "Well, I suppose," said
I, "that if there are such creatures, Tony, they must
wear their looking-glasses and combs fastened on somehow—like fins to a fish." "See!" said Tony, chuckling
with delight; "what a thing it is to know the Scriptures like your reverence. I never should have found
it out. But there's another point, sir, I should like to
know, if you please; I've been bothered about it in my
mind hundreds of times. Here be I, that have gone
up and down Holacombe cliffs and streams fifty years
come next Candlemas, and I've gone and watched the
water by moonlight and sunlight, days and nights, on
purpose, in rough weather and smooth (even Sundays
too, saving your presence), and my sight as good as
most men's, and yet I never could come to see a merry-
maid in all my life! How's that, sir?" "Are you sure,
Tony," I rejoined, "that there are such things in existence at all?" "Oh, sir, my old father seen her twice!
He was out once by night for wreck (my father watched
the coast like most of the old people formerly), and it
came to pass that he was down by the duck-pool on
the sand at low-water tide, and all at once he heard

music in the sea. Well, he croped on behind a rock, like a coastguard-man watching a boat, and got very near the noise. He couldn't make out the words, but the sound was exactly like Bill Martin's voice, that singed second counter in church. At last he got very near, and there was the merry-maid very plain to be seen, swimming about upon the waves like a woman bathing—and singing away. But my father said it was very sad and solemn to hear—more like the tune of a funeral hymn than a Christmas carol by far—but it was so sweet that it was as much as he could do to hold back from plunging into the tide after her. And he an old man of sixty-seven, with a wife and a house-ful of children at home! The second time was down here by Holacombe Pits. He had been looking out for spars: there was a ship breaking up in the Chan-nel, and he saw some one move just at half-tide mark. So he went on very softly, step and step, till he got nigh the place, and there was the merry-maid sitting on a rock, the bootifullest merry-maid that eye could behold, and she was twisting about her long hair, and dressing it just like one of our girls getting ready for her sweetheart on the Sabbath-day. The old man made sure he should greep hold of her before ever she found him out, and he had got so near that a couple of paces more and he would have caught her by the hair as sure as tithe or tax, when, lo and behold! she looked back and glimpsed him. So in one moment she dived head-foremost off the rock, and then tumbled herself topsy-turvy about in the waters, and cast a look at my poor father, and grinned like a seal!"

HUMPHREY VIVIAN.

AMONG the changes that have passed over the face of our land with such torrent-like rapidity in this wondrous nineteenth century of marvel and miracle, none are more striking and complete than that which has transformed the torpid clergy of past periods into the active and energetic ministers of our own Church and time. The country incumbent of Macaulay's History, the guests at the second table of the patron and the squire—the Trullibers and the Parson Adams of Fielding and Smollett—would find no deuterotype in the present day. But in the transition period of our ecclesiastical history there are here and there fossil memorials of the former men that would enable a thoughtful mind to construct singular specimens of character which, while embodying the past, would also indicate the future lineaments of gradual change and improvement. Among these is one, a personal friend of the writer when he first entered the ministry, whose kindliness of heart and originality of character may supply sundry graphic and interesting reminiscences.

As old Johnson would have said, had he written his life, so let me say of Humphrey Vivian, that he was at once the stately priest, the genial companion, and the faithful, facetious friend. Let me indulge some of these recollections, and gather up some materials of personal history, which are by no means wanting. For it was his great delight, when a guest at my table, after he had done more than justice to the viands set before him, when his gold snuff-box had been produced and ceremoniously offered to all around, and his glass filled with his favourite wine—" sound old Tory port " —to recall in whole volumes the events of his youth and manhood, and to dilate with emphatic gusto on the contrasts of the age and times.

The personal aspect of my friend presented an imposing solemnity to the eye. Tall, even to the measure of six feet two inches, but slender withal as the bole of a poplar-tree, with small features and twinkling eye, and a round undersized head, and yet with a demeanour so pompous, such a frequency of condescending bows, and such a roll of words, that he took immediate rank as a gentleman of the old school. And as to his mental endowments, be it enough to record that there were few men as wise as he looked. His garb was that of a pluralised clergyman of the days of the Georges,—fine black broadcloth, that hung around him in festive moments like mourning on a Maypole. His vest was of rich silk with wide pockets, roomy enough to hold the inevitable snuff-box, the gold *étui*, and the small cock-fighter's saw, which was used to cut away the natural spur of the bird when it was replaced with steel. This last was a common equipment of a country gentleman, lay or clerical, in those days. His apparel terminated in black silk stockings and nether garments, buckled

with gold or silver at the knee. Buckles also clasped
his shoes.   Thus attired, he was no unfit representative
of the clergy who ruled and reigned in their parochial
domain in the west of England in the early part of the
eighteenth century.   His conversational powers were
ample and amusing; but it was when he could be
brought to dilate on his own adventures and history in
earlier life that he most surely riveted and requited
the attention of his auditors.

At my table one day the topic of discourse was the
marriage of the clergy. " The young curates," said he,
" should always marry, and that as soon as ever they
are ordained.   Nothing brightens up a parsonage like
the ribbons of a merry wife.   I, you know, have buried
three Mrs Vivians; and when I come to look back, I
really can hardly decide which it was that made the
happiest home.   If I had to live my life over again, I
should certainly marry all three.   And yet I did not
win my first love, after all.   Her grumpy old father
came between us and blighted our days, as the Psalmist
puts it.   Ah! the very sound of her name is like a
charm to me still.   Bridget Morrice!   But ' Biddy'
she was always called at home; and very soon she
was ' Biddy dear' to me.

" I was at Oxford then, and when I came down for
the ' Long' I used to be very duly at church, because
there I could see Biddy.   Her pew was opposite to
mine; and there was I in full rig as we used to dress
in those days,—long scarlet coat, silk waistcoat with a
figured pattern, and tights.   One Sunday after prayers
up comes old Morrice, roaring like a bull.   ' Mr Vivian,'
he growled, ' I'll trouble you to take your eyes off my
daughter's face in church.   I saw you, sir, when you
pretended to be bowing in the Creed.   You were bow-

ing to Biddy, my daughter, sir, across the aisle; and
that you call attending divine service, do you, sir?'
However, in spite of the old dragon, we used to meet
in the garden, and there, in the arbour, what fruit
Biddy used to give me! Such peaches, plums, and
sometimes cheesecakes and tarts! Talk of a sweet
tooth! I think that in those days I had a whole set;
and now I have but one left of any kind, and that is a
stump. But Biddy treated me very unkindly after all.
There was a regiment of soldiers stationed in the town,
and of course lots of gay young officers fluttering about
in feathers and lace. Well, one day it was rumoured
about that old Morrice and his wife were going to give
a spread, and these captain fellows were to be there,
head and chief. There were to be dinner and a dance,
and I of course thought that, somehow or other, Biddy
would manage with her mother to get me a card and a
corner. I waited and watched; but no—none came.
So at last away I went to the house, angry and fierce,
and determined to have matters cleared up. Old Morrice, luckily, was out, and his wife with him; but there
was Biddy, up to her elbows in jellies and jams, fussing
and fuming like a maid to get things nice and tooth-
some for cockering up those red rascals, that I hated
like grim death. 'Well, Biddy,' I said, 'do you call
this pretty, to serve me so? Here you ask everybody
to your feasts and your junkets—yes, every one in the
town but me!' And what with the vexation and the
smell of the cookery, I actually burst out sobbing
like a boy. This made Biddy cry too, and there was
a scene, sure enough. 'It is father's fault, Henry,
utterly and entirely: he is so mad against you because
he thinks you want me for the sake of his money.'
'Money, Biddy dear!' I said—'money! Now I do

think that if I bring blood your father ought to bring
groats !'

"Just then some one lifted the latch, and poor
Biddy began to scream: 'O Henry, dear! what shall I
do? That's father come back. He'll surely kill you
or me, or do some rash deed. What can I do? Here,
here,' she said, opening a kind of closet-door, 'step in,
that's a dear, and wait till I can get you out. Don't
cough or sneeze, but keep quiet and still as a mouse
till I come to call you.' In I went, and Biddy shut
the door. Well, do you know, I found she had put me
in a sort of storeroom, where they kept the sweets ;
and on a long table there was such a spread : raspberry-
creams, ices, jellies, all kinds of flummery, and in the
middle a thing I never could resist—a fine sugary cake.
Didn't I help myself ! and when I began to think that
all these niceties were got up to fill up the waistcoats
of those rollicking fellows that had cut me out of my
Biddy's heart, it did make me half mad. However,
when I thought of that cake, I said to myself, 'Not
one crumb of that lovely thing shall go down their
horrid throats after all—see if it does !' We wore long
wide pockets in those days, big enough to hold a
Christmas pie. So in went the cake ; and there was
room besides for a whole plate of macaroons. Pres-
ently Biddy was at the door, and in such a way.
'Make haste, Henry, dear—quick ; and do go straight
home ! I would not have you meet father for the
world !' You may guess how I scudded away through
the streets with my skirts bulging out, and the boys
shouting after me, 'There goes the Oxford scholar with
his humps slipped down !'

"Next time I met Biddy, it was coming out of
church. She could hardly tell whether to laugh or

cry. 'How could you, Henry, dear?' she said,—'how could you carry off our beautiful cake?' 'How? Biddy dear,' said I; 'why, in my pocket, to be sure.'

"But the worst of all was that Biddy was cold to me from that very time; and when I came home from college the next year I heard that she was engaged to a Captain Upjohns, and she was married to him not long after. So he had Biddy and I had the cake. But she was my first love; and I do think, after all, notwithstanding the three Mrs Vivians, she was verily my last love also. People say that Queen Mary declared that if she was opened after her death, Calais would be found graven on her heart. And I, too, say often, that if my dead bosom were examined, it would be found that Biddy Morrice was carved on mine.

"Well, well; time passed away—years upon years. I was ordained, and served half-a-dozen curacies— three at once for some time; and then I got, one after another, my two first livings. I was a widower. I had lost the first—no, no, I am sorry to say the second Mrs Vivian, when one day I heard that Biddy Morrice was a rich widow. Old Upjohns, it seems, had died and left her no end of money. And then the thought occurred to me that we two might come together after all. ''Twould be like a romance,' I said. I found out that she was settled in great style at Bath. So up I went and found, sure enough, she had a splendid house. A fine formal old butler received me, and I sent up my name. I was shown into a splendid drawing-room, with rich furniture, like a bishop's palace, all velvet and gold. I sat down, thinking over old times, when Biddy used to come to meet me with her rosy cheeks and her strawberry mouth, and a waist you might span with your hand. At last the door opened, and in she came. But alack, alas! such a cat! oh dear, oh dear! and with such a bow-window: it was surprising,—more like old Mrs Morrice than my Biddy. I was aghast. I never kissed her, as I intended, but I stood staring like a gawky. I remember I offered her a pinch of snuff, which she took. We had a talk, but it was all prisms and prunes with Biddy. However, she invited me to dinner the next day, and I went. Everything first-rate,—turbot and haunch, and so on, all upon sil- ver; fine old Madeira, and glorious port; and that sleek fellow, the butler, ruling over all! There was a moderate dessert, and on the middle dish there was such a cake! 'I remember,' said Biddy, but without the shadow of a smile —'I remember that you are fond of cake.' Well, after the cloth was removed, I felt all the better for my dinner, and it is at that time I always have most courage, particularly after the third glass. As I looked on the sleek butler and his pompous ways, I thought to myself, 'I should like to dethrone that rule, and reign myself over her cellar.'

"So I broached the subject of my wishes. 'Don't you think, Biddy dear,' said I, 'now that my second Mrs V. has gone, and old Upjohns also out of the way, that we two——?' 'O Henry, Henry,' she broke in; 'the old Adam is still, I see, strong as ever in you. As sweet Mr Cheekey says at our Bethesda, "We are all criminally minded to our dying day."' Never believe me if Bridget had not turned Methodist, and all that. And so, in short, she cut me dead. However, she sent me this snuff-box, and I had her picture put under the lid. Sweet face, isn't it? But then it was taken thirty years before that dinner at Bath."

But it was when the conversation turned upon curacies, and stipends, and the usual topers among clerical guests, that our friend Humphrey's remembrances became of chief interest and value. "Oh, the changes that I have lived to see!" was his favourite phrase. "I remember so well when I was ordained deacon, and came down in my brand-new bombasine bachelor's gown, and a hood that made me look behind like a two-year-old goat, and bands half-a-yard long, what a swell I used to think myself to be! Talk of your one good curacy! why, when I began to work I served four. Ay, and I had £10 apiece for them, and thought myself in paradise. I remember there were three of us. John Braddon—he had two curacies and the evening lecture; and Millerford we thought very low down—he had two and no more. We all lived, sir, in the town, and boarded and lodged together. £20 a-year each we paid the unfortunate fellow that took us in. Our first landlord was old Geake, the grocer. He stood it twelve months, and then broke all to pieces, and was made bankrupt by his creditors. He actually said in court that we had eaten and drunk all his substance. Well, then, a man called Stag undertook us. He was a market-gardener; and, do you know, after a time he went too! He said it was not so much the meat we consumed, but he had no more vegetables to sell. So we cut him. At last an old fellow named Brewer came forward, and said he would try his luck with us. He stood it pretty well, but then his wife had private property of her own; but she used to say it all went under the waistcoats of the young clergy. She had no family; but she said she would rather have had six children of her own than keep us three. But, no doubt, she exaggerated. Women will do so sometimes."

"Did you live well, Mr Vivian?" we interposed.

"Like fighting-cocks, sir. We insisted on good break-
fasts, plain joints and plenty for dinner, and nice hot
suppers. We didn't care much about tea—nobody did
in those days. But then, behind the parlour door there
was always a keg of brandy on tap, and we had a right
to go with our little tin cups and draw the spigot twice
a-day."

"No doubt, Mr Vivian, you worked hard in those
days?"

"Didn't we? To be sure it was only on Sundays,
but it was enough for all the week. We used to start
in the morning and travel on foot to all the points of
the compass, every man of us with his umbrella. My
first service was at nine o'clock in the morning, prayers
and sermon. Then on to Tregare at half-past eleven,
West Lariston at two o'clock, and Kimovick at four,
and home in the evening, pretty well done up. Braddon and Millerford just the same tramp. But then,
how we did enjoy our roast goose, sirloin, or leg of
mutton afterwards! We bargained expressly for a hot
dinner on Sundays, and we had it too. Then what fun
afterwards! Every man had something to tell about
his parish. I remember Millerford had to call and see
an old woman, a reputed witch. He was to examine
her mouth, and see if the roof had the five black marks
that stamped an old woman as a witch. He wished to
save her, and he declared that she had but four, and
one of them doubtful. One day Braddon had cbris-
tened a man-child, as he thought, Thomas; but the
next week the father came in great perplexity. ''Twas
the mistake of the nurse. 'Tis a girl. How shall us
do? Us can never call a maid Tom. You must christen
her over again, sir.' As this could not be, we had to
put our heads together, and at last we advised Braddon

to alter the name to Thomasine (pronounced Tamzine), and so he just saved her sex.

"One day I had a good story of my own to relate about a pinch of snuff. It was always the custom in those days for the clergyman after the marriage to salute the bride first, before any other person. Well, it was so that I had just married a very buxom, rosy young lady, and when it was over I proceeded to observe the usual ceremony. But I had just before taken an enormous finger-and-thumb-ful of snuff; so no sooner had the bride received my kiss—and I gave her a smart kiss for her good looks—than she began to sneeze. The bridegroom kissed her, of course, and he began also. Then the best man advanced to the privilege. Better he hadn't, for he began to sneeze awfully; and by-and-by the bridesmaids also, for they were all kissed in turn, till the whole party went sneezing down the aisle, and the last thing I heard outside the church door was 'tchu, 'tchu, 'tchu, till the noise was drowned by the bells from the tower."

"But I suppose, Mr Vivian, you did not remain long a curate; you must have received some of your several livings at an early period of life?"

"So I did, sir, sure enough. My text on such subjects was, '*Ask not, and you shall never receive.*' First of all, I had the vicarage of Percombe, up towards the moors. This came from a private friend. Next, the Duchy gave me the rectory of South Wingley. I had trouble enough to get it. I went up to London, and besieged the Council two or three times a-day. People said they gave me the living to get rid of me from town. But it wasn't so. Next I had Trelegh from the second Mrs Vivian's uncle. Yes, yes, preferment enough for one man. By the by, did you ever hear how near

M

I was once to the lawn-sleeves and the bench? That was a close shave! I was staying in Bath, at the York House, and there I always dined in the coffee-room. Well, one day a gentleman came in and ordered dinner in the next box to mine—a sole and a chop. I observed a bottle of Madeira wine; and from his nicety and parlour ways, I judged him to be some big-wig, and very rich. I saw he looked about for a news 'Gazette,' so I offered him mine, and exchanged a few words by way of getting known to him. He offered me a glass of wine, and of course I took it, and sat down to converse. We grew very friendly, and by-and-by it turned out that his name was Vivian, and spelt exactly like mine. It was growing late, and he took leave, but, to my surprise, invited me to dine with him the next day at Lansdowne Crescent. I was only too glad to go. It was a noble house, with a troop of servants and superb furniture, and, what was most to the purpose, a glorious feed. After dinner, at dessert-time, while we were talking over our wine, I saw, over the mantelpiece, a fine picture of Perceval, the Prime Minister at that time. So I ventured to ask, 'Is Mr Perceval, sir, a relative of your family?' 'No, sir, no,' he said. 'I have his picture because I like his politics, and respect him as a Minister and as a man. I have been introduced to him, however, and I can claim some personal acquaintance with him.' 'Have you, my friend?' thought I. 'Then, take my word for it, I will make use of you as a stepping-stone in life.' So, when it was nearly time to wish him good night, I said, 'I have a favour to ask you, sir. I am going to town in a. day or two, and I shall be deeply obliged if you will write a letter to Mr Perceval, merely telling him that the bearer is a friend of yours, a clergyman in quest of

some preferment, and that as he is the patron of so
many good things in the Church, you will be much
obliged to him if he will bestow something valuable on
your friend.' He looked rather glum at this, and
twirled his fingers a bit, and at length said, 'Why, no,
Mr Vivian, I can't go so far as that. Consider, I have
known you only a few hours, and have never heard you
officiate—although, no doubt, you are well qualified to
hold preferment in the Church. But I'll tell you what
I will do. I have a friend, the rector of the parish
where Mr Perceval lives, and I know he always attends
his church. I will give you a letter to him, and he
may suggest some opportunity of promoting your plan.'
Of course I jumped at this, took my letter, and was off
by the mail the very next day. The first man I called
on was, of course, the clergyman. It was on a Saturday, and by good luck he had been taken ill. I was
shown in where he lay on a sofa, looking quite ghastly.
'Have you got a sermon with you, Mr Vivian?' said
he; 'anything will do.' I always took with me, wherever I went, some half-dozen, and I said so. 'Because,
as you see, I cannot go to church to-morrow, and a
friend who was to have taken my duty has disappointed
me. I shall be indeed thankful if you will undertake
the work.' This was the very thing; and accordingly
I was in the vestry-hall the next morning, an hour
before time, rigged out in full canonicals, hired for the
day—silk and sarcenet—and my hair well frizzed, as
you may suppose. Just before service I said to the
clerk, 'I am told that Mr Perceval attends your church;
can you point out to me his pew?' 'That I can, sir,'
said he, 'in a moment. There it is in full front of the
desk and pulpit, the third pew down, with the brass
rods and silk curtains.' Well, the service began; but

the said pew was empty till the end of the Belief, when,
lo and behold! in came the beadle, marching with great
pomp, and after him Mr Perceval and some friends.
You may guess after that what eyes and ears I had for
the rest of the congregation. There was the Prime
Minister; I see him now, in his purple coat and cuffs,
silk waistcoat—fine as Sisera's—and with a wig that
looked like wisdom itself. He was very attentive. I
watched him, and saw how careful he was to keep time
with all the service. At length came the last psalm,
and up I went. The pulpit fitted me as if it had been
made for me; and the cushion, I remember, was all
velvet and gold. My text was, 'Where is the wise
man? where is the scribe? where is the disputer?'
&c. I saw that Mr Perceval never took his eyes off
my face all through the discourse. It was one of my
very best sermons. I saw that he was delighted with
it; and when I came to the end, I observed that he
turned round and looked up at me, and whispered
something to a gentleman who was with him, and then
they both looked up at me, and smiled. Said I to
myself, 'Humphrey, the golden ball is cast; thy fortune
is made, as sure as rates and taxes. Look out for a
bishopric, and that soon!' I never was so happy in
all my life. I dined that night at the Mitre in Fleet
Street, on a rump-steak; and I often caught myself
smiling and slapping my thigh and muttering. I saw
the waiter stare when I said to myself, but in an
audible voice, 'Done for a guinea! Make way for my
lord!' Next day I went into the City to meet ——,
who was in town on business. After he had settled
what he came to do, he walked some way home with
me. Well, sir, when we came to the Strand there was
a dreadful uproar, people talking very low and seriously.

At length a gentleman said to my companion, ' Have you heard the dreadful news ? A rascal called Bellingham has shot Mr Perceval dead in the lobby of the House of Commons !' It was like a deathblow to me. Poor fellow ! It cut me through like a knife. I was indeed a crushed man, clean dissolved, as the psalm says. And from that very hour I have been convinced and persuaded—ay, I do believe it like the Creed—that the very same ball that shot poor Perceval cut away a mitre from my head as clean as a whistle. Yes, I have never swerved from that belief all these years; and up to this day, when I say my prayers, as I do after I am in bed, I always begin with the Confirmation, from ' Defend, &c., this Thy servant.' "

OLD TREVARTEN:

A TALE OF THE PIXIES.

Mount and follow ! stout and cripple !
  Horse and hattock, "but and ben" ;
Horses for the Pixie people,
  Hattock for the Brownie men.
          —R. S. HAWKER.

PEOPLE may talk if they please about the march of
agriculture, and they may boast that by the discoveries of science a man will soon be able to carry
into a large field enough manure for its soil in his coat-
pocket, but there has been the ready answer, "Yes, and
bring away the produce in his fob." I am half inclined
to agree with an old parishioner of mine, who used often
to say, "It was an unlucky time for England when the
phrase 'gentleman farmer' came up, and folks began
to try their new-fangled plans—such as clover for
horses and turnips for sheep." "Rents," he declared,
"were never lower than when a tenant would pare

and burn,[1] and take their crops out of every field, so
as to carry off the land as much as he brought on it"
—a theory on which, being a renter himself, he had
thriven, and put by money for full fifty years. Equally
original, by the way, were the devices cherished by my
aged friend for the repair of roads. When Macadam
had driven his first turnpike through the West, a public
dinner was given in honour of the event; and being
presented with a free ticket, and well coaxed into the
bargain, Old Trevarten made his appearance as a guest.
But it was observed that, amid all the jingling of glasses
and cheering of toasts, he sat motionless and mute, if
not actually sulky. At length the engineer, somewhat
piqued at his silence, said, during a pause, "Why, sir,
I am afraid that I have not had the honour of gaining
your approval in this undertaking of mine."

"To tell you the truth, sir," was the slow and
sturdy answer, "I don't like your road at all, by no
means."

"Well, but what are your reasons, sir, for disliking
what most people are pleased with?"

"Why, sir, you have had a brave lot of money out of
the country, and there's nothing as I see to show for it
—'tis all gone!"

"Gone, sir, gone! Why, bless me, isn't there the
road—the fine, wide, level road?"

"Well, yes, sartainly; but where's they matereyals
that cost such a sight of taxes? You've smashed mun
to nort: there's pilm [dust] in the drought, and there's
mucks [mud] in the rain, but nowt else that I see.
Now, when I wor waywarden of Wide Widger, I let

[1] A reference to a custom, still followed to some extent in South
Devon and Cornwall, of paring the turf of grass-fields and burning the
sods.

the farmers have something to show for their money. Why, sir, 'tis ten year agone come Candlemas that I wor in office for the ways, and I put down stones as big as beehives, and there they be now!"

Access to such a living volume of bygone usages and notions was an advantage not to be despised; and it was long my custom to resort to "mine ancient" for information difficult to be obtained elsewhere. Once " I do remember me" that I encountered him in the middle of a reedy marsh on his farm. He paused, and awaited my approach, leaning on his staff just where the path crossed a bed of the cotton-rush, then in full bloom. I had gathered a handful of the stalks, each with its pod of fine white gossamer threads, like a bunch of snowy silk.

" Ha!" said he, with a kind of half alarm, " you beant afeared to pick that there ?"

" Afraid ? No; why should I be ?"

" Why, some people think it's unlucky to carry off the pisky wool; but perhaps you know from the Scriptures how to keep off any harm."

I did know better than to reason against such fancies with a Cornish yeoman of threescore and fifteen, and I thought it a good opening for a saw or ancient instance. " Pixies!" was my leading answer; " and who are they ?"

" Ancient inhabitants," was the grave reply—"folks that used to live in the land before us Christians comed here. So, at least, I've heerd my mother say. They are a small people."

" And what about this wool ? What use do they make of it."

" Why, they spin it for clothing, and to keep 'em warm by night. They'd do a power of work for the farmers, and for a very small matter to eat and drink, too ; and they would sing, evenings—sing and crowdie like a Christmas choir."

The solemn tones of his voice, and the grim gravity of visage with which old Trevarten made known these mysteries, attested his own deep belief in their reality and truth. " Had I never seen those rings on the grass upon Hennacleare Hill—circles about a foot wide, of a darker colour than the rest of the turf ? " he inquired, well knowing that I had, but rather rejoicing in an opportunity of enlightening me with scientific revelations of his own. " Did I know how they came there, and who made them ? "

" No."

" Well, that was surprising: he thought that the college teached such things, or why did it cost so much money to go there to learn ? Howsomever, *he* would let me know about they rings. The piskies made mun, dancing hand-in-hand by night. They rise about midnight, and they put on their Sunday clothes, and they agree to meet in such or such a spot, and there one will crowdie and the others daunce, and beat out the time with their feet, till they've worn the shape of a roundabout in the grass, and nort will wear out that ring for evermore ! "

Deeply grateful for this information, I ventured to inquire, " And did you ever see any of these pixy people yourself ? "

" Why, I can't say for sartain that I didno seed mun ; my mother hath—so I've yeerd her tell divers times. No; but I've seed their works, such as tying up the manes of the colts in stirrups for riding by night, and terrifying the cows into the clover till they wor jist a bosted with the wet grass. And I've been pisky-eyed

more than once coming home from the market or fair ;
and I've yeerd mun at their rollicking night-times fray-
quently, but I can't say that I ever seed their faytures,
so as to know 'em again another time."

"Well," said I, as a sort of closing and clenching
remark, "all I can say is that I wish I could lay hold
of one of these pixies, just to look at—that's all."

"Do you ?" was his quick rejoinder ; "do you really
desire it ? I daresay I can oblige you one day. It is
not a month agone that I'd all but catched one."

"Indeed !" said I, half bewildered. "How ? Where
was it ?"

"Why, sir, you see the case was this. I'd a bin to
Simon Jude fair, and I stayed rather latish settling with
the jobber Brown for some sheep, and so it wor past
twelve o'clock at night before I come through Stowe
wood ; and just as I crossed Combe Water, sure enough
I yeerd the piskies. I know'd very well where their
ring was close by the gate, and so I stopped my horse
and got off. Well, on I croped afoot till there was
nothing but a gap between me and the pisky ring, and
I could hear every word they said. One had got the
crowder, and he was working away his elbow to the
tune of ' Green Slieves ' bravely, and the rest wor daunc-
ing and singing and merrymaking like a stage-play. It
made me just 'mazed in my head to look at 'em. Well,
I thort to myself, if I could but catch one of these
chaps to carry home. I've yeerd that there's nothing
so lucky in a house as a tame pisky. So I stooped
down and I picked up a stone, oh, as big as my two fistes,
and I swinged my arm and I scrashed the stone right
into the ring. What a screech there was ! Such a
yell ! and one in pertickler I yeerd screaming and
hopping with a leg a-brok like a drashel. That one I

was pretty sure of. But still, as it was very late, and my wife would be looking for me home, and it was dark also, so I thout I might as well come down and fetch my pisky in the morning by daylight. Well, sure enough, soon as I rose, I took one of these baskets with a cover that the women have invented—a ridicule they call it—and down I goes to the ring. And do you know, sir, they'd a be so cunning—they'd a had the art for to carry their comrade clear off, and there wasn't so much as a screed of one left! But, however," said my venerable friend, seeing that I did not look quite satisfied with the evidence—"however, there the stone was that I drashed in amongst mun!"

Alas! alas! how often in after-days, when I have encountered the theories of men learned in the 'ologies, and pondering the prodigious inferences which they had deduced from a stratum here and a deposit there, —how irresistibly have my thoughts recurred to old Trevarten and his amount of proof, "There the stone was that I drashed in amongst mun!"

THE END.

PRINTED BY WILLIAM BLACKWOOD AND SONS.

IT IS HOPED SHORTLY TO PUBLISH,

UNIFORM WITH THE PRESENT VOLUME,

THE COLLECTED POETICAL WORKS OF
REV. R. S. HAWKER.

WILLIAM BLACKWOOD & SONS, EDINBURGH AND LONDON.

Catalogue

of

Messrs Blackwood & Sons'

Publications

PHILOSOPHICAL CLASSICS FOR ENGLISH READERS.

EDITED BY WILLIAM KNIGHT, LL.D.,
Professor of Moral Philosophy in the University of St Andrews.

In crown 8vo Volumes, with Portraits, price 3s. 6d.

Contents of the Series.

DESCARTES, by Professor Mahaffy, Dublin.—BUTLER, by Rev. W. Lucas Collins, M.A.—BERKELEY, by Professor Campbell Fraser.—FICHTE, by Professor Adamson, Glasgow. — KANT, by Professor Wallace, Oxford.—HAMILTON, by Professor Veitch, Glasgow.—HEGEL, by the Master of Balliol.—LEIBNIZ, by J. Theodore Merz.—VICO by Professor Flint, Edinburgh.—HOBBES, by Professor Croom Robertson. — HUME, by the Editor. — SPINOZA, by the Very Rev. Principal Caird, Glasgow.— BACON : Part 1. The Life, by Professor Nichol.—BACON : Part II. Philosophy, by the same Author.—LOCKE, by Professor Campbell Fraser.

FOREIGN CLASSICS FOR ENGLISH READERS.
EDITED BY MRS OLIPHANT.

In crown 8vo, 2s. 6d.

Contents of the Series.

DANTE, by the Editor. — VOLTAIRE, by General Sir E. B. Hamley, K.C.B.—PASCAL, by Principal Tulloch. — PETRARCH, by Henry Reeve, C.B.—GOETHE, by A. Hayward, Q.C.—MOLIÈRE, by the Editor and F. Tarver, M.A.—MONTAIGNE, hy Rev. W. L. Collins, M.A.—RABELAIS, by Sir Walter Besant. — CALDERON, by E. J. Hasell. — SAINT SIMON, hy Clifton W. Collins, M.A.—CERVANTES, by the Editor. — CORNEILLE AND RACINE, by Henry M. Trollope. — MADAME DE SÉVIGNÉ, by Miss Thackeray.—LA FONTAINE, AND OTHER FRENCH FABULISTS, by Rev. W. Lucas Collins, M.A.—SCHILLER, by James Sime, M.A., Author of 'Lessing, his Life and Writings.'—TASSO, by E. J. Hasell. — ROUSSEAU, hy Henry Grey Graham. — ALFRED DE MUSSET, by C. F. Oliphant.

ANCIENT CLASSICS FOR ENGLISH READERS.
EDITED BY THE REV. W. LUCAS COLLINS, M.A.

CHEAP RE-ISSUE. In limp cloth, fcap. 8vo, price 1s. each.

Two Volumes will be issued Monthly in the following order :—

HOMER: ILIAD,	. . The Editor.	*Ready.*	HESIOD AND THEOGNIS, J. Davies.		*Ready.*
HOMER: ODYSSEY,	The Editor.		PLAUTUS AND TERENCE, The Editor.		
HERODOTUS,	. . G. C. Swayne.	*Ready.*	TACITUS, . . .	W. B. Donne.	*Ready.*
CÆSAR, . .	Anthony Trollope.		LUCIAN, .	. The Editor.	
VIRGIL, .	. . . . The Editor.	*Ready.*	PLATO, . . .	C. W. Collins.	*Ready.*
HORACE, .	Sir Theodore Martin.		GREEK ANTHOLOGY, Lord Neaves.		
ÆSCHYLUS, .	Bishop Copleston.	*Ready.*	LIVY, . .	. . The Editor.	*Ready.*
XENOPHON, . .	Sir Alex. Grant.		OVID, ...	Rev. A. Church.	
CICERO, .	. . The Editor.	*Ready.*	CATULLUS, TIBULLUS, AND PROPERTIUS, . . . J. Davies.		1898. *Jan.*
SOPHOCLES, .	. . C. W. Collins.		DEMOSTHENES, . W. J. Brodribb.		
PLINY, .	Church and Brodribb.	*Ready.*	ARISTOTLE, .	Sir Alex. Grant.	*Feb.*
EURIPIDES,	. . W. B. Donne.		THUCYDIDES, .	. The Editor.	
JUVENAL, . .	. . E. Walford.	*Ready.*	LUCRETIUS, .	W. H. Mallock.	*March.*
ARISTOPHANES, .	. The Editor.		PINDAR, . .	Rev. F. D. Morice.	

CATALOGUE

OF

MESSRS BLACKWOOD & SONS'

PUBLICATIONS.

ALISON.
    History of Europe. By Sir ARCHIBALD ALISON, Bart., D.C.L.
    1. From the Commencement of the French Revolution to
      the Battle of Waterloo.
      LIBRARY EDITION, 14 vols., with Portraits. Demy 8vo, £10, 10s.
      ANOTHER EDITION, in 20 vols. crown 8vo, £6.
      PEOPLE'S EDITION. 13 vols. crown 8vo, £2, 11s.
    2. Continuation to the Accession of Louis Napoleon.
      LIBRARY EDITION, 8 vols. 8vo, £6, 7s. 6d.
      PEOPLE'S EDITION, 8 vols. crown 8vo. 34s.
    Epitome of Alison's History of Europe. Thirtieth Thou-
    sand, 7s. 6d.
    Atlas to Alison's History of Europe. By A. Keith Johnston.
      LIBRARY EDITION, demy 4to, £3, 3s.
      PEOPLE'S EDITION, 31s. 6d.
    Life of John Duke of Marlborough. With some Account of
    his Contemporaries, and of the War of the Succession. Third Edition. 2 vols.
    8vo. Portraits and Maps, 30s.
    Essays : Historical, Political, and Miscellaneous. 3 vols.
    demy 8vo, 45s.

ACROSS FRANCE IN A CARAVAN: BEING SOME ACCOUNT
    OF A JOURNEY FROM BORDEAUX TO GENOA IN THE "ESCAROOT," taken in the Winter
    1889-90. By the Author of 'A Day of my Life at Eton.' With fifty Illustrations
    by John Wallace, after Sketches by the Author, and a Map. Cheap Edition,
    demy 8vo, 7s. 6d.

ACTA SANCTORUM HIBERNIÆ ; Ex Codice Salmanticensi.
    Nunc primum integre edita opera CAROLI DE SMEDT et JOSEPHI DE BACKER, e
    Soc. Jesu, Hagiographorum Bollandianorum ; Auctore et Sumptus Largiente
    JOANNE PATRICIO MARCHIONE BOTHÆ. In One handsome 4to Volume, bound in
    half roxburghe, £2, 2s.; in paper cover, 31s. 6d.

ADOLPHUS. Some Memories of Paris. By F. ADOLPHUS.
    Crown 8vo, 6s.

AFLALO. A Sketch of the Natural History (Vertebrates) of
    the British Islands. By F. G. AFLALO, F.R.G.S., F.Z.S., Author of 'A Sketch
    of the Natural History of Australia,' &c. With numerous Illustrations by Lodge
    and Bennett. In 1 vol. crown 8vo.   *[In the press.*

AIKMAN.
    Manures and the Principles of Manuring. By C. M. AIKMAN,
    D.Sc., F.R.S.E., &c., Professor of Chemistry, Glasgow Veterinary College;
    Examiner in Chemistry, University of Glasgow, &c. Crown 8vo, 6s. 6d.
    Farmyard Manure : Its Nature, Composition, and Treatment.
    Crown 8vo, 1s. 6d.

BLACKWOOD.

New Educational Series. *See separate Catalogue.*

New Uniform Series of Novels (Copyright).
Crown 8vo, cloth. Price 3s. 6d. each. Now ready :—

THE MAID OF SKER. By R. D. Blackmore.
WENDERHOLME. By P. G. Hamerton.
THE STORY OF MARORÉDEL. By D. Storrar Meldrum.
MISS MARJORIBANKS. By Mrs Oliphant.
THE PERPETUAL CURATE, and THE RECTOR. By the Same.
SALEM CHAPEL, and THE DOCTOR'S FAMILY. By the Same.
A SENSITIVE PLANT. By E. D. Gerard.
LADY LEE'S WIDOWHOOD. By General Sir E. B. Hamley.
KATIE STEWART, and other Stories. By Mrs Oliphant.
VALENTINE AND HIS BROTHER. By the Same.
SONS AND DAUGHTERS. By the Same.
MARMORNE. By P. G. Hamerton.

REATA. By E. D. Gerard.
BEGGAR MY NEIGHBOUR. By the Same.
THE WATERS OF HERCULES. By the Same.
FAIR TO SEE. By L. W. M. Lockhart.
MINE IS THINE. By the Same.
DOUBLES AND QUITS. By the Same.
ALTIORA PETO. By Laurence Oliphant.
PICCADILLY. By the Same. With Illustrations.
LADY BABY. By D. Gerard.
THE BLACKSMITH OF VOE. By Paul Cushing.
THE DILEMMA. By the Author of 'The Battle of Dorking.'
MY TRIVIAL LIFE AND MISFORTUNE. By A Plain Woman.
POOR NELLIE. By the Same.

Standard Novels. Uniform in size and binding. Each complete in one Volume.

FLORIN SERIES, Illustrated Boards. Bound in Cloth, 2s. 6d.

TOM CRINGLE'S LOG. By Michael Scott.
THE CRUISE OF THE MIDGE. By the Same.
CYRIL THORNTON. By Captain Hamilton.
ANNALS OF THE PARISH. By John Galt.
THE PROVOST, &c. By the Same.
SIR ANDREW WYLIE. By the Same.
THE ENTAIL. By the Same.
MISS MOLLY. By Beatrice May Butt.
REGINALD DALTON. By J. G. Lockhart.

PEN OWEN. By Dean Hook.
ADAM BLAIR. By J. G. Lockhart.
LADY LEE'S WIDOWHOOD. By General Sir E. B. Hamley.
SALEM CHAPEL. By Mrs Oliphant.
THE PERPETUAL CURATE. By the Same.
MISS MARJORIBANKS. By the Same.
JOHN : A Love Story. By the Same.

SHILLING SERIES, Illustrated Cover. Bound in Cloth, 1s. 6d.

THE RECTOR, and THE DOCTOR'S FAMILY. By Mrs Oliphant.
THE LIFE OF MANSIE WAUCH. By D. M. Moir.
PENINSULAR SCENES AND SKETCHES. By F. Hardman.

SIR FRIZZLE PUMPKIN, NIGHTS AT MESS, &c.
THE SUBALTERN.
LIFE IN THE FAR WEST. By G. F. Ruxton.
VALERIUS : A Roman Story. By J. G. Lockhart.

BON GAULTIER'S BOOK OF BALLADS. Fifteenth Edition. With Illustrations by Doyle, Leech, and Crowquill. Fcap. 8vo, 5s.

BOWHILL. Questions and Answers in the Theory and Practice of Military Topography. By Major J. H. BOWHILL. In 1 vol. crown 8vo. With Atlas containing 34 working plans and diagrams. [*In the press.*

BRADDON. Thirty Years of Shikar. By Sir EDWARD BRADDON, K.C.M.G. With Illustrations by G. D. Giles, and Map of Oudh Forest Tracts and Nepal Terai. Demy 8vo, 18s.

BROUGHAM. Memoirs of the Life and Times of Henry Lord Brougham. Written by HIMSELF. 3 vols. 8vo, £2, 8s. The Volumes are sold separately, price 16s. each.

BROWN. The Forester : A Practical Treatise on the Planting and Tending of Forest-trees and the General Management of Woodlands. By JAMES BROWN, LL.D. Sixth Edition, Enlarged. Edited by JOHN NISBET, D.Œc., Author of 'British Forest Trees,' &c. In 2 vols. royal 8vo, with 350 Illustrations, 42s. net.

Also being issued in 15 Monthly parts, price 2s. 6d. net each.
[*Parts 1 to 11 ready.*

BROWN. A Manual of Botany, Anatomical and Physiological. For the Use of Students. By ROBERT BROWN, M.A., Ph.D. Crown 8vo, with numerous Illustrations, 12s. 6d.

BRUCE.

In Clover and Heather. Poems by WALLACE BRUCE. New and Enlarged Edition. Crown 8vo, 3s. 6d.
A limited number of Copies of the First Edition, on large hand-made paper, 12s. 6d.

Here's a Hand. Addresses and Poems. Crown 8vo, 5s.
Large Paper Edition, limited to 100 copies, price 21s.

BUCHAN. Introductory Text-Book of Meteorology. By ALEXANDER BUCHAN, LL.D., F.R.S.E., Secretary of the Scottish Meteorological Society, &c. New Edition. Crown 8vo, with Coloured Charts and Engravings.
[*In preparation.*

BURBIDGE.

Domestic Floriculture, Window Gardening, and Floral Decorations. Being Practical Directions for the Propagation, Culture, and Arrangement of Plants and Flowers as Domestic Ornaments. By F. W. BURBIDGE. Second Edition. Crown 8vo, with numerous Illustrations, 7s. 6d.

Cultivated Plants: Their Propagation and Improvement. Including Natural and Artificial Hybridisation, Raising from Seed, Cuttings and Layers, Grafting and Budding, as applied to the Families and Genera in Cultivation. Crown 8vo, with numerous Illustrations, 12s. 6d.

BURGESS. The Viking Path: A Tale of the White Christ. By J. J. HALDANE BURGESS, Author of 'Rasmie's Büddie,' 'Shetland Sketches,' &c. Crown 8vo, 6s.

BURKE. The Flowering of the Almond Tree, and other Poems. By CHRISTIAN BURKE. Pott 4to, 5s.

BURROWS.

Commentaries on the History of England, from the Earliest Times to 1865. By MONTAGU BURROWS, Chichele Professor of Modern History in the University of Oxford; Captain R.N.; F.S.A., &c.; "Officier de l'Instruction Publique," France. Crown 8vo, 7s. 6d.

The History of the Foreign Policy of Great Britain. Demy 8vo, 12s.

BURTON.

The History of Scotland: From Agricola's Invasion to the Extinction of the last Jacobite Insurrection. By JOHN HILL BURTON, D.C.L., Historiographer-Royal for Scotland. Cheaper Edition. In 8 vols. Crown 8vo, 3s. 6d. each.

History of the British Empire during the Reign of Queen Anne. In 3 vols. 8vo. 36s.

The Scot Abroad. Third Edition. Crown 8vo, 10s. 6d.

The Book-Hunter. New Edition. With Portrait. Crown 8vo, 7s. 6d.

BUTCHER. Armenosa of Egypt. A Romance of the Arab Conquest. By the Very Rev. Dean BUTCHER, D.D., F.S.A., Chaplain at Cairo. Crown 8vo, 6s.

BUTE. The Altus of St Columba. With a Prose Paraphrase and Notes. In paper cover, 2s. 6d.

BUTE, MACPHAIL, AND LONSDALE. The Arms of the Royal and Parliamentary Burghs of Scotland. By JOHN, MARQUESS OF BUTE, K.T., J. R. N. MACPHAIL, and H. W. LONSDALE. With 131 Engravings on wood, and 11 other Illustrations. Crown 4to, £2, 2s. net.

BUTLER. The Ancient Church and Parish of Abernethy, Perthshire. A Historical Study. By Rev. D. BUTLER, M.A., Minister of the Parish. With Collotype Illustrations. In 1 vol. crown 4to. [*In the press.*

BUTT.

Theatricals: An Interlude. By BEATRICE MAY BUTT. Crown 8vo, 6s.

Miss Molly. Cheap Edition, 2s.

Eugenie. Crown 8vo, 6s. 6d.

BUTT.
Elizabeth, and other Sketches. Crown 8vo, 6s.
Delicia. New Edition. Crown 8vo, 2s. 6d.

CAIRD. Sermons. By JOHN CAIRD, D.D., Principal of the
University of Glasgow. Seventeenth Thousand. Fcap. 8vo, 5s.

CALDWELL. Schopenhauer's System in its Philosophical Significance (the Shaw Fellowship Lectures, 1893). By WILLIAM CALDWELL, M.A.,
D.Sc., Professor of Moral and Social Philosophy, Northwestern University,
U.S.A.; formerly Assistant to the Professor of Logic and Metaphysics, Edin.,
and Examiner in Philosophy in the University of St Andrews. Demy 8vo,
10s. 6d. net.

CALLWELL. The Effect of Maritime Command on Land
Campaigns since Waterloo. By Major C. E. CALLWELL, R.A. With Plans.
Post 8vo, 6s. net.

CANTON. A Lost Epic, and other Poems. By WILLIAM
CANTON. Crown 8vo, 5s.

CARSTAIRS.
Human Nature in Rural India. By R. CARSTAIRS. Crown
8vo, 6s.
British Work in India. Crown 8vo, 6s.

CAUVIN. A Treasury of the English and German Languages.
Compiled from the best Authors and Lexicographers in both Languages. By
JOSEPH CAUVIN, LL.D. and Ph.D., of the University of Göttingen, &c. Crown
8vo, 7s. 6d.

CHARTERIS. Canonicity; or, Early Testimonies to the Exist-
ence and Use of the Books of the New Testament. Based on Kirchhoffer's
'Quellensammlung.' Edited by A. H. CHARTERIS, D.D., Professor of Biblical
Criticism in the University of Edinburgh. 8vo, 18s.

CHENNELLS. Recollections of an Egyptian Princess. By
her English Governess (Miss E. CHENNELLS). Being a Record of Five Years'
Residence at the Court of Ismael Pasha, Khédive. Second Edition. With Three
Portraits. Post 8vo, 7s. 6d.

CHESNEY. The Dilemma. By General Sir GEORGE CHESNEY,
K.C.B., M.P., Author of 'The Battle of Dorking,' &c. New Edition. Crown
8vo, 3s. 6d.

CHRISTISON. Early Fortifications in Scotland: Motes, Camps,
and Forts. Being the Rhind Lectures in Archæology for 1893. By DAVID
CHRISTISON, M.D. With numerous Illustrations and Maps. In 1 vol. pott 4to.
[*In the press.*

CHRISTISON. Life of Sir Robert Christison, Bart., M.D.,
D.C.L. Oxon., Professor of Medical Jurisprudence in the University of Edin-
burgh. Edited by his SONS. In 2 vols. 8vo. Vol. I.—Autobiography. 16s.
Vol. II.—Memoirs. 16s.

CHURCH. Chapters in an Adventurous Life. Sir Richard
Church in Italy and Greece. By E. M. CHURCH. With Photogravure
Portrait. Demy 8vo, 10s. 6d.

CHURCH SERVICE SOCIETY.
A Book of Common Order: being Forms of Worship issued
by the Church Service Society. Seventh Edition, carefully revised. In 1 vol.
crown 8vo, cloth, 3s. 6d.; French morocco, 5s. Also in 2 vols. crown 8vo,
cloth, 4s.; French morocco, 6s. 6d.
Daily Offices for Morning and Evening Prayer throughout
the Week. Crown 8vo, 3s. 6d.

CHURCH SERVICE SOCIETY. Order of Divine Service for Children. Issued by the Church Service Society. With Scottish Hymnal. Cloth, 3d.

CLOUSTON. Popular Tales and Fictions: their Migrations and Transformations. By W. A. CLOUSTON, Editor of 'Arabian Poetry for English Readers,' &c. 2 vols. post 8vo, roxburghe binding, 25s.

COCHRAN. A Handy Text-Book of Military Law. Compiled chiefly to assist Officers preparing for Examination; also for all Officers of the Regular and Auxiliary Forces. Comprising also a Synopsis of part of the Army Act. By Major F. COCHRAN, Hampshire Regiment Garrison Instructor, North British District. Crown 8vo, 7s. 6d.

COLQUHOUN. The Moor and the Loch. Containing Minute Instructions in all Highland Sports, with Wanderings over Crag and Corrie, Flood and Fell. By JOHN COLQUHOUN. Cheap Edition. With Illustrations. Demy 8vo, 10s. 6d.

COLVILE. Round the Black Man's Garden. By Lady Z. COLVILE, F.R.G.S. With 2 Maps and 50 Illustrations from Drawings by the Author and from Photographs. Demy 8vo, 16s.

CONDER. The Bible and the East. By Lieut.-Col. C. R. CONDER, R.E., LL.D., D.C.L., M.R.A.S., Author of 'Tent Work in Palestine,' &c. With Illustrations and a Map. Crown 8vo, 5s.

CONSTITUTION AND LAW OF THE CHURCH OF SCOTLAND. With an Introductory Note by the late Principal Tulloch. New Edition, Revised and Enlarged. Crown 8vo, 3s. 6d.

COTTERILL. Suggested Reforms in Public Schools. By C. C. COTTERILL, M.A. Crown 8vo, 3s. 6d.

COUNTY HISTORIES OF SCOTLAND. In demy 8vo volumes of about 350 pp. each. With Maps. Price 7s. 6d. net.

Fife and Kinross. By ÆNEAS J. G. MACKAY, LL.D., Sheriff of these Counties.

Dumfries and Galloway. By Sir HERBERT MAXWELL, Bart., M.P.

Moray and Nairn. By CHARLES RAMPINI, LL.D., Sheriff-Substitute of these Counties.

Inverness. By J. CAMERON LEES, D.D. [*Others in preparation.*

CRAWFORD. Saracinesca. By F. MARION CRAWFORD, Author of 'Mr Isaacs,' &c., &c. Cheap Edition. Crown 8vo, 3s. 6d.

CRAWFORD.

The Doctrine of Holy Scripture respecting the Atonement. By the late THOMAS J. CRAWFORD, D.D., Professor of Divinity in the University of Edinburgh. Fifth Edition. 8vo, 12s.

The Fatherhood of God, Considered in its General and Special Aspects. Third Edition, Revised and Enlarged. 8vo, 9s.

The Preaching of the Cross, and other Sermons. 8vo, 7s. 6d.

The Mysteries of Christianity. Crown 8vo, 7s. 6d.

CROSS. Impressions of Dante, and of the New World; with a Few Words on Bimetallism. By J. W. CROSS, Editor of 'George Eliot's Life, as related in her Letters and Journals.' Post 8vo, 6s.

CUMBERLAND. Sport on the Pamirs and Turkistan Steppes. By Major C. S. CUMBERLAND. With Map and Frontispiece. Demy 8vo, 10s. 6d.

CURSE OF INTELLECT. Third Edition. Fcap. 8vo, 2s. 6d. net.

CUSHING. The Blacksmith of Voe. By PAUL CUSHING, Author of 'The Bull i' th' Thorn,' 'Cut with his own Diamond.' Cheap Edition. Crown 8vo, 3s. 6d.

DARBISHIRE. Physical Maps for the use of History Students.
By BERNHARD V. DARBISHIRE, M.A., Trinity College, Oxford. Two Series :—
Ancient History (9 maps); Modern History (12 maps). *[In the press.*

DAVIES. Norfolk Broads and Rivers ; or, The Waterways,
Lagoons, and Decoys of East Anglia. By G. CHRISTOPHER DAVIES. Illustrated
with Seven full-page Plates. New and Cheaper Edition. Crown 8vo, 6s.

DE LA WARR. An Eastern Cruise in the 'Edeline.' By the
Countess DE LA WARR. In Illustrated Cover. 2s.

DESCARTES. The Method, Meditations, and Principles of Philo-
sophy of Descartes. Translated from the Original French and Latin. With a
New Introductory Essay, Historical and Critical, on the Cartesian Philosophy.
By Professor VEITCH, LL.D., Glasgow University. Eleventh Edition. 6s. 6d.

DOGS, OUR DOMESTICATED : Their Treatment in reference
to Food, Diseases, Habits, Punishment, Accomplishments. By 'MAGENTA.'
Crown 8vo, 2s. 6d.

DOUGLAS.
The Ethics of John Stuart Mill. By CHARLES DOUGLAS,
M.A., D.Sc., Lecturer in Moral Philosophy, and Assistant to the Professor of
Moral Philosophy in the University of Edinburgh. Post 8vo, 6s. net.
John Stuart Mill: A Study of his Philosophy. Crown 8vo,
4s. 6d. net.

DOUGLAS. Chinese Stories. By ROBERT K. DOUGLAS. With
numerous Illustrations by Parkinson, Forestier, and others. New and Cheaper
Edition. Small demy 8vo, 5s.

DOUGLAS. Iras: A Mystery. By THEO. DOUGLAS, Author of
'A Bride Elect.' Cheaper Edition, in Paper Cover specially designed by Womrath.
Crown 8vo, 1s. 6d.

DU CANE. The Odyssey of Homer, Books I.-XII. Translated
into English Verse. By Sir CHARLES DU CANE, K.C.M.G. 8vo, 10s. 6d.

DUDGEON. History of the Edinburgh or Queen's Regiment
Light Infantry Militia, now 3rd Battalion The Royal Scots ; with an Account of
the Origin and Progress of the Militia, and a Brief Sketch of the Old Royal
Scots. By Major R. C. DUDGEON, Adjutant 3rd Battalion the Royal Scots.
Post 8vo, with Illustrations, 10s. 6d.

DUNSMORE. Manual of the Law of Scotland as to the Relations between Agricultural Tenants and the Landlords, Servants, Merchants, and
Bowers. By W. DUNSMORE. 8vo, 7s. 6d.

DZIEWICKI. Entombed in Flesh. By M. H. DZIEWICKI. In
1 vol. crown 8vo. *[In the press.*

ELIOT.
George Eliot's Life, Related in Her Letters and Journals.
Arranged and Edited by her husband, J. W. CROSS. With Portrait and other
Illustrations. Third Edition. 3 vols. post 8vo, 42s.
George Eliot's Life. With Portrait and other Illustrations.
New Edition, in one volume. Crown 8vo, 7s. 6d.
Works of George Eliot (Standard Edition). 21 volumes,
crown 8vo. In buckram cloth, gilt top, 2s. 6d. per vol. ; or in roxburghe
binding, 3s. 6d. per vol.
    ADAM BEDE. 2 vols.—THE MILL ON THE FLOSS. 2 vols.—FELIX HOLT, THE
RADICAL. 2 vols.—ROMOLA. 2 vols.—SCENES OF CLERICAL LIFE. 2 vols.—
MIDDLEMARCH. 3 vols.—DANIEL DERONDA. 3 vols.—SILAS MARNER. 1 vol.
—JUBAL. 1 vol.—THE SPANISH GIPSY. 1 vol.—ESSAYS. 1 vol.—THEOPHRAS-
TUS SUCH. 1 vol.
Life and Works of George Eliot (Cabinet Edition). 24
volumes, crown 8vo, price £6. Also to be had handsomely bound in half and full
calf. The Volumes are sold separately, bound in cloth, price 5s. each.

ELIOT.
>Novels by George Eliot. Cheap Edition. New issue in
>Monthly Volumes. Printed on fine laid paper, and uniformly bound. In course
>of publication.
>>Adam Bede. 3s. 6d.—The Mill on the Floss. 3s. 6d.—Scenes of Clerical
>>Life. 3s.—Silas Marner; the Weaver of Raveloe. 2s. 6d.—Felix Holt, the
>>Radical. 3s. 6d.—Romola. 3s. 6d.—Middlemarch. 7s. 6d.—Daniel Deronda.
>>7s. 6d.
>Essays. New Edition. Crown 8vo, 5s.
>Impressions of Theophrastus Such. New Edition. Crown
>8vo, 5s.
>The Spanish Gypsy. New Edition. Crown 8vo, 5s.
>The Legend of Jubal, and other Poems, Old and New.
>New Edition. Crown 8vo, 5s.
>Scenes of Clerical Life. Popular Edition. Royal 8vo, in
>paper cover, price 6d.
>Wise, Witty, and Tender Sayings, in Prose and Verse. Selected
>from the Works of GEORGE ELIOT. New Edition. Fcap. 8vo, 3s. 6d.

ESSAYS ON SOCIAL SUBJECTS. Originally published in
>the 'Saturday Review.' New Edition. First and Second Series. 2 vols. crown
>8vo, 6s. each.

FAITHS OF THE WORLD, The. A Concise History of the
>Great Religious Systems of the World. By various Authors. Crown 8vo, 5s.

FALKNER. The Lost Stradivarius. By J. MEADE FALKNER.
>Second Edition. Crown 8vo, 6s.

FENNELL AND O'CALLAGHAN. A Prince of Tyrone. By
>CHARLOTTE FENNELL and J. P. O'CALLAGHAN. Crown 8vo, 6s.

FERGUSON. Sir Samuel Ferguson in the Ireland of his Day.
>By LADY FERGUSON, Author of 'The Irish before the Conquest,' 'Life of William
>Reeves, D.D., Lord Bishop of Down, Connor, and Dromore,' &c., &c. With
>Two Portraits. 2 vols. post 8vo, 21s.

FERRIER.
>Philosophical Works of the late James F. Ferrier, B.A.
>Oxon., Professor of Moral Philosophy and Political Economy, St Andrews.
>New Edition. Edited by Sir ALEXANDER GRANT, Bart., D.C.L., and Professor
>LUSHINGTON. 3 vols. crown 8vo, 34s. 6d.
>Institutes of Metaphysic. Third Edition. 10s. 6d.
>Lectures on the Early Greek Philosophy. 4th Edition. 10s. 6d.
>Philosophical Remains, including the Lectures on Early
>Greek Philosophy. New Edition. 2 vols. 24s.

FLINT.
>Historical Philosophy in France and French Belgium and
>Switzerland. By ROBERT FLINT, Corresponding Member of the Institute of
>France, Hon. Member of the Royal Society of Palermo, Professor in the Univer-
>sity of Edinburgh, &c. 8vo, 21s.
>Agnosticism. Being the Croall Lecture for 1887-88.
>[In the press.
>Theism. Being the Baird Lecture for 1876. Ninth Edition,
>Revised. Crown 8vo, 7s. 6d
>Anti-Theistic Theories. Being the Baird Lecture for 1877.
>Fifth Edition. Crown 8vo, 10s. 6d.

FOREIGN CLASSICS FOR ENGLISH READERS. Edited
>by Mrs OLIPHANT. Price 2s. 6d. For List of Volumes, see page 2.

FOSTER. The Fallen City, and other Poems. By WILL FOSTER.
>Crown 8vo, 6s.

FRANCILLON.   Gods and Heroes ; or, The Kingdom of Jupiter.
By R. E. FRANCILLON. With 8 Illustrations. Crown 8vo, 5s.

FRANCIS.   Among the Untrodden Ways.   By M. E. FRANCIS
(Mrs Francis Blundell), Author of ' In a North Country Village,' 'A Daughter of
the Soil,' 'Frieze and Fustian,' &c. Crown 8vo, 3s. 6d.

FRASER.
Philosophy of Theism.   Being the Gifford Lectures delivered
before the University of Edinburgh in 1894-95. First Series. By ALEXANDER
CAMPBELL FRASER, D.C.L. Oxford ; Emeritus Professor of Logic and Metaphysics in the University of Edinburgh. Post 8vo, 7s. 6d. net.

Philosophy of Theism.   Being the Gifford Lectures delivered
before the University of Edinburgh in 1895-96. Second Series. Post 8vo,
7s. 6d. net.

FRASER.   St Mary's of Old Montrose : A History of the Parish
of Maryton. By the Rev. WILLIAM RUXTON FRASER, M.A., F.S.A. Scot.,
Emeritus Minister of Maryton ; Author of ' History of the Parish and Burgh of
Laurencekirk.' Crown 8vo, 3s. 6d.

FULLARTON.
Merlin : A Dramatic Poem.   By RALPH MACLEOD FULLARTON.
Crown 8vo, 5s.

Tanhäuser.   Crown 8vo, 6s.

Lallan Sangs and German Lyrics.   Crown 8vo, 5s.

GALT.
Novels by JOHN GALT.   With General Introduction and
Prefatory Notes by S. R. CROCKETT. The Text Revised and Edited by D.
STORRAR MELDRUM, Author of 'The Story of Margrédel.' With Photogravure
Illustrations from Drawings by John Wallace. Fcap. 8vo, 3s. net each vol.

ANNALS OF THE PARISH, and THE AYRSHIRE LEGATEES. 2 vols.—SIR ANDREW
WYLIE. 2 vols.—THE ENTAIL ; or, The Lairds of Grippy. 2 vols.—THE PRO-
VOST, and THE LAST OF THE LAIRDS. 2 vols.

See also STANDARD NOVELS, *p. 6.*

GENERAL ASSEMBLY OF THE CHURCH OF SCOTLAND.
Scottish Hymnal, With Appendix Incorporated.   Published
for use in Churches by Authority of the General Assembly. 1. Large type,
cloth, red edges, 2s. 6d.; French morocco, 4s.   2. Bourgeois type, limp cloth, 1s.;
French morocco, 2s.   3. Nonpareil type, cloth, red edges, 6d.; French morocco,
1s. 4d.   4. Paper covers, 3d.   5. Sunday-School Edition, paper covers, 1d.,
cloth, 2d.   No. 1, bound with the Psalms and Paraphrases, French morocco, 8s.
No. 2, bound with the Psalms and Paraphrases, cloth, 2s.; French morocco, 3s.

Prayers for Social and Family Worship.   Prepared by a
Special Committee of the General Assembly of the Church of Scotland. Entirely
New Edition, Revised and Enlarged. Fcap. 8vo, red edges, 2s.

Prayers for Family Worship.   A Selection of Four Weeks'
Prayers. New Edition. Authorised by the General Assembly of the Church of
Scotland. Fcap. 8vo, red edges, 1s. 6d.

One Hundred Prayers.   Prepared by the Committee on Aids
to Devotion. 16mo, cloth limp, 6d.

Morning and Evening Prayers for Affixing to Bibles.   Prepared
by the Committee on Aids to Devotion. 1d. for 6, or 1s. per 100.

GERARD.
Reata : What's in a Name.   By E. D. GERARD.   Cheap
Edition. Crown 8vo, 3s. 6d.

Beggar my Neighbour.   Cheap Edition.   Crown 8vo, 3s. 6d.

The Waters of Hercules.   Cheap Edition.   Crown 8vo, 3s. 6d.

A Sensitive Plant.   Crown 8vo, 3s. 6d.

GERARD.
A Foreigner. An Anglo-German Study. By E. GERARD.
Crown 8vo, 6s.
The Land beyond the Forest. Facts, Figures, and Fancies
from Transylvania. With Maps and Illustrations. 2 vols. post 8vo, 25s.
Bis : Some Tales Retold. Crown 8vo, 6s.
A Secret Mission. 2 vols. crown 8vo, 17s.
An Electric Shock, and other Stories. Crown 8vo, 6s.
GERARD.
A Spotless Reputation. By DOROTHEA GERARD. Third
Edition. Crown 8vo, 6s.
The Wrong Man. Second Edition. Crown 8vo, 6s.
Lady Baby. Cheap Edition. Crown 8vo, 3s. 6d.
Recha. Second Edition. Crown 8vo, 6s.
The Rich Miss Riddell. Second Edition. Crown 8vo, 6s.
GERARD. Stonyhurst Latin Grammar. By Rev. JOHN GERARD.
Second Edition. Fcap. 8vo, 3s.
GORDON CUMMING.
At Home in Fiji. By C. F. GORDON CUMMING. Fourth
Edition, post 8vo. With Illustrations and Map. 7s. 6d.
A Lady's Cruise in a French Man-of-War. New and Cheaper
Edition. 8vo. With Illustrations and Map. 12s. 6d.
Fire-Fountains. The Kingdom of Hawaii : Its Volcanoes,
and the History of its Missions. With Map and Illustrations. 2 vols. 8vo, 25s.
Wanderings in China. New and Cheaper Edition. 8vo, with
Illustrations, 10s.
Granite Crags : The Yō-semité Region of California. Illus-
trated with 8 Engravings. New and Cheaper Edition. 8vo, 8s. 6d.
GRAHAM. Manual of the Elections (Scot.) (Corrupt and Illegal
Practices) Act, 1890. With Analysis, Relative Act of Sederunt, Appendix con-
taining the Corrupt Practices Acts of 1883 and 1885, and Copious Index. By J.
EDWARD GRAHAM, Advocate. 8vo, 4s. 6d.
GRAND.
A Domestic Experiment. By SARAH GRAND, Author of
'The Heavenly Twins,' 'Ideals : A Study from Life.' Crown 8vo, 6s.
Singularly Deluded. Crown 8vo, 6s.
GRANT. Bush-Life in Queensland. By A. C. GRANT. New
Edition. Crown 8vo, 6s.
GRIER.
In Furthest Ind. The Narrative of Mr EDWARD CARLYON of
Ellswether, in the County of Northampton, and late of the Honourable East India
Company's Service, Gentleman. Wrote by his own hand in the year of grace 1697.
Edited, with a few Explanatory Notes, by SYDNEY C. GRIER. Post 8vo, 6s.
His Excellency's English Governess. Crown 8vo, 6s.
An Uncrowned King : A Romance of High Politics. Second
Edition. Crown 8vo, 6s.
Peace with Honour. Crown 8vo, 6s.
GUTHRIE-SMITH. Crispus : A Drama. By H. GUTHRIE-
SMITH. Fcap. 4to, 5s.

HAGGARD. Under Crescent and Star. By Lieut.-Col. ANDREW
HAGGARD, D.S.O., Author of 'Dodo and I,' 'Tempest Torn,' &c. With a
Portrait. Second Edition. Crown 8vo, 6s.
HALDANE. Subtropical Cultivations and Climates. A Handy
Book for Planters, Colonists, and Settlers. By R. C. HALDANE. Post 8vo, 9s.

HAMERTON.

Wenderholme: A Story of Lancashire and Yorkshire Life.
By P. G. HAMERTON, Author of 'A Painter's Camp.' New Edition. Crown 8vo, 3s. 6d.

Marmorne. New Edition. Crown 8vo, 3s. 6d.

HAMILTON.

Lectures on Metaphysics. By Sir WILLIAM HAMILTON,
Bart., Professor of Logic and Metaphysics in the University of Edinburgh. Edited by the Rev. H. L. MANSEL, B.D., LL.D., Dean of St Paul's; and JOHN VEITCH, M.A., LL.D., Professor of Logic and Rhetoric, Glasgow. Seventh Edition. 2 vols. 8vo, 24s.

Lectures on Logic. Edited by the SAME. Third Edition,
Revised. 2 vols., 24s.

Discussions on Philosophy and Literature, Education and
University Reform. Third Edition. 8vo, 21s.

Memoir of Sir William Hamilton, Bart., Professor of Logic
and Metaphysics in the University of Edinburgh. By Professor VEITCH, of the University of Glasgow. 8vo, with Portrait, 18s.

Sir William Hamilton: The Man and his Philosophy. Two
Lectures delivered before the Edinburgh Philosophical Institution, January and February 1883. By Professor VEITCH. Crown 8vo, 2s.

HAMLEY.

The Operations of War Explained and Illustrated. By
General Sir EDWARD BRUCE HAMLEY, K.C.B., K.C.M.G. Fifth Edition, Revised throughout. 4to, with numerous Illustrations, 30s.

National Defence; Articles and Speeches. Post 8vo, 6s.

Shakespeare's Funeral, and other Papers. Post 8vo, 7s. 6d.

Thomas Carlyle: An Essay. Second Edition. Crown 8vo,
2s. 6d.

On Outposts. Second Edition. 8vo, 2s.

Wellington's Career; A Military and Political Summary.
Crown 8vo, 2s.

Lady Lee's Widowhood. New Edition. Crown 8vo, 3s. 6d.
Cheaper Edition, 2s. 6d.

Our Poor Relations. A Philozoic Essay. With Illustrations,
chiefly by Ernest Griset. Crown 8vo, cloth gilt, 3s. 6d.

The Life of General Sir Edward Bruce Hamley, K.C.B.,
K.C.M.G. By ALEXANDER INNES SHAND. With two Photogravure Portraits and other Illustrations. Cheaper Edition. With a Statement by Mr EDWARD HAMLEY. 2 vols. demy 8vo, 10s. 6d.

HANNAY. The Later Renaissance. By DAVID HANNAY. Being
the second volume of 'Periods of European Literature.' Edited by Professor Saintsbury. In 1 vol. crown 8vo. *[In the press.*

HARE. Down the Village Street: Scenes in a West Country
Hamlet. By CHRISTOPHER HARE. Second Edition. Crown 8vo, 6s.

HARRADEN.

In Varying Moods: Short Stories. By BEATRICE HARRADEN,
Author of 'Ships that Pass in the Night.' Twelfth Edition Crown 8vo, 3s. 6d.

Hilda Strafford, and The Remittance Man. Two Californian
Stories. Tenth Edition. Crown 8vo, 3s. 6d.

Untold Tales of the Past. With 40 Illustrations by H. R. Millar.
Square crown 8vo, gilt top, 6s.

HARRIS.

From Batum to Baghdad, *viâ* Tiflis, Tabriz, and Persian
Kurdistan. By WALTER B. HARRIS, F.R.G.S., Author of 'The Land of an African Sultan; Travels in Morocco,' &c. With numerous Illustrations and 2 Maps. Demy 8vo, 12s.

HARRIS.
Tafilet. The Narrative of a Journey of Exploration to the
Atlas Mountains and the Oases of the North-West Sahara. With Illustrations
by Maurice Romberg from Sketches and Photographs by the Author, and Two
Maps. Demy 8vo, 12s.
A Journey through the Yemen, and some General Remarks
upon that Country. With 3 Maps and numerous Illustrations by Forestier and
Wallace from Sketches and Photographs taken by the Author. Demy 8vo, 16s.
Danovitch, and other Stories. Crown 8vo, 6s.

HAWKER. The Prose Works of Rev. R. S. HAWKER, Vicar of
Morwenstow. Including 'Footprints of Former Men in Far Cornwall.' Re-edited,
with Sketches never before published. With a Frontispiece. Crown 8vo, 3s. 6d.

HAY. The Works of the Right Rev. Dr George Hay, Bishop of
Edinburgh. Edited under the Supervision of the Right Rev. Bishop STRAIN.
With Memoir and Portrait of the Author. 5 vols. crown 8vo, bound in extra
cloth, £1, 1s. The following Volumes may be had separately—viz.:
The Devout Christian Instructed in the Law of Christ from the Written
Word. 2 vols., 8s.—The Pious Christian Instructed in the Nature and Practice
of the Principal Exercises of Piety. 1 vol., 3s.

HEATLEY.
The Horse-Owner's Safeguard. A Handy Medical Guide for
every Man who owns a Horse. By G. S. HEATLEY, M.R.C.V.S. Crown 8vo, 5s.
The Stock-Owner's Guide. A Handy Medical Treatise for
every Man who owns an Ox or a Cow. Crown 8vo, 4s. 6d.

HEDDERWICK. Lays of Middle Age; and other Poems. By
JAMES HEDDERWICK, LL.D., Author of 'Backward Glances.' Price 3s. 6d.

HEMANS.
The Poetical Works of Mrs Hemans. Copyright Editions.
Royal 8vo, 5s. The Same with Engravings, cloth, gilt edges, 7s. 6d.
Select Poems of Mrs Hemans. Fcap., cloth, gilt edges, 3s.

HERKLESS. Cardinal Beaton: Priest and Politician. By
JOHN HERKLESS, Professor of Church History, St Andrews. With a Portrait.
Post 8vo, 7s. 6d.

HEWISON. The Isle of Bute in the Olden Time. With Illus-
trations, Maps, and Plans. By JAMES KING HEWISON, M.A., F.S.A. (Scot.),
Minister of Rothesay. Vol. I., Celtic Saints and Heroes. Crown 4to, 15s. net.
Vol. II., The Royal Stewards and the Brandanes. Crown 4to, 15s. net.

HIBBEN. Inductive Logic. By JOHN GRIER HIBBEN, Ph.D.,
Assistant Professor of Logic in Princeton University, U.S.A. Crown 8vo,
3s. 6d. net.

HILDEBRAND. The Early Relations between Britain and
Scandinavia. Being the Rhind Lectures in Archæology for 1896. By Dr HANS
HILDEBRAND, Royal Antiquary of Sweden. With Illustrations. In 1 vol.
post 8vo. [*In the press.*

HOME PRAYERS. By Ministers of the Church of Scotland
and Members of the Church Service Society. Second Edition. Fcap. 8vo, 3s.

HORNBY. Admiral of the Fleet Sir Geoffrey Phipps Hornby,
G.C.B. A Biography. By Mrs FRED. EGERTON. With Three Portraits. Demy
8vo, 16s.

HUTCHINSON. Hints on the Game of Golf. By HORACE G.
HUTCHINSON. Ninth Edition, Enlarged. Fcap. 8vo, cloth, 1s.

HYSLOP. The Elements of Ethics. By JAMES H. HYSLOP,
Ph.D., Instructor in Ethics, Columbia College, New York, Author of 'The
Elements of Logic.' Post 8vo, 7s. 6d. net.

IDDESLEIGH. Life, Letters, and Diaries of Sir Stafford North-
cote, First Earl of Iddesleigh. By ANDREW LANG. With Three Portraits and a
View of Pynes. Third Edition. 2 vols. post 8vo, 31s. 6d.
POPULAR EDITION. With Portrait and View of Pynes. Post 8vo, 7s. 6d.

INDEX GEOGRAPHICUS: Being a List, alphabetically arranged, of the Principal Places on the Globe, with the Countries and Subdivisions of the Countries in which they are situated, and their Latitudes and Longitudes. Imperial 8vo, pp. 676, 21s.

JEAN JAMBON. Our Trip to Blunderland; or, Grand Excursion to Blundertown and Back. By JEAN JAMBON. With Sixty Illustrations designed by CHARLES DOYLE, engraved by DALZIEL. Fourth Thousand. Cloth, gilt edges, 6s. 6d. Cheap Edition, cloth, 3s. 6d. Boards, 2s. 6d.

JEBB. A Strange Career. The Life and Adventures of JOHN GLADWYN JEBB. By his Widow. With an Introduction by H. RIDER HAGGARD, and an Electrogravure Portrait of Mr Jebb. Third Edition. Demy 8vo, 10s. 6d. CHEAP EDITION. With Illustrations by John Wallace. Crown 8vo, 3s. 6d.

Some Unconventional People. By Mrs GLADWYN JEBB, Author of 'Life and Adventures of J. G. Jebb.' With Illustrations. Crown 8vo, 3s. 6d.

JERNINGHAM.

Reminiscences of an Attaché. By HUBERT E. H. JERNINGHAM. Second Edition. Crown 8vo, 5s

Diane de Breteuille. A Love Story. Crown 8vo, 2s. 6d.

JOHNSTON.

The Chemistry of Common Life. By Professor J. F. W. JOHNSTON. New Edition, Revised. By ARTHUR HERBERT CHURCH, M.A. Oxon.; Author of 'Food: its Sources, Constituents, and Uses,' &c. With Maps and 102 Engravings. Crown 8vo, 7s. 6d.

Elements of Agricultural Chemistry. An entirely New Edition from the Edition by Sir CHARLES A. CAMERON, M.D., F.R.C.S.I., &c. Revised and brought down to date by C. M. AIKMAN, M.A., B.Sc., F.R.S.E., Professor of Chemistry, Glasgow Veterinary College. 17th Edition. Crown 8vo, 6s. 6d.

Catechism of Agricultural Chemistry. An entirely New Edition from the Edition by Sir CHARLES A. CAMERON. Revised and Enlarged by C. M. AIKMAN, M.A., &c. 95th Thousand. With numerous Illustrations. Crown 8vo, 1s.

JOHNSTON. Agricultural Holdings (Scotland) Acts, 1883 and 1889; and the Ground Game Act, 1880. With Notes, and Summary of Procedure, &c. By CHRISTOPHER N. JOHNSTON, M.A., Advocate. Demy 8vo, 5s.

JOKAI. Timar's Two Worlds. By MAURUS JOKAI. Authorised Translation by Mrs HEGAN KENNARD. Cheap Edition. Crown 8vo, 6s.

KEBBEL. The Old and the New: English Country Life. By T. E. KEBBEL, M.A., Author of 'The Agricultural Labourers,' 'Essays in History and Politics,' 'Life of Lord Beaconsfield.' Crown 8vo, 5s.

KERR. St Andrews in 1645-46. By D. R. KERR. Crown 8vo, 2s. 6d.

KINGLAKE.

History of the Invasion of the Crimea. By A. W. KINGLAKE. Cabinet Edition, Revised. With an Index to the Complete Work. Illustrated with Maps and Plans. Complete in 9 vols., crown 8vo, at 6s. each.

—— Abridged Edition for Military Students. Revised by Lieut.-Col. Sir GEORGE SYDENHAM CLARKE, K.C.M.G., R.E. In 1 vol. demy 8vo. [*In the press.*

History of the Invasion of the Crimea. Demy 8vo. Vol. VI. Winter Troubles. With a Map, 16s. Vols. VII. and VIII. From the Morrow of Inkerman to the Death of Lord Raglan With an Index to the Whole Work. With Maps and Plans. 28s.

Eothen. A New Edition, uniform with the Cabinet Edition of the 'History of the Invasion of the Crimea.' 6s. CHEAPER EDITION. With Portrait and Biographical Sketch of the Author. Crown 8vo, 3s. 6d. Popular Edition, in paper cover, 1s net.

KIRBY. In Haunts of Wild Game: A Hunter-Naturalist's
Wanderings from Kahlamba to Libombo. By FREDERICK VAUGHAN KIRBY,
F.Z.S. (Maqaqamba). With numerous Illustrations by Charles Whymper, and a
Map. Large demy 8vo, 25s.

KNEIPP. My Water-Cure. As Tested through more than
Thirty Years, and Described for the Healing of Diseases and the Preservation of
Health. By SEBASTIAN KNEIPP, Parish Priest of Wörishofen (Bavaria). With a
Portrait and other Illustrations. Authorised English Translation from the
Thirtieth German Edition, by A. de F. Cheap Edition. With an Appendix, con-
taining the Latest Developments of Pfarrer Kneipp's System, and a Preface by
E. Gerard. Crown 8vo, 3s. 6d.

KNOLLYS. The Elements of Field-Artillery. Designed for
the Use of Infantry and Cavalry Officers. By HENRY KNOLLYS, Colonel Royal
Artillery; Author of 'From Sedan to Saarbrück,' Editor of 'Incidents in the
Sepoy War,' &c. With Engravings. Crown 8vo, 7s. 6d.

LANG.
Life, Letters, and Diaries of Sir Stafford Northcote, First
Earl of Iddesleigh. By ANDREW LANG. With Three Portraits and a View of
Pynes. Third Edition. 2 vols. post 8vo, 31s. 6d.
POPULAR EDITION. With Portrait and View of Pynes. Post 8vo, 7s. 6d.
The Highlands of Scotland in 1750. From Manuscript 104
in the King's Library, British Museum. With an Introduction. In 1 vol. crown
8vo. [*In the press.*

LANG. The Expansion of the Christian Life. The Duff Lecture for 1897. By the Rev. J. MARSHALL LANG, D.D Crown 8vo, 5s.

LEES. A Handbook of the Sheriff and Justice of Peace Small
Debt Courts. With Notes, References, and Forms. By J. M. LEES, Advocate,
Sheriff of Stirling, Dumbarton, and Clackmannan. 8vo, 7s. 6d.

LINDSAY.
Recent Advances in Theistic Philosophy of Religion. By Rev.
JAMES LINDSAY, M.A., B.D., B.Sc., F.R.S.E., F.G.S., Minister of the Parish of
St Andrew's, Kilmarnock. Demy 8vo, 12s. 6d. net.
The Progressiveness of Modern Christian Thought. Crown
8vo, 6s.
Essays, Literary and Philosophical. Crown 8vo, 3s. 6d.
The Significance of the Old Testament for Modern Theology.
Crown 8vo, 1s. net.
The Teaching Function of the Modern Pulpit. Crown 8vo,
1s. net.

LOCKHART.
Doubles and Quits. By LAURENCE W. M. LOCKHART. New
Edition. Crown 8vo, 3s. 6d.
Fair to See. New Edition. Crown 8vo, 3s. 6d.
Mine is Thine. New Edition. Crown 8vo, 3s. 6d.

LOCKHART.
The Church of Scotland in the Thirteenth Century. The
Life and Times of David de Bernham of St Andrews (Bishop), A.D. 1239 to 1253.
With List of Churches dedicated by him, and Dates. By WILLIAM LOCKHART,
A.M., D.D., F.S.A. Scot., Minister of Colinton Parish. 2d Edition. 8vo, 6s.
Dies Tristes: Sermons for Seasons of Sorrow. Crown 8vo, 6s.

LORIMER.
The Institutes of Law: A Treatise of the Principles of Jurisprudence as determined by Nature. By the late JAMES LORIMER, Professor of
Public Law and of the Law of Nature and Nations in the University of Edinburgh. New Edition, Revised and much Enlarged. 8vo, 18s.

LORIMER.
The Institutes of the Law of Nations. A Treatise of the Jural Relation of Separate Political Communities. In 2 vols. 8vo. Volume I., price 16s. Volume II., price 20s.

LUGARD. The Rise of our East African Empire : Early Efforts in Uganda and Nyassaland. By F. D. LUGARD, Captain Norfolk Regiment. With 130 Illustrations from Drawings and Photographs under the personal superintendence of the Author, and 14 specially prepared Maps. In 2 vols. large demy 8vo, 42s.

M'CHESNEY.
Miriam Cromwell, Royalist : A Romance of the Great Rebellion. By DORA GREENWELL M'CHESNEY. Crown 8vo, 6s.

Kathleen Clare : Her Book, 1637-41. With Frontispiece, and five full-page Illustrations by James A. Shearman. Crown 8vo, 6s.

M'COMBIE. Cattle and Cattle-Breeders. By WILLIAM M'COMBIE, Tillyfour. New Edition, Enlarged, with Memoir of the Author by JAMES MACDONALD, F.R.S.E., Secretary Highland and Agricultural Society of Scotland. Crown 8vo, 3s. 6d.

M'CRIE.
Works of the Rev. Thomas M'Crie, D.D. Uniform Edition. 4 vols. crown 8vo, 24s.

Life of John Knox. Crown 8vo, 6s. Another Edition, 3s. 6d.

Life of Andrew Melville. Crown 8vo, 6s.

History of the Progress and Suppression of the Reformation in Italy in the Sixteenth Century. Crown 8vo, 4s.

History of the Progress and Suppression of the Reformation in Spain in the Sixteenth Century. Crown 8vo, 3s. 6d.

M'CRIE. The Public Worship of Presbyterian Scotland. Historically treated. With copious Notes, Appendices, and Index. The Fourteenth Series of the Cunningham Lectures. By the Rev. CHARLES G. M'CRIE, D.D. Demy 8vo, 10s. 6d.

MACDONALD. A Manual of the Criminal Law (Scotland) Procedure Act, 1887. By NORMAN DORAN MACDONALD. Revised by the LORD JUSTICE-CLERK. 8vo, 10s. 6d.

MACDONALD AND SINCLAIR. History of Polled Aberdeen and Angus Cattle. Giving an Account of the Origin, Improvement, and Characteristics of the Breed. By JAMES MACDONALD and JAMES SINCLAIR. Illustrated with numerous Animal Portraits. Post 8vo, 12s. 6d.

MACDOUGALL AND DODDS. A Manual of the Local Government (Scotland) Act, 1894. With Introduction, Explanatory Notes, and Copious Index. By J. PATTEN MACDOUGALL, Legal Secretary to the Lord Advocate, and J. M. DODDS. Tenth Thousand, Revised. Crown 8vo, 2s. 6d. net.

MACINTYRE. Hindu - Koh : Wanderings and Wild Sports on and beyond the Himalayas. By Major-General DONALD MACINTYRE, V.C., late Prince of Wales' Own Goorkhas, F.R.G.S. *Dedicated to H.R.H. The Prince of Wales.* New and Cheaper Edition, Revised, with numerous Illustrations. Post 8vo, 3s. 6d.

MACKAY.
Elements of Modern Geography. By the Rev. ALEXANDER MACKAY, LL.D., F.R.G.S. 55th Thousand, Revised to the present time. Crown 8vo, pp. 300, 3s.

The Intermediate Geography. Intended as an Intermediate Book between the Author's 'Outlines of Geography' and 'Elements of Geography.' Eighteenth Edition, Revised. Fcap. 8vo, pp. 238, 2s.

Outlines of Modern Geography. 191st Thousand, Revised to the present time. Fcap. 8vo, pp. 128, 1s.

Elements of Physiography. New Edition. Rewritten and Enlarged. With numerous Illustrations. Crown 8vo.   [*In the press.*

MACKENZIE. Studies in Roman Law. With Comparative
Views of the Laws of France, England, and Scotland. By Lord MACKENZIE,
one of the Judges of the Court of Session in Scotland. Sixth Edition, Edited
by JOHN KIRKPATRICK, M.A., LL.B., Advocate, Professor of History in the
University of Edinburgh. 8vo, 12s.

MACPHERSON. Glimpses of Church and Social Life in the
Highlands in Olden Times. By ALEXANDER MACPHERSON, F.S.A. Scot. With
6 Photogravure Portraits and other full-page Illustrations. Small 4to, 25s.

M'PHERSON. Golf and Golfers. Past and Present. By J.
GORDON M'PHERSON, Ph.D., F.R.S.E. With an Introduction by the Right Hon.
A. J. BALFOUR, and a Portrait of the Author. Fcap. 8vo, 1s. 6d.

MACRAE. A Handbook of Deer-Stalking. By ALEXANDER
MACRAE, late Forester to Lord Henry Bentinck. With Introduction by Horatio
Ross, Esq. Fcap. 8vo, with 2 Photographs from Life. 3s. 6d.

MAIN. Three Hundred English Sonnets. Chosen and Edited
by DAVID M. MAIN. New Edition. Fcap. 8vo, 3s. 6d.

MAIR. A Digest of Laws and Decisions, Ecclesiastical and
Civil, relating to the Constitution, Practice, and Affairs of the Church of Scot-
land. With Notes and Forms of Procedure. By the Rev. WILLIAM MAIR, D.D.,
Minister of the Parish of Earlston. New Edition, Revised. Crown 8vo, 9s. net.

MARCHMONT AND THE HUMES OF POLWARTH. By
One of their Descendants. With numerous Portraits and other Illustrations.
Crown 4to, 21s. net.

MARSHMAN. History of India. From the Earliest Period to
the present time. By JOHN CLARK MARSHMAN, C.S.I. Third and Cheaper
Edition. Post 8vo, with Map, 6s.

MARTIN.
The Æneid of Virgil. Books I.-VI. Translated by Sir THEO-
DORE MARTIN, K.C.B. Post 8vo, 7s. 6d.
Goethe's Faust. Part I. Translated into English Verse.
Second Edition, crown 8vo, 6s. Ninth Edition, fcap. 8vo, 3s. 6d.
Goethe's Faust. Part II. Translated into English Verse.
Second Edition, Revised. Fcap. 8vo, 6s.
The Works of Horace. Translated into English Verse, with
Life and Notes. 2 vols. New Edition. Crown 8vo, 21s.
Poems and Ballads of Heinrich Heine. Done into English
Verse. Third Edition. Small crown 8vo, 5s.
The Song of the Bell, and other Translations from Schiller,
Goethe, Uhland, and Others. Crown 8vo, 7s. 6d.
Madonna Pia : A Tragedy ; and Three Other Dramas. Crown
8vo, 7s. 6d.
Catullus. With Life and Notes. Second Edition, Revised
and Corrected. Post 8vo, 7s. 6d.
The 'Vita Nuova' of Dante. Translated, with an Introduction
and Notes. Third Edition. Small crown 8vo, 5s.
Aladdin : A Dramatic Poem. By ADAM OEHLENSCHLAEGER.
Fcap. 8vo, 5s.
Correggio : A Tragedy. By OEHLENSCHLAEGER. With Notes.
Fcap. 8vo, 3s.

MARTIN. On some of Shakespeare's Female Characters. By
HELENA FAUCIT, Lady MARTIN. Dedicated by permission to Her Most Gracious
Majesty the Queen. Fifth Edition. With a Portrait by Lehmann. Demy
8vo, 7s. 6d.

MARWICK. Observations on the Law and Practice in regard
to Municipal Elections and the Conduct of the Business of Town Councils and
Commissioners of Police in Scotland. By Sir JAMES D. MARWICK, LL.D.,
Town-Clerk of Glasgow. Royal 8vo, 30s.

MATHESON.
Can the Old Faith Live with the New ? or, The Problem of Evolution and Revelation. By the Rev. GEORGE MATHESON, D.D. Third Edition. Crown 8vo, 7s. 6d.

The Psalmist and the Scientist ; or, Modern Value of the Religious Sentiment. Third Edition. Crown 8vo, 5s.

Spiritual Development of St Paul. Fourth Edition. Cr. 8vo, 5s.

The Distinctive Messages of the Old Religions. Second Edition. Crown 8vo, 5s.

Sacred Songs. New and Cheaper Edition. Crown 8vo, 2s. 6d.

MATHIESON. The Supremacy and Sufficiency of Jesus Christ our Lord, as set forth in the Epistle to the Hebrews. By J. E. MATHIESON, Superintendent of Mildmay Conference Hall, 1880 to 1890. Second Edition. Crown 8vo, 3s. 6d.

MAURICE. The Balance of Military Power in Europe. An Examination of the War Resources of Great Britain and the Continental States. By Colonel MAURICE, R.A., Professor of Military Art and History at the Royal Staff College. Crown 8vo, with a Map, 6s.

MAXWELL.
A Duke of Britain. A Romance of the Fourth Century. By Sir HERBERT MAXWELL, Bart., M.P., F.S.A., &c., Author of 'Passages in the Life of Sir Lucian Elphin.' Fourth Edition. Crown 8vo, 6s.

Life and Times of the Rt. Hon. William Henry Smith, M.P. With Portraits and numerous Illustrations by Herbert Railton, G. L. Seymour, and Others. 2 vols. demy 8vo, 25s.
POPULAR EDITION. With a Portrait and other Illustrations. Crown 8vo, 3s. 6d.

Scottish Land-Names : Their Origin and Meaning. Being the Rhind Lectures in Archæology for 1893. Post 8vo, 6s.

Meridiana : Noontide Essays. Post 8vo, 7s. 6d.

Post Meridiana : Afternoon Essays. Post 8vo, 6s.

Dumfries and Galloway. Being one of the Volumes of the County Histories of Scotland. With Four Maps. Demy 8vo, 7s. 6d. net.

MELDRUM.
The Story of Margrédel : Being a Fireside History of a Fifeshire Family. By D. STORRAR MELDRUM. Cheap Edition. Crown 8vo, 3s. 6d.

Grey Mantle and Gold Fringe. Crown 8vo, 6s.

MELLONE. Studies in Philosophical Criticism and Construction. By SYDNEY HERBERT MELLONE, M.A. Lond., D.Sc. Edin. Post 8vo. 10s. 6d. net.

MERZ. A History of European Thought in the Nineteenth Century. By JOHN THEODORE MERZ. Vol. I., post 8vo, 10s. 6d. net.

MICHIE.
The Larch : Being a Practical Treatise on its Culture and General Management. By CHRISTOPHER Y. MICHIE, Forester, Cullen House. Crown 8vo, with Illustrations. New and Cheaper Edition, Enlarged, 5s.

The Practice of Forestry. Crown 8vo, with Illustrations. 6s.

MIDDLETON. The Story of Alastair Bhan Comyn ; or, The Tragedy of Dunphail. A Tale of Tradition and Romance. By the Lady MIDDLETON. Square 8vo, 10s. Cheaper Edition, 5s.

MIDDLETON. Latin Verse Unseens. By G. MIDDLETON, M.A., Lecturer in Latin, Aberdeen University ; late Scholar of Emmanuel College. Cambridge ; Joint-Author of 'Student's Companion to Latin Authors.' Crown 8vo, 1s. 6d.

MILLER. The Dream of Mr H——, the Herbalist. By HUGH MILLER, F.R.S.E., late H.M. Geological Survey, Author of 'Landscape Geology.' With a Photogravure Frontispiece. Crown 8vo, 2s. 6d.

MILLS. Greek Verse Unseens. By T. R. MILLS, M.A., late Lecturer in Greek, Aberdeen University ; formerly Scholar of Wadham College, Oxford ; Joint-Author of 'Student's Companion to Latin Authors. In 1 vol. crown 8vo.   *[In the press.*

MINTO.

A Manual of English Prose Literature, Biographical and Critical: designed mainly to show Characteristics of Style.. By W. MINTO, M.A., Hon. LL.D. of St Andrews; Professor of Logic in the University of Aberdeen. Third Edition, Revised. Crown 8vo, 7s. 6d.

Characteristics of English Poets, from Chaucer to Shirley. New Edition, Revised. Crown 8vo, 7s. 6d.

Plain Principles of Prose Composition. Crown 8vo, 1s. 6d.

The Literature of the Georgian Era. Edited, with a Biographical Introduction, by Professor KNIGHT, St Andrews. Post 8vo, 6s.

MOIR.

Life of Mansie Wauch, Tailor in Dalkeith. By D. M. MOIR. With CRUIKSHANK's Illustrations. Cheaper Edition. Crown 8vo, 2s. 6d. Another Edition, without Illustrations, fcap. 8vo, 1s. 6d.

Domestic Verses. Centenary Edition. With a Portrait. Crown 8vo, 3s. 6d.

MOLE. For the Sake of a Slandered Woman. By MARION MOLE. Fcap. 8vo, 2s. 6d. net.

MOMERIE.

Defects of Modern Christianity, and other Sermons. By Rev. ALFRED WILLIAMS MOMERIE, M.A., D.Sc., LL.D. Fifth Edition. Crown 8vo, 5s.

The Basis of Religion. Being an Examination of Natural Religion. Third Edition. Crown 8vo, 2s. 6d.

The Origin of Evil, and other Sermons. Eighth Edition, Enlarged. Crown 8vo, 5s.

Personality. The Beginning and End of Metaphysics, and a Necessary Assumption in all Positive Philosophy. Fifth Ed., Revised. Cr. 8vo, 3s.

Agnosticism. Fourth Edition, Revised. Crown 8vo, 5s.

Preaching and Hearing; and other Sermons. Fourth Edition, Enlarged. Crown 8vo, 5s.

Belief in God. Third Edition. Crown 8vo, 3s.

Inspiration; and other Sermons. Second Edition, Enlarged. Crown 8vo, 5s.

Church and Creed. Third Edition. Crown 8vo, 4s. 6d.

The Future of Religion, and other Essays. Second Edition. Crown 8vo, 3s. 6d.

The English Church and the Romish Schism. Second Edition. Crown 8vo, 2s. 6d.

MONCREIFF.

The Provost-Marshal. A Romance of the Middle Shires. By the Hon. FREDERICK MONCREIFF. Crown 8vo, 6s.

The X Jewel. A Romance of the Days of James VI. Cr. 8vo, 6s.

MONTAGUE. Military Topography. Illustrated by Practical Examples of a Practical Subject. By Major-General W. E. MONTAGUE, C.B., P.S.C., late Garrison Instructor Intelligence Department, Author of 'Campaigning in South Africa.' With Forty-one Diagrams. Crown 8vo, 5s.

MONTALEMBERT. Memoir of Count de Montalembert. A Chapter of Recent French History. By Mrs OLIPHANT, Author of the 'Life of Edward Irving,' &c. 2 vols. crown 8vo, £1, 4s.

MORISON.

Doorside Ditties. By JEANIE MORISON. With a Frontispiece. Crown 8vo, 3s. 6d.

Æolus. A Romance in Lyrics. Crown 8vo, 3s.

There as Here. Crown 8vo, 3s. *** A limited impression on hand-made paper, bound in vellum, 7s. 6d.

Selections from Poems. Crown 8vo, 4s. 6d.

Sordello. An Outline Analysis of Mr Browning's Poem. Crown 8vo, 3s.

MORISON.

Of "Fifine at the Fair," "Christmas Eve and Easter Day, and other of Mr Browning's Poems. Crown 8vo, 3s.

The Purpose of the Ages. Crown 8vo, 9s.

Gordon : An Our-day Idyll. Crown 8vo, 3s.

Saint Isadora, and other Poems. Crown 8vo, 1s. 6d.

Snatches of Song. Paper, 1s. 6d. ; cloth, 3s.

Pontius Pilate. Paper, 1s. 6d. ; cloth, 3s.

Mill o' Forres. Crown 8vo, 1s.

Ane Booke of Ballades. Fcap. 4to, 1s.

MUNRO. The Lost Pibroch, and other Sheiling Stories. By NEIL MUNRO. Crown 8vo, 6s.

MUNRO.

Rambles and Studies in Bosnia-Herzegovina and Dalmatia. With an Account of the Proceedings of the Congress of Archæologists and Anthropologists held at Ssrajevo in 1894. By ROBERT MUNRO, M.A., M.D., F.R.S.E., Author of 'The Lake-Dwellings of Europe,' &c. With numerous Illustrations. Demy 8vo, 12s. 6d. net.

Prehistoric Problems. With numerous Illustrations. Demy 8vo, 10s. net.

MUNRO. On Valuation of Property. By WILLIAM MUNRO, M.A., Her Majesty's Assessor of Railways and Canals for Scotland. Second Edition, Revised and Enlarged. 8vo, 3s. 6d.

MURDOCH. Manual of the Law of Insolvency and Bankruptcy : Comprehending a Summary of the Law of Insolvency, Notour Bankruptcy, Composition - Contracts, Trust - Deeds, Cessios, and Sequestrations ; and the Winding-up of Joint-Stock Companies in Scotland ; with Annotations on the various Insolvency and Bankruptcy Statutes ; and with Forms of Procedure applicable to these Subjects. By JAMES MURDOCH, Member of the Faculty of Procurators in Glasgow. Fifth Edition, Revised and Enlarged. 8vo, 12s. net.

MURRAY. A Popular Manual of Finance. By SYDNEY J. MURRAY. In 1 vol. crown 8vo. [In the press.

MYERS. A Manual of Classical Geography. By JOHN L. MYERS, M.A., Fellow of Magdalene College ; Lecturer and Tutor, Christ Church, Oxford. In 1 vol. crown 8vo. [In the press.

MY TRIVIAL LIFE AND MISFORTUNE: A Gossip with no Plot in Particular. By A PLAIN WOMAN. Cheap Edition. Crown 8vo, 3s. 6d.

By the SAME AUTHOR.

POOR NELLIE. Cheap Edition. Crown 8vo, 3s. 6d.

NAPIER. The Construction of the Wonderful Canon of Logarithms. By JOHN NAPIER of Merchiston. Translated, with Notes, and a Catalogue of Napier's Works, by WILLIAM RAE MACDONALD. Small 4to, 15s. *A few large-paper copies on Whatman paper*, 30s.

NEAVES. Songs and Verses, Social and Scientific. By An Old Contributor to 'Maga.' By the Hon. Lord NEAVES. Fifth Edition. Fcap. 8vo, 4s.

NICHOLSON.

A Manual of Zoology, for the Use of Students. With a General Introduction on the Principles of Zoology. By HENRY ALLEYNE NICHOLSON, M.D., D.Sc., F.L.S., F.G.S., Regius Professor of Natural History in the University of Aberdeen. Seventh Edition, Rewritten and Enlarged. Post 8vo, pp. 956, with 555 Engravings on Wood, 18s.

Text-Book of Zoology, for Junior Students. Fifth Edition, Rewritten and Enlarged. Crown 8vo, with 358 Engravings on Wood, 10s. 6d.

Introductory Text-Book of Zoology. By PROFESSOR H. A. NICHOLSON and ALEXANDER BROWN, M.A., M.B., B.Sc., Lecturer on Zoology in the University of Aberdeen. New Edition, Revised and Enlarged. [In the press.

NICHOLSON.
A Manual of Palæontology, for the Use of Students. With a
General Introduction on the Principles of Palæontology. By Professor H.
ALLEYNE NICHOLSON and RICHARD LYDEKKER, B.A. Third Edition, entirely
Rewritten and greatly Enlarged. 2 vols. 8vo, £3, 3s.
The Ancient Life-History of the Earth. An Outline of the
Principles and Leading Facts of Palæontological Science. Crown 8vo, with 276
Engravings, 10s. 6d.
On the "Tabulate Corals" of the Palæozoic Period, with
Critical Descriptions of Illustrative Species. Illustrated with 15 Lithographed
Plates and numerous Engravings. Super-royal 8vo, 21s.
Synopsis of the Classification of the Animal Kingdom. 8vo,
with 106 Illustrations, 6s.
On the Structure and Affinities of the Genus Monticulipora
and its Sub-Genera, with Critical Descriptions of Illustrative Species. Illustrated
with numerous Engravings on Wood and Lithographed Plates. Super-royal
8vo, 18s.

NICHOLSON.
Thoth. A Romance. By JOSEPH SHIELD NICHOLSON, M.A.,
D.Sc., Professor of Commercial and Political Economy and Mercantile Law in
the University of Edinburgh. Third Edition. Crown 8vo, 4s. 6d.
A Dreamer of Dreams. A Modern Romance. Second Edi-
tion. Crown 8vo, 6s.

NICOLSON AND MURE. A Handbook to the Local Govern-
ment (Scotland) Act, 1889. With Introduction, Explanatory Notes, and Index.
By J. BADENACH NICOLSON, Advocate, Counsel to the Scotch Education
Department, and W. J. MURE, Advocate, Legal Secretary to the Lord Advocate
for Scotland. Ninth Reprint. 8vo, 5s.

OLIPHANT.
Masollam : A Problem of the Period. A Novel. By LAURENCE
OLIPHANT. 3 vols. post 8vo, 25s. 6d.
Scientific Religion; or, Higher Possibilities of Life and
Practice through the Operation of Natural Forces. Second Edition. 8vo, 16s.
Altiora Peto. Cheap Edition. Crown 8vo, boards, 2s. 6d. ;
cloth, 3s. 6d. Illustrated Edition. Crown 8vo, cloth, 6s.
Piccadilly. With Illustrations by Richard Doyle. New Edi-
tion, 3s. 6d. Cheap Edition, boards, 2s. 6d.
Traits and Travesties ; Social and Political. Post 8vo, 10s. 6d.
Episodes in a Life of Adventure ; or, Moss from a Rolling
Stone. Cheaper Edition. Post 8vo, 3s. 6d.
Haifa : Life in Modern Palestine. Second Edition. 8vo, 7s. 6d.
The Land of Gilead. With Excursions in the Lebanon.
With Illustrations and Maps. Demy 8vo, 21s.
Memoir of the Life of Laurence Oliphant, and of Alice
Oliphant, his Wife. By Mrs M. O. W. OLIPHANT. Seventh Edition. 2 vols.
post 8vo, with Portraits. 21s.
POPULAR EDITION. With a New Preface. Post 8vo, with Portraits. 7s. 6d.

OLIPHANT.
Annals of a Publishing House. William Blackwood and his
Sons ; Their Magazine and Friends. By Mrs OLIPHANT. With Four Portraits.
Third Edition. Demy 8vo. Vols. 1. and II. £2, 2s.
Who was Lost and is Found. Second Edition. Crown
8vo, 6s.
Miss Marjoribanks. New Edition. Crown 8vo, 3s. 6d.
The Perpetual Curate, and The Rector. New Edition. Crown
8vo, 3s. 6d.

OLIPHANT.
Salem Chapel, and The Doctor's Family. New Edition.
Crown 8vo, 3s. 6d
Chronicles of Carlingford. 3 vols. crown 8vo, in uniform
binding, gilt top, 3s. 6d. each.
Katie Stewart, and other Stories. New Edition. Crown 8vo,
cloth, 3s. 6d.
Katie Stewart. Illustrated boards, 2s. 6d.
Valentine and his Brother. New Edition. Crown 8vo, 3s. 6d.
Sons and Daughters. Crown 8vo, 3s. 6d.
Two Stories of the Seen and the Unseen. The Open Door
—Old Lady Mary. Paper covers, 1s.
OLIPHANT. Notes of a Pilgrimage to Jerusalem and the Holy
Land. By F. R. OLIPHANT. Crown 8vo, 3s. 6d.
OSWALD. By Fell and Fjord; or, Scenes and Studies in Ice-
land. By E. J. OSWALD. Post 8vo, with Illustrations. 7s. 6d.

PAGE.
Introductory Text-Book of Geology. By DAVID PAGE, LL.D.,
Professor of Geology in the Durham University of Physical Science, Newcastle.
With Engravings and Glossarial Index. New Edition. Revised by Professor
LAPWORTH of Mason Science College, Birmingham. [*In preparation.*
Advanced Text-Book of Geology, Descriptive and Industrial.
With Engravings, and Glossary of Scientific Terms. New Edition. Revised by
Professor LAPWORTH. [*In preparation.*
Introductory Text-Book of Physical Geography. With Sketch-
Maps and Illustrations. Edited by Professor LAPWORTH, LL.D., F.G.S., &c.,
Mason Science College, Birmingham. Thirteenth Edition, Revised and Enlarged.
2s. 6d.
Advanced Text-Book of Physical Geography. Third Edition.
Revised and Enlarged by Professor LAPWORTH. With Engravings. 5s.
PATERSON. A Manual of Agricultural Botany. From the
German of Dr A. B. FRANK, Professor in the Royal Agricultural College, Berlin.
Translated by JOHN W. PATERSON, B.Sc., Ph.D., Free Life Member of the High-
land and Agricultural Society of Scotland, and of the Royal Agricultural Society
of England. With over 100 Illustrations. In 1 vol. crown 8vo. [*In the press.*
PATON.
Spindrift. By Sir J. NOEL PATON. Fcap., cloth, 5s.
Poems by a Painter. Fcap., cloth, 5s.
PATRICK. The Apology of Origen in Reply to Celsus. A Chap-
ter in the History of Apologetics. By the Rev. J. PATRICK, D.D. Post 8vo, 7s. 6d.
PAUL. History of the Royal Company of Archers, the Queen's
Body-Guard for Scotland. By JAMES BALFOUR PAUL, Advocate of the Scottish
Bar. Crown 4to, with Portraits and other Illustrations. £2, 2s.
PEILE. Lawn Tennis as a Game of Skill. By Lieut.-Col. S. C.
F. PEILE, B.S.C. Revised Edition, with new Scoring Rules. Fcap. 8vo, cloth, 1s.
PETTIGREW. The Handy Book of Bees, and their Profitable
Management. By A. PETTIGREW. Fifth Edition, Enlarged, with Engravings.
Crown 8vo, 3s. 6d.
PFLEIDERER. Philosophy and Development of Religion.
Being the Edinburgh Gifford Lectures for 1894. By OTTO PFLEIDERER, D.D.
Professor of Theology at Berlin University. In 2 vols. post 8vo, 15s. net.
PHILLIPS. The Knight's Tale. By F. EMILY PHILLIPS, Author
of 'The Education of Antonia.' Crown 8vo, 3s. 6d.
PHILOSOPHICAL CLASSICS FOR ENGLISH READERS.
Edited by WILLIAM KNIGHT, LL.D., Professor of Moral Philosophy, University
of St Andrews. In crown 8vo volumes, with Portraits, price 3s. 6d.
[*For List of Volumes, see page 2.*

POLLARD. A Study in Municipal Government : The Corpora-
tion of Berlin. By JAMES POLLARD, C.A., Chairman of the Edinburgh Public
Health Committee, and Secretary of the Edinburgh Chamber of Commerce.
Second Edition, Revised. Crown 8vo, 3s. 6d.

POLLOK. The Course of Time : A Poem. By ROBERT POLLOK,
A.M. Cottage Edition, 32mo, 8d. The Same, cloth, gilt edges, 1s. 6d. Another
Edition, with Illustrations by Birket Foster and others, fcap., cloth, 3s. 6d., or
with edges gilt, 4s.

PORT ROYAL LOGIC. Translated from the French ; with
Introduction, Notes, and Appendix. By THOMAS SPENCER BAYNES, LL.D., Professor in the University of St Andrews. Tenth Edition, 12mo, 4s.

POTTS AND DARNELL.

Aditus Faciliores : An Easy Latin Construing Book, with
Complete Vocabulary By A. W. POTTS, M.A., LL.D., and the Rev. C. DARNELL,
M.A., Head-Master of Cargilfield Preparatory School Edinburgh. Tenth Edition,
fcap. 8vo, 3s. 6d.

Aditus Faciliores Graeci. An Easy Greek Construing Book,
with Complete Vocabulary. Fifth Edition, Revised. Fcap. 8vo, 3s.

POTTS. School Sermons. By the late ALEXANDER WM. POTTS
LL.D., First Head-Master of Fettes College. With a Memoir and Portrait
Crown 8vo, 7s. 6d.

PRINGLE. The Live Stock of the Farm. By ROBERT O.
PRINGLE. Third Edition. Revised and Edited by JAMES MACDONALD. Crown
8vo, 7s. 6d.

PUBLIC GENERAL STATUTES AFFECTING SCOTLAND
from 1707 to 1847, with Chronological Table and Index. 3 vols. large 8vo, £3, 3s.

PUBLIC GENERAL STATUTES AFFECTING SCOTLAND,
COLLECTION OF. Published Annually, with General Index.

RAMSAY. Scotland and Scotsmen in the Eighteenth Century.
Edited from the MSS. of JOHN RAMSAY, Esq. of Ochtertyre, by ALEXANDER
ALLARDYCE, Author of 'Memoir of Admiral Lord Keith, K.B.,' &c. 2 vols.
8vo, 31s. 6d.

RANJITSINHJI. The Jubilee Book of Cricket. By PRINCE
RANJITSINHJI.
ÉDITION DE LUXE. Limited to 350 Copies, printed on hand made paper, and
handsomely bound in buckram. Crown 4to, with 22 Photogravures and 85
full-page Plates. Each copy signed by Prince Ranjitsinhji. Price £5, 5s. net.
FINE PAPER EDITION. Medium 8vo, with Photogravure Frontispiece and 106
full-page Plates on art paper. 25s. net.
POPULAR EDITION. With 107 full-page Illustrations. Fifth Edition. Large
crown 8vo, 6s.

RANKIN.

A Handbook of the Church of Scotland. By JAMES RANKIN,
D.D., Minister of Muthill; Author of 'Character Studies in the Old Testament,
&c. An entirely New and much Enlarged Edition. Crown 8vo, with 2 Maps,
7s. 6d.

The First Saints. Post 8vo, 7s. 6d.

The Creed in Scotland. An Exposition of the Apostles'
Creed. With Extracts from Archbishop Hamilton's Catechism of 1552, John
Calvin's Catechism of 1556, and a Catena of Ancient Latin and other Hymns.
Post 8vo, 7s. 6d.

The Worthy Communicant. A Guide to the Devout Observance of the Lord's Supper. Limp cloth, 1s. 3d.

The Young Churchman. Lessons on the Creed, the Com-
mandments, the Means of Grace, and the Church. Limp cloth, 1s. 3d.

First Communion Lessons. 25th Edition. Paper Cover, 2d.

RANKINE. A Hero of the Dark Continent. Memoir of Rev.
Wm. Affleck Scott, M.A., M.B., C.M., Church of Scotland Missionary at Blantyre,
British Central Africa. By W. HENRY RANKINE, B.D., Minister at Titwood.
With a Portrait and other Illustrations. Cheap Edition. Crown 8vo, 2s.

ROBERTSON. The Early Religion of Israel. As set forth by
Biblical Writers and Modern Critical Historians. Being the Baird Lecture for
1888-89. By JAMES ROBERTSON, D.D., Professor of Oriental Languages in the
University of Glasgow. Fourth Edition. Crown 8vo, 10s. 8d.

ROBERTSON.
Orellana, and other Poems. By J. LOGIE ROBERTSON,
M.A. Fcap. 8vo. Printed on hand-made paper. 6s.

A History of English Literature. For Secondary Schools.
With an Introduction by Professor MASSON, Edinburgh University. Cr. 8vo, 3s.

English Verse for Junior Classes. In Two Parts. Part I.—
Chaucer to Coleridge. Part II.—Nineteenth Century Poets. Crown 8vo, each
1s. 6d. net.

Outlines of English Literature for Young Scholars. With
Illustrative Specimens. Crown 8vo, 1s. 6d.

ROBINSON. Wild Traits in Tame Animals. Being some
Familiar Studies in Evolution. By LOUIS ROBINSON, M.D. With Illustrations
by STEPHEN T. DADD. Demy 8vo, 10s. 6d. net.

RODGER. Aberdeen Doctors at Home and Abroad. The Story
of a Medical School. By ELLA HILL BURTON RODGER. Demy 8vo, 10s. 8d.

ROSCOE. Rambles with a Fishing-Rod. By E. S. ROSCOE.
Crown 8vo, 4s. 6d.

ROSS AND SOMERVILLE. Beggars on Horseback: A Riding
Tour in North Wales. By MARTIN ROSS and E. Œ. SOMERVILLE. With Illustrations by E. Œ. SOMERVILLE. Crown 8vo, 3s. 6d.

RUTLAND.
Notes of an Irish Tour in 1846. By the DUKE OF RUTLAND,
G.C.B. (Lord JOHN MANNERS). New Edition. Crown 8vo, 2s. 6d.

Correspondence between the Right Honble. William Pitt
and Charles Duke of Rutland, Lord-Lieutenant of Ireland, 1781-1787. With
Introductory Note by JOHN DUKE OF RUTLAND. 8vo, 7s. 8d.

RUTLAND.
Gems of German Poetry. Translated by the DUCHESS OF
RUTLAND (Lady JOHN MANNERS). [*New Edition in preparation.*

Impressions of Bad-Homburg. Comprising a Short Account
of the Women's Associations of Germany under the Red Cross. Crown 8vo, 1s. 6d.

Some Personal Recollections of the Later Years of the Earl
of Beaconsfield, K.G. Sixth Edition. 6d.

Employment of Women in the Public Service. 6d.

Some of the Advantages of Easily Accessible Reading and
Recreation Rooms and Free Libraries. With Remarks on Starting and Main-
taining them. Second Edition. Crown 8vo, 1s.

A Sequel to Rich Men's Dwellings, and other Occasional
Papers. Crown 8vo, 2s. 6d.

Encouraging Experiences of Reading and Recreation Rooms,
Aims of Guilds, Nottingham Social Guide, Existing Institutions, &c., &c.
Crown 8vo, 1s.

SAINTSBURY. The Flourishing of Romance and the Rise of
Allegory (12th and 13th Centuries). By GEORGE SAINTSBURY, M.A., Professor of
Rhetoric and English Literature in Edinburgh University. Being the first vol-
ume issued of "PERIODS OF EUROPEAN LITERATURE." Edited by Professor
SAINTSBURY. Crown 8vo, 5s. net.

SCHEFFEL. The Trumpeter. A Romance of the Rhine. By
JOSEPH VICTOR VON SCHEFFEL. Translated from the Two Hundredth German
Edition by JESSIE BECK and LOUISA LORIMER. With an Introduction by Sir
THEODORE MARTIN, K.C.B. Long 8vo, 8s. 6d.

SCHILLER. Wallenstein. A Dramatic Poem. By FRIEDRICH
VON SCHILLER. Translated by C. G. N. LOCKHART. Fcap. 8vo, 7s. 8d

SCOTT. Tom Cringle's Log. By MICHAEL SCOTT. New Edition.
With 19 Full-page Illustrations. Crown 8vo, 3s. 6d.

SCOUGAL. Prisons and their Inmates; or, Scenes from a
Silent World. By FRANCIS SCOUGAL. Crown 8vo, boards, 2s.

SELKIRK. Poems. By J. B. SELKIRK, Author of 'Ethics and
Æsthetics of Modern Poetry,' 'Bible Truths with Shakespearian Parallels,' &c.
New and Enlarged Edition. Crown 8vo, printed on antique paper, 6s.

SELLAR'S Manual of the Acts relating to Education in Scotland. By J. EDWARD GRAHAM, B.A. Oxon., Advocate. Ninth Edition. Demy
8vo, 12s. 6d.

SETH.
Scottish Philosophy. A Comparison of the Scottish and
German Answers to Hume. Balfour Philosophical Lectures, University of
Edinburgh. By ANDREW SETH, LL.D., Professor of Logic and Metaphysics in
Edinburgh University. Second Edition. Crown 8vo, 5s.

Hegelianism and Personality. Balfour Philosophical Lectures.
Second Series. Second Edition. Crown 8vo, 5s.

Man's Place in the Cosmos, and other Essays. Post 8vo,
7s. 6d. net.

Two Lectures on Theism. Delivered on the occasion of the
Sesquicentennial Celebration of Princeton University. Crown 8vo, 2s. 6d.

SETH. A Study of Ethical Principles. By JAMES SETH, M.A.,
Professor of Philosophy in Cornell University, U.S.A. New Edition, Revised.
In 1 vol. post 8vo. [*In the press.*

SHADWELL. The Life of Colin Campbell, Lord Clyde. Illustrated by Extracts from his Diary and Correspondence. By Lieutenant-General
SHADWELL C.B. With Portrait, Maps, and Plans. 2 vols. 8vo, 36s.

SHAND.
The Life of General Sir Edward Bruce Hamley, K.C.B.,
K.C.M.G. By ALEX. INNES SHAND, Author of 'Kilcarra,' 'Against Time,' &c.
With two Photogravure Portraits and other Illustrations. Cheaper Edition, with
a Statement by Mr Edward Hamley. 2 vols. demy 8vo, 10s. 6d.

Letters from the West of Ireland. Reprinted from the
'Times.' Crown 8vo, 5s.

SHARPE. Letters from and to Charles Kirkpatrick Sharpe.
Edited by ALEXANDER ALLARDYCE, Author of 'Memoir of Admiral Lord Keith,
K.B.,' &c. With a Memoir by the Rev. W. K. R. BEDFORD. In 2 vols. 8vo.
Illustrated with Etchings and other Engravings. £2, 12s. 6d.

SIM. Margaret Sim's Cookery. With an Introduction by L. B.
WALFORD, Author of 'Mr Smith: A Part of his Life,' &c. Crown 8vo, 5s.

SIMPSON. The Wild Rabbit in a New Aspect; or, Rabbit-
Warrens that Pay. A book for Landowners, Sportsmen, Land Agents, Farmers,
Gamekeepers, and Allotment Holders. A Record of Recent Experiments con-
ducted on the Estate of the Right Hon. the Earl of Wharncliffe at Wortley Hall.
By J. SIMPSON. Second Edition, Enlarged. Small crown 8vo, 5s.

SIMPSON. Side-Lights on Siberia. With an Account of a
Journey on the Great Siberian Iron Road. By J. Y. SIMPSON. With numerous
Illustrations. In 1 vol. demy 8vo. [*In the press.*

SINCLAIR. Audrey Craven. By MAY SINCLAIR. Second
Edition. Crown 8vo, 6s.

SKELTON.
The Table-Talk of Shirley. By JOHN SKELTON, Advocate,
C.B., LL.D., Author of 'The Essays of Shirley.' With a Frontispiece. Sixth
Edition, Revised and Enlarged. Post 8vo, 7s. 6d.

The Table-Talk of Shirley. Second Series. Summers and
Winters at Balmawhapple. With Illustrations. Two Volumes. Second Edition.
Post 8vo, 10s. net.

SKELTON.

Maitland of Lethington ; and the Scotland of Mary Stuart.
A History. Limited Edition, with Portraits. Demy 8vo, 2 vols., 28s. net.

The Handbook of Public Health. A New Edition, Revised by
JAMES PATTEN MACDOUGALL, Advocate, Legal Member of the Local Government
Board for Scotland, Joint-Author of 'The Parish Council Guide for Scotland,'
and ABIJAH MURRAY, Chief Clerk of the Local Government Board for Scotland.
In Two Parts. Crown 8vo.. Part I.—The Public Health (Scotland) Act, 1897,
with Notes. Part II.—Circulars of the Local Government Board, &c. The
Parts will be issued separately, and also complete in one Volume.

The Local Government (Scotland) Act in Relation to Public
Health. A Handy Guide for County and District Councillors, Medical Officers,
Sanitary Inspectors, and Members of Parochial Boards. Second Edition. With
a new Preface on appointment of Sanitary Officers. Crown 8vo, 2s.

SKRINE.   Columba : A Drama.   By JOHN HUNTLEY SKRINE,
Warden of Glenalmond ; Author of 'A Memory of Edward Thring.' Fcap. 4to, 6s.

SMITH.

Thorndale ; or, The Conflict of Opinions. By WILLIAM SMITH,
Author of 'A Discourse on Ethics,' &c. New Edition. Crown 8vo, 10s. 6d.

Gravenhurst ; or, Thoughts on Good and Evil.   Second Edi-
tion. With Memoir and Portrait of the Author. Crown 8vo, 8s.

The Story of William and Lucy Smith.   Edited by GEORGE
MERRIAM. Large post 8vo, 12s. 6d.

SMITH.   Memoir of the Families of M'Combie and Thoms,
originally M'Intosh and M'Thomas. Compiled from History and Tradition. By
WILLIAM M'COMBIE SMITH. With Illustrations. 8vo, 7s. 6d.

SMITH.   Greek Testament Lessons for Colleges, Schools, and
Private Students, consisting chiefly of the Sermon on the Mount and the Parables
of our Lord. With Notes and Essays. By the Rev. J. HUNTER SMITH, M.A.,
King Edward's School, Birmingham. Crown 8vo, 6s.

SMITH.   The Secretary for Scotland.   Being a Statement of the
Powers and Duties of the new Scottish Office. With a Short Historical Intro-
duction, and numerous references to important Administrative Documents. By
W. C. SMITH, LL.B., Advocate. 8vo, 6s.

"SON OF THE MARSHES, A."

From Spring to Fall ; or, When Life Stirs.   By "A SON OF
THE MARSHES." Cheap Uniform Edition. Crown 8vo, 3s. 6d.

Within an Hour of London Town : Among Wild Birds and
their Haunts. Edited by J. A. OWEN. Cheap Uniform Edition. Crown 8vo,
3s. 6d.

With the Woodlanders and by the Tide.   Cheap Uniform
Edition. Crown 8vo, 3s. 6d.

On Surrey Hills.   Cheap Uniform Edition.   Crown 8vo, 3s. 6d.

Annals of a Fishing Village.   Cheap Uniform Edition.   Crown
8vo, 3s. 6d.

SORLEY.   The Ethics of Naturalism.   Being the Shaw Fellow-
ship Lectures, 1884. By W. R. SORLEY, M.A., Fellow of Trinity College, Cambridge, Professor of Moral Philosophy in the University of Aberdeen. Crown
8vo, 6s.

SPROTT.   The Worship and Offices of the Church of Scotland.
By GEORGE W. SPROTT, D.D., Minister of North Berwick. Crown 6vo, 6s.

STATISTICAL ACCOUNT OF SCOTLAND.   Complete, with
Index. 15 vols. 8vo, £16, 16s.

STEEVENS.

The Land of the Dollar.   By G. W. STEEVENS, Author of
Naval Policy,' &c. Crown 8vo, 6s.

With the Conquering Turk.   With 4 Maps.   Demy 8vo, 10s. 6d.

STEPHENS.

The Book of the Farm; detailing the Labours of the Farmer,
Farm-Steward, Ploughman, Shepherd, Hedger, Farm-Labourer, Field-Worker,
and Cattle-man. Illustrated with numerous Portraits of Animals and Engravings
of Implements, and Plans of Farm Buildings. Fourth Edition. Revised, and
in great part Re-written, by JAMES MACDONALD, F.R.S.E., Secretary Highland
and Agricultural Society of Scotland. Complete in Six Divisional Volumes,
bound in cloth, each 10s. 6d., or handsomely bound, in 3 volumes, with leather
back and gilt top, £3, 3s.
  ** Also being issued in 20 monthly Parts, price 2s. 6d. net each.
        [*Parts I.-VII. ready.*

Catechism of Practical Agriculture. 22d Thousand. Revised
by JAMES MACDONALD, F.R.S.E. With numerous Illustrations. Crown 8vo, 1s.

The Book of Farm Implements and Machines. By J. SLIGHT
and R. SCOTT BURN, Engineers. Edited by HENRY STEPHENS. Large 8vo, £2, 2s.

STEVENSON. British Fungi. (Hymenomycetes.) By Rev.
JOHN STEVENSON, Author of 'Mycologia Scotica,' Hon. Sec. Cryptogamic Society
of Scotland. Vols. I. and II., post 8vo, with Illustrations, price 12s. 6d. net each.

STEWART. Advice to Purchasers of Horses. By JOHN
STEWART, V.S. New Edition. 2s. 6d.

STODDART.

John Stuart Blackie: A Biography. By ANNA M. STODDART.
With 3 Plates. Third Edition. 2 vols. demy 8vo, 21s.
      POPULAR EDITION, with Portrait. Crown 8vo, 6s.

Sir Philip Sidney: Servant of God. Illustrated by MARGARET
L. HUGGINS. With a New Portrait of Sir Philip Sidney. Small 4to, with a
specially designed Cover. 5s.

STORMONTH.

Dictionary of the English Language, Pronouncing, Etymological, and Explanatory. By the Rev. JAMES STORMONTH. Revised by the
Rev. P. H. PHELP. Library Edition. New and Cheaper Edition, with Supplement. Imperial 8vo, handsomely bound in half morocco, 18s. net.

Etymological and Pronouncing Dictionary of the English
Language. Including a very Copious Selection of Scientific Terms. For use in
Schools and Colleges, and as a Book of General Reference. The Pronunciation
carefully revised by the Rev. P. H. PHELP, M.A. Cantab. Thirteenth Edition,
with Supplement. Crown 8vo, pp. 800. 7s. 6d.

The School Dictionary. New Edition, Revised.
        [*In preparation.*

STORY. The Apostolic Ministry in the Scottish Church (The
Baird Lecture for 1897). By ROBERT HERBERT STORY, D.D. (Edin.), F.S.A.
Scot., Professor of Ecclesiastical History in the University of Glasgow; Principal
Clerk of the General Assembly; and Chaplain to the Queen. Crown 8vo, 7s. 6d.

STORY.

Nero; A Historical Play. By W. W. STORY, Author of
'Roba di Roma.' Fcap. 8vo, 6s.

Vallombrosa. Post 8vo, 5s.

Poems. 2 vols., 7s. 6d.

Fiammetta. A Summer Idyl. Crown 8vo, 7s. 6d.

Conversations in a Studio. 2 vols. crown 8vo, 12s. 6d.

Excursions in Art and Letters. Crown 8vo, 7s. 6d.

A Poet's Portfolio: Later Readings. 18mo, 3s. 6d.

STRACHEY. Talk at a Country House. Fact and Fiction.
By Sir EDWARD STRACHEY, Bart. With a Portrait of the Author. Crown 8vo,
4s. 6d. net.

STURGIS. Little Comedies, Old and New. By JULIAN STURGIS.
Crown 8vo, 7s. 6d.

SUTHERLAND. Handbook of Hardy Herbaceous and Alpine Flowers, for General Garden Decoration. Containing Descriptions of upwards of 1000 Species of Ornamental Hardy Perennial and Alpine Plants; along with Concise and Plain Instructions for their Propagation and Culture. By WILLIAM SUTHERLAND, Landscape Gardener; formerly Manager of the Herbaceous Department at Kew. Crown 8vo, 7s. 6d.

TAYLOR. The Story of my Life. By the late Colonel MEADOWS TAYLOR, Author of 'The Confessions of a Thug,' &c., &c. Edited by his Daughter. New and Cheaper Edition. being the Fourth. Crown 8vo. 6s.

THOMAS. The Woodland Life. By EDWARD THOMAS. With a Frontispiece. Square 8vo, 6s.

THOMSON.
The Diversions of a Prime Minister. By Basil Thomson. With a Map, numerous Illustrations by J. W. Cawston and others, and Reproductions of Rare Plates from Early Voyages of Sixteenth and Seventeenth Centuries. Small demy 8vo, 15s.

South Sea Yarns. With 10 Full-page Illustrations. Cheaper Edition. Crown 8vo, 3s. 6d.

THOMSON.
Handy Book of the Flower-Garden: Being Practical Directions for the Propagation, Culture, and Arrangement of Plants in Flower-Gardens all the year round. With Engraved Plans. By DAVID THOMSON, Gardener to his Grace the Duke of Buccleuch, K.T., at Drumlanrig. Fourth and Cheaper Edition. Crown 8vo, 6s.

The Handy Book of Fruit-Culture under Glass: Being a series of Elaborate Practical Treatises on the Cultivation and Forcing of Pines, Vines, Peaches, Figs, Melons, Strawberries, and Cucumbers. With Engravings of Hothouses, &c. Second Edition, Revised and Enlarged. Crown 8vo, 7s. 6d.

THOMSON. A Practical Treatise on the Cultivation of the Grape Vine. By WILLIAM THOMSON, Tweed Vineyards. Tenth Edition. 8vo, 5s.

THOMSON. Cookery for the Sick and Convalescent. With Directions for the Preparation of Poultices, Fomentations, &c. By BARBARA THOMSON. Fcap. 8vo, 1s. 6d.

THORBURN. Asiatic Neighbours. By S. S. THORBURN, Bengal Civil Service, Author of 'Bannú; or, Our Afghan Frontier,' 'David Leslie: A Story of the Afghan Frontier,' 'Musalmans and Money-Lenders in the Panjab.' With Two Maps. Demy 8vo, 10s. 6d. net.

THORNTON. Opposites. A Series of Essays on the Unpopular Sides of Popular Questions. By LEWIS THORNTON. 8vo, 12s. 6d.

TIELE. Elements of the Science of Religion. Part I.—Morphological. Being the Gifford Lectures delivered before the University of Edinburgh in 1896. By C. P. TIELE, Theol. D., Litt.D. (Bonon.), Hon. M.R.A.S., &c., Professor of the Science of Religion in the University of Leiden. In 2 vols. Vol. I. post 8vo, 7s. 6d. net.

TOKE. French Historical Unseens. For Army Classes By N. E. TOKE, B.A In 1 vol. crown 8vo.   [*In the press.*

TRANSACTIONS OF THE HIGHLAND AND AGRICUL-TURAL SOCIETY OF SCOTLAND. Published annually, price 5s.

TRAVERS.
Mona Maclean, Medical Student. A Novel. By GRAHAM TRAVERS. Twelfth Edition. Crown 8vo, 6s.

Fellow Travellers. Fourth Edition. Crown 8vo, 6s.

TRYON. Life of Vice-Admiral Sir George Tryon, K.C.B. By Rear-Admiral C. C. PENROSE FITZGERALD. With Two Portraits and numerous Illustrations. Second Edition. Demy 8vo, 21s.

TULLOCH.
Rational Theology and Christian Philosophy in England in the Seventeenth Century. By JOHN TULLOCH, D.D., Principal of St Mary's College in the University of St Andrews, and one of her Majesty's Chaplains in Ordinary in Scotland. Second Edition. 2 vols. 8vo, 16s.

TULLOCH.
Modern Theories in Philosophy and Religion. 8vo, 15s.
Luther, and other Leaders of the Reformation. Third Edition, Enlarged. Crown 8vo, 3s. 6d.
Memoir of Principal Tulloch, D.D., LL.D. By Mrs OLIPHANT, Author of 'Life of Edward Irving.' Third and Cheaper Edition. 8vo, with Portrait, 7s. 6d.

TWEEDIE. The Arabian Horse: His Country and People. By Major-General W. TWEEDIE, C.S.I., Bengal Staff Corps; for many years H.B.M.'s Consul-General, Baghdad, and Political Resident for the Government of India in Turkish Arabia. In one vol. royal 4to, with Seven Coloured Plates and other Illustrations, and a Map of the Country. Price £3, 3s. net.

TYLER. The Whence and the Whither of Man. A Brief History of his Origin and Development through Conformity to Environment. The Morse Lectures of 1895. By JOHN M. TYLER, Professor of Biology, Amherst College, U.S.A. Post 8vo, 6s. net.

VEITCH.
Memoir of John Veitch, LL.D., Professor of Logic and Rhetoric, University of Glasgow. By MARY R. L. BRYCE. With Portrait and 3 Photogravure Plates. Demy 8vo, 7s. 6d.
Border Essays. By JOHN VEITCH, LL.D., Professor of Logic and Rhetoric, University of Glasgow. Crown 8vo, 4s. 6d. net.
The History and Poetry of the Scottish Border: their Main Features and Relations. New and Enlarged Edition. 2 vols. demy 8vo, 16s.
Institutes of Logic. Post 8vo, 12s. 6d.
The Feeling for Nature in Scottish Poetry. From the Earliest Times to the Present Day. 2 vols. fcap. 8vo, in roxburghe binding, 15s.
Merlin and other Poems. Fcap. 8vo, 4s. 6d.
Knowing and Being. Essays in Philosophy. First Series. Crown 8vo, 5s.
Dualism and Monism; and other Essays. Essays in Philosophy. Second Series. With an Introduction by R. M. Wenley. Crown 8vo, 4s. 6d. net.

VIRGIL. The Æneid of Virgil. Translated in English Blank Verse by G. K. RICKARDS, M.A., and Lord RAVENSWORTH. 2 vols. fcap. 8vo, 10s.

WACE. Christianity and Agnosticism. Reviews of some Recent Attacks on the Christian Faith. By HENRY WACE, D.D., Principal of King's College, London; Preacher of Lincoln's Inn; Chaplain to the Queen. Second Edition. Post 8vo, 10s. 6d. net.

WADDELL. An Old Kirk Chronicle: Being a History of Auldhams, Tyninghams, and Whitekirk, in East Lothian. From Session Records, 1615 to 1850. By Rev. P. HATELY WADDELL, B.D., Minister of the United Parish. Small Paper Edition, 200 Copies. Price £1. Large Paper Edition, 50 Copies. Price £1, 10s.

WALDO. The Ban of the Gubbe. By CEDRIC DANE WALDO. Crown 8vo, 2s. 6d.

WALFORD. Four Biographies from 'Blackwood': Jane Taylor, Hannah More, Elizabeth Fry, Mary Somerville. By L. B. WALFORD. Crown 8vo, 5s.

WARREN'S (SAMUEL) WORKS:—
Diary of a Late Physician. Cloth, 2s. 6d.; boards, 2s
Ten Thousand A-Year. Cloth, 3s. 6d.; boards, 2s. 6d.
Now and Then. The Lily and the Bee. Intellectual and Moral Development of the Present Age. 4s. 6d.
Essays: Critical, Imaginative, and Juridical. 5s.

WENLEY.
Socrates and Christ : A Study in the Philosophy of Religion.
By R. M. WENLEY, M.A., D.Sc., D.Phil., Professor of Philosophy in the University of Michigan, U.S.A. Crown 8vo, 6s.
Aspects of Pessimism. Crown 8vo, 6s.

WHITE.
The Eighteen Christian Centuries. By the Rev. JAMES WHITE. Seventh Edition. Post 8vo, with Index, 6s.
History of France, from the Earliest Times. Sixth Thousand.
Post 8vo, with Index, 6s.

WHITE.
Archæological Sketches in Scotland—Kintyre and Knapdale.
By Colonel T. P. WHITE, R.E., of the Ordnance Survey. With numerous Illustrations. 2 vols. folio, £4, 4s. Vol. I., Kintyre, sold separately, £2, 2s.
The Ordnance Survey of the United Kingdom. A Popular Account. Crown 8vo, 5s.

WILKES. Latin Historical Unseens. For Army Classes. By
L. C. VAUGHAN WILKES, M.A. In 1 vol. crown 8vo. [*In the press.*

WILLIAMSON. The Horticultural Handbook and Exhibitor's Guide. A Treatise on Cultivating, Exhibiting, and Judging Plants, Flowers, Fruits, and Vegetables. By W. WILLIAMSON, Gardener. Revised by MALCOLM DUNN, Gardener to his Grace the Duke of Buccleuch and Queensberry, Dalkeith Park. New and Cheaper Edition, enlarged. Crown 8vo, paper cover, 2s. ; cloth, 2s. 6d.

WILLIAMSON. Poems of Nature and Life. By DAVID R.
WILLIAMSON, Minister of Kirkmaiden. Fcap. 8vo, 3s.

WILLS. Behind an Eastern Veil. A Plain Tale of Events occurring in the Experience of a Lady who had a unique opportunity of observing the Inner Life of Ladies of the Upper Class in Persia. By C. J. WILLS, Author of ' In the Land of the Lion and Sun,' ' Persia as it is,' &c., &c. Cheaper Edition. Demy 8vo, 5s.

WILSON.
Works of Professor Wilson. Edited by his Son-in-Law, Professor FERRIER. 12 vols. crown 8vo, £2, 8s.
Christopher in his Sporting-Jacket. 2 vols., 8s.
Isle of Palms, City of the Plague, and other Poems. 4s.
Lights and Shadows of Scottish Life, and other Tales. 4s.
Essays, Critical and Imaginative. 4 vols., 16s.
The Noctes Ambrosianæ. 4 vols., 16s.
Homer and his Translators, and the Greek Drama. Crown 8vo, 4s.

WORSLEY.
Homer's Odyssey. Translated into English Verse in the Spenserian Stanza. By PHILIP STANHOPE WORSLEY, M.A. New and Cheaper Edition. Post 8vo, 7s. 6d. net.
Homer's Iliad. Translated by P. S. Worsley and Prof. Conington. 2 vols. crown 8vo, 21s.

YATE. England and Russia Face to Face in Asia. A Record of Travel with the Afghan Boundary Commission. By Captain A. C. YATE, Bombay Staff Corps. 8vo, with Maps and Illustrations, 21s.

YATE. Northern Afghanistan ; or, Letters from the Afghan Boundary Commission. By Colonel C. E. YATE, C.S.I., C.M.G., Bombay Staff Corps, F.R.G.S. 8vo, with Maps, 18s.

YULE. Fortification : For the use of Officers in the Army, and Readers of Military History. By Colonel Sir HENRY YULE, Bengal Engineers. 8vo, with Numerous Illustrations, 10s.

www.ingramcontent.com/pod-product-compliance
Lightning Source LLC
Chambersburg PA
CBHW030323270326
41926CB00010B/1480